**Dare to search for your questions,
Dare to face them,
And Dare to live authentically by your own answers!**

I

Dare to search for your questions,
Dare to face them,
And Dare to live authentically by your own answers!

Waeil BORHAN

Translation
Dr. Sara Enany

NEXT CENTURY
PUBLISHING

I

Dare to search for your questions,
Dare to face them,
And Dare to live authentically by your own answers!

ISBN: 978-1-68102-629-9
LOC: 2017908793
Printed in the United States of America

God-centrism:
Observations on Civilization

Table of Contents

I

**Dare to search for your questions,
Dare to face them,
And Dare to live authentically by your own answers!**

Preface

This is a book about the ultimate graven image, Self. Dear reader, I will accompany you through this book to talk about civilizations, paradigms, human beings, the Self, individual and collective ego, and their relationship to God Almighty.

This is a book about being proactive, not reactive. To move from being an object to being a subject, you must have choices: this book is also about those choices. To have choices, you must find your own questions, or you will be merely adopting those of others who have found theirs. This is, therefore, also a book about questions. By asking questions, I aim to assist you in generating your own, dear Reader, and in transforming your life into a series of questions.

This is a book about questions, not about answers. I believe that asking the right questions is more important than finding the right answers; every innovation and invention in human history started with a question, driven by a rebellion against the answers of the age.

Dear reader, in this book I will do everything I can to challenge your heart, to lead you from the shadow of safe answers to the light of questions. Answers lead more to endings; questions lead more to beginnings.

This is a book not about the clarity of black and white, but the deceptiveness of grey. It is also a book about courage: the courage to call things by name. The courage to diagnose accurately. The courage to find a cure, to confront and tame the Self, to move from being an object to being a subject, to shift from unconsciousness to awareness, to seek your own questions, the courage to choose, the courage to try. The courage to fail, again and again and again, to learn from failure, and turn it into success.

This is a book about common ground: how to find it, how to build on it. It's about turning 'or' into 'and'. This is a book about the future. We will revisit the past so as to learn about the present, look at the present in order to diagnose it, and find out what choices to make and what roles to play in the future. Naturally, since this is a book about the future, it is addressed to those who will live most of their lives in that future: the young. This book calls upon young people to do more than live in the future: it calls upon you to shape and create it.

Most importantly, this is a book about God, and God's purpose for you. I plan to ask you some questions, and present some theories. My own answers to these questions are not THE answers; they're my own attempt at answers, right or wrong. I am not presenting them to you for your agreement, but rather, to generate new questions within you. Even if you do agree with me, please set my own answers aside, and try to find yours. Why? Because my ultimate goal is for us to move our current civilization – which I believe is at a turning-point in history – forward. The alternative is to allow it to lead us somewhere unthinkable.

This may seem odd; not many people call for establishing a new civilization. Past civilizations have been extensively studied, while active, or after their fall. But what gives me the courage to make this call is that humanity has never been so advanced, and especially, never so immediately and directly connected. This will not come about unless there is a critical mass of people with the courage to seek out their own questions and, through their answers, move the world forward into a civilization of the future. This book, I hope, will be a tool to form this critical mass.

I would like to alert the reader to something else: I plan to offer you a different perspective on ideas and situations you may already know. All I will do is ask you to move to a different vantage-point. You will then be completely free to remain in the new location, or return to where you were. The greatest achievement, naturally, would be for you to move to a third location, and teach us all something new from this fresh viewpoint.

The Golden Rule

It is very important to remember the golden rule as we journey together through this book: The aim of searching for questions is to ask them to yourself, not to use them to judge others.

Dear reader, this book is yours. What it offers you is designed to generate your questions, followed by your answers. Part of its design is that every section is followed by blank pages for you to write down your questions and impressions.

I would like to offer a few words of advice for you on your reading journey. Write down what occurs to you as it comes to mind. Thoughts are often like comets: they glow briefly, then are gone. Don't overthink: jot down what you have in mind quickly, without editing. Some thoughts come from deeper than your conscious mind: it is useful to listen to what comes from those depths, and write it down. Write down what you think: here, you can think and analyze, then make a note of your conclusions. (Note: When you find instructions to think and contemplate, what I mean is for you to write on both levels: the shooting stars of thoughts that flash by, and your in-depth analysis.) Make a note of all your questions: don't try to find answers until you have read the whole book.

For best results, be honest with yourself. Try to go through the feelings in your heart and mind, and write them down. Don't try to set down what you "should" feel. When you are done, read over the notes you made on your journey. Try to find out what your words are saying to you.

On the back cover of this book, you will find a blank space where you can make a note of the effect this journey has had on you. Interact with groups of people like yourself who have read the book – I repeat, after you have read the entire book – and discuss your questions, impressions and feelings. This will generate new questions and impressions within you. Make a note of all of these, too, in your copy. The editorial team of *Yours* is currently creating an electronic portal to communicate with you, and keep readers posted on future events, lectures and workshops about what you have read and written.

Introduction and Terminology

This book uses some terms which I think it may be useful to define at the start to avoid confusion. A given term may have multiple meanings depending on the reader's background; therefore, my intended sense is given in this section.

1. Divine Spirit

By this, I mean the divine part of every one of us, the one the Lord has breathed into us. Specialists and scientists have researched this and arrived at a more precise definition, but for this book, the simple meaning will suffice: the divine part within every human being. The how and why of it is not the issue under examination; there is no need to delve deeper. Divine Spirit is meant not as an adjective but as a possessive, as one would say God's earth or God's creatures.

Here is the definition of Divine Spirit offered by Dr. Amr Wardani, Secretary General of the Egyptian Fatwa Council:

> The Divine Spirit is gentle, placed by God in human beings, and made by Him to be the repository of all good things and virtuous behaviors. It is one of God's creations; just as hearing is created within the ear, souls are created within bodies. It is pure and untainted ....It is not, as some might believe, part of God placed within His creations; it is claimed by God in His Word,

"I have breathed my spirit into it," thus honoring the spirit, and doing honor to us as well.

2. Civilization

My search for a definition of civilization led me to the following definitions which I would like to share with the reader. Before I start, to avoid confusion, I would like to distinguish three terms which are often confused in meaning: culture, progress, and civilization.

a) Culture: Culture is popularly understood to mean a certain refinement of thought and sensibility, including in the areas of law, politics and history, in addition to comportment, conduct, and other ideological and abstract matters.

b) Progress: This refers to the practical, concrete application of theory, as made manifest in medicine, architecture, industry and agriculture, and other practical applications.

c) Civilization: By civilization, what is meant is a combination of progress in both fields: the theoretical/intellectual, and the experimental/applied, in concert.

Culture is a liberating and refining force upon humanity. Culture makes the rules and ideological framework by which people's lives are organized; progress is humanity's gradual exertion of control over the universe around us and the things we use, including technological advances for our convenience. The stability generated by such a lifestyle enables us to produce what is known as civilization.

However, as to the exact meaning of 'civilization, experts disagree. There are two camps, each adhering to a certain ideology. The first, espoused by the German philosophers Keyserling, Ratano and Thomas, views civilization as a collection of ideological phenomena in society. Upon closer examination, the masters of this theory appear to exclude what has to do with arts, industry, polytechnics and mathematics from their definition. More succinctly, they confine it to the theoretical framework alone: to them, civilization is indistinguishable from culture.

The second camp, espoused by McIver, Albert Schweitzer and Edward Taylor, defines civilization as 'the achievement of a given society in arts, sciences and architecture'. McIver defines civilization as "the thing we are, not the things we use, manifest in arts, literature, theology and morality." Albert Schweitzer calls civilization "the material and spiritual advancement of individuals and groups." They appear to confine their definition to the material production of a given nation: their definition of civilization is closer to the definition of progress, above.

Ibn Khaldun on Civilization

> Civilization is a form of sedentary living, where villages and towns spring up, giving their inhabitants regular arts of living, working, socializing, learning, industry, managing life's affairs, government, and organizing the means of diversion and entertainment.

He goes on to say,

> Kingdoms and states are the ultimate goal of bands [of tribes]; civilization is the aim of Bedouins; and all civilizations, Bedouin or civilized, like their rulers and commoners, have a limited lifespan.

This discourse evidently refers to the succession of civilizations. Dr. Ahmad Abd el-Razzak defines civilization as

> a collection of concepts shared by a group of people, and the resulting ideals, traditions, thoughts, systems, laws and mechanisms of settling the disputes of this group.

Will Durant defines civilization as

> social order promoting cultural creation. Four elements constitute it: economic provision, political organization, moral traditions and the pursuit of knowledge and the arts.

Another expert defines civilization as "an expression of the system of beliefs, values and principles, the result of human activity in every field of thought, literature, science and art as a whole, in which all arts are equal." Tarek Sowidan defines it as "the ideological methodology of a given nation, manifested in material and abstract productions such as the theoretical study of history, literature, ethics and morals and practical sciences such as medicine, chemistry, industry and so forth. It follows that science is the most important basis for civilizations."

Having attempted a definition, we can now try to start a discussion. When we speak of a certain civilization, we speak of a broad framework that may mean many things, chosen by a group of people to be the melting-pot that brings them together. Civilization – any civilization – comprises within it a number of cultures, each with its own languages, religions, and ethnicities.

Western Civilization

Western civilization is the result of the cross-pollination of previous civilizations, from Ancient Egypt to the present, through Greco-Roman and Islamic times. Western civilization comprises, among others, British, French, Spanish, German and American cultures. All of these are a manifestation of the spirit of a given culture, as well as the specific musical, culinary and temperamental heritage that differ from culture to culture. Western civilization is made up of diverse ethnicities: Anglo-Saxon, Mediterranean, Scandinavian and so on, each with its own language, and diverse religions such as Judaism, different sects of Christianity, different sects of Islam, and others.

Western civilization is, in sum, a broad framework bringing together all of the above, giving it a distinct flavor, yet keeping the specific flavor of each of its separate ingredients. If a German and a Spaniard meet, both under the umbrella of Western civilization, they may discuss the differences between the art, music and cuisine of their respective cultures; at the same time, each of them can move their place of abode to any location within what is loosely defined as Western civilization without undue discomfort. Either can move from Spain to Germany (or to France, England, Canada, Australia, or the United States) if offered a suitable job, without expecting to find insurmountable hardships in adapting to that country's lifestyle, and without missing any of the comfortably predictable institutions that make their way of life possible – schools, hospitals, banks, places of entertainment, public libraries, shopping centers and so on – and which were present in their country of origin. That is not to say that there are no cultural differences; but there are no fundamental differences between where one was, and where one finds oneself.

In contrast, the fundamental differences will be something else altogether if the Spaniard and the German in the previous example encountered a person from Egypt, the Emirates, Tunisia, India or China, for example. The differences between them go beyond the cultural: they are differences of civilization. If the Spaniard or the German – members of Western civilization – move to India or China, or vice versa, they will sense a great wrench between life at home and abroad, and suffer alienation. This is because each of the two parties has moved to a civilizationally different location; this is where the greatest difference lies.

It is important here to make a distinction between the broad understanding of 'Western civilization' as a whole and the empires that rose and fell throughout its long history. The greatest empire history has known, namely the British Empire, rose and fell within this civilization: at its peak, it ruled one-third of the known world, and about one-quarter of its inhabitants (450 million people); similar in type if not in scale were the French and Spanish empires, and others. The American Empire flourishes even today. This wonderful civilization, with all its pros and cons, has a number of epistemological paradigms, but one above all: hierarchy. This has remained the prevailing characteristic of Western civilization.

Islamic civilization

This great civilization flourished about 1400 years ago, and continued to do so for around a thousand years. Like Western civilization, Islamic civilization stretched westwards as far as the Atlantic Ocean and eastwards as far as Indonesia, from Western Asia northwards to the Sahara Desert in the south. Like its modern counterpart, it comprised diverse cultures, languages, religions, ethnicities and races. Arabs, Persians, Amazigh, Saharan populations, Turks, Central and Western Asian populations, the inhabitants of Western China, Malawi Islanders and Indians, were part of it, with their vast array of languages and ethnicities, and of course the three

Abrahamic religions, as well as others, such as Hindus, Sikhs, Zoroastrians, Buddhists, and so on.

Like Western civilization after it, Islamic civilization was the superstructure, the unifying framework bringing all of these diverse elements together. Moving from place to place in this civilization was to a great extent similar to the above example about Western civilization, taking into account, of course, the great developments since then in technology and communications, etc. The flourishing of science and culture in this civilization was thanks to individuals and groups, not all of whom were Muslims, but of different Abrahamic and non-Abrahamic religions, different peoples, cultures and ethnicities; it was this rich diversity that made a civilization of it.

From East Asia to Western Europe, from Central Asia to the Sahara, arts and sciences flourished. Muslims, for whom the civilization was named, were not even a majority in Islamic civilization. Muslims were in fact a tiny minority in the countries with relatively high populations at the time, such as Egypt and India, comprising for a long time no more than 5% of their respective societies. It is important to make a distinction between Islamic proto-empires and states, and the Islamic World itself: examples of the former were the Umayyad, Abbasid and Ottoman empires, as well as the Indian Muslims, the Seljuks in Anatolia, and Andalusia on the Iberian Peninsula, whereas the latter, the Islamic World was the civilization that prevailed at that time, the lighthouse of the world. It is an error to confuse the larger concept of civilization with the narrower concept of empire, blaming civilization for crimes for which it is not responsible.

While Islamic civilization had a number of intellectual paradigms, the main one was built on assimilation and synthesis of all the cultures within it, which lent it its unique character and flavor. This was the case at the civilization's peak, before its decline, passing the torch to the next – Western civilization.

The Intellectual Paradigm

According to the late philosopher Dr. Abd el-Wahab el-Messiri,

> The intellectual paradigm attempts to reach a complete and final formulation of human existence. The

term "complete" in this encyclopedia means total, overarching and universal, while "final" means a thing's decisive conclusion, and its ultimate end. The paradigms have three main elements: The Lord, Nature, and Humanity.

There are, of course, other definitions of a paradigm; however, I think the above is the closest to this book's purposes. Adding "The Other" to the three main elements, and defining said other as part of humanity, will provide us with a suitable entry-point.

To simplify the concept of a paradigm, we shall ask three questions and provide an example of our solar system.

First: The Three Great Questions

I believe it is important for each of us to ask themselves (alone) these questions, and seek the answers alone.

Question One: Where did you come from?

Question Two: What is my purpose in this world, and what is the nature, and form, of my relationship with God, the Other, and the Environment in this life?

Question Three: Where am I headed after this life in this world is over?

Your answers to these questions will help you pinpoint the paradigm you wish to live by.

PARADIGM ONE: The questions and answers are as follows:

Question One: Where did you come from?

Answer: From God.

Question Three: Where are you headed?

Answer: To God.

Question Two: What is your purpose here?

Answer: I am free so long as I serve God, and my relationship with myself, the Other, and the Environment follows what God wants of me not what I want for myself.

These short answers are an indicator of a life under the paradigm of God-centrism.

PARADIGM TWO: The questions and answers are as follows:

Question One: Where did you come from?

Answer: I came from Adam or as a result of Darwin's theory of evolution. I actually don't waste a lot of time on this.

Question Three: Where are you headed after your journey in this life is done?

Answer: Either I will expire, or I am going to another life with God, and I don't waste much time on this, either.

Question Two: What is your purpose in this life, and what is the nature of your relationship with God, the Other, and the Environment in this life?

Answer: Yes! This is the question I care about, and this is the area where I spend most of my mental energy. My answer is that I am a completely free person, and within this freedom, I want to be happy. I have developed relationships with the Other based on a framework of virtuous principles, which provide both my Self and the Other's Self with an enjoyable life.

I believe in God, and have devoted certain places and set times to practice my worship of Him in the form that makes my Self the most comfortable.

The above answers are an indicator of a life under the paradigm of Self-Centeredness.

Having examined the above questions and answers, the Three Main Questions, and the two types of answers in the light of different paradigms, in order to form a clear picture, it is time for the example of the Solar System.

(It is suggested that you ask yourself the Three Main Questions and write the answers down in this space. "I don't know" is a valid answer.)

I

Second: The Solar System Example

We know that the sun is the center of the solar system; it moves, while the planets of the solar system orbit it, and some of these in turn, like Earth, have moons that orbit them; however, the center is reserved for the Sun.

In the God-centric paradigm, I choose of my own free will, fully conscious and aware that God is the center of my life, like the Sun. My self, the environment, and the Other, are planets orbiting this sun. My life's journey entire is a submission to the center of my creation, which is God; I do His will and fulfil His wishes in every aspect of my life. Under God-centrism, I choose to put God's will above my own, His purpose above my own, and His wants above before my own.

Under self-centeredness, the "I" takes the position of the sun, whether I do this of my own free will or because I have unconsciously or unknowingly placed my Self at the center of my universe. We can situate the rest of the relationships, such as the Other, the Environment, and God, in place of the planets that orbit the sun. In fact, I might add that this self-centeredness leads to a delusion: instead of perceiving that we approach or retreat from God, we instead believe that we are capable of pushing the Almighty away and pulling Him back to us at our whim.

Under self-centeredness, the Self makes short shrift of God, treating Him as a source of emotional and mental comfort, not unlike yoga or meditation. Under self-centeredness, the Self creates its own definitions of God, and not the concept of God as He has revealed Himself to us. The Self does not deny God's existence; but in practice, God's desires are subordinated to the Self's, His will to the Self's, and His purpose to the Self's.

Does this mean that Self-Centeredness does not believe in God?

On the contrary! It believes in God, and the Self obeys God's orders insofar as they concern matters of worship; however, in the details of everyday life, that's another matter. The Self places itself and its desires in the forefront; it creates an illusion that it can take what it wants from the Almighty, pulling Him nearer or farther, as it wills. Its search for happiness leads each person's Self to develop a relationship with the Self of each individual in society, creating a magnificent paradigm of humanistic values, such as liberty with responsibility, efficiency, truthfulness, honesty, cleanliness, and others. These values have organized society and borne stunning real-life fruit; however, we have crafted this exceptional system of living for ourselves, not for God.

The Development of the Current Paradigm of Self-Centeredness

Every civilization has its own philosophy, created by its philosophers. It is then adopted by its thinkers, who convert it to ideas that can change reality; studied by politicians, media professionals, and intellectuals, who simplify it for the rest of us; and adopted by artists, who translate it into paintings, stories, novels, films, songs, and so on. Thus, the above play their roles like instruments in an orchestra playing variations on the theme of the same paradigm.

Ancient history is rife with evidence of self-centeredness. The current paradigm, however, is our concern, inasmuch is it prevails in present times – Western civilization. This paradigm crystallized into its current form over hundreds of years. There was an extremely important event that marked its beginnings: what I shall call *rejection*.

Before the Renaissance, Europe was in the Dark Ages, rife with ignorance and injustice; an alliance formed between the church, capital, and political power. This alliance revolved around greed, power and money. With great skill, some men of the Church fused God, religion and priests into one great indistinguishable ingot of charlatanism, controlled by the clerics.

This ingot was used to confer divine legitimacy upon the unholy alliance's avaricious goals, and to oppress and torment the serfs – all in the name of God, and in fulfilment of His will, as these charlatans claimed. This gave rise to hundreds of years of conflicts, wars and massacres, claiming millions of victims, while millions more fled Europe to escape oppression and tyranny. This was the legacy Renaissance philosophers encountered; it was this they had to confront when they laid the foundation-stone for what we now know as Western civilization.

As a result of this painful legacy, the greedy men of the Church were rejected by all and sundry; but this alliance had been so skillfully forged that people's rejection of the churchmen's practices was accompanied by an aversion not only to religion, but to God Himself.

This attitude found expression in the writing of Renaissance thinkers: there is hardly a mention of the Almighty to be found in the works of the political thinkers, economists, and sociologists of that era. This is what I meant by Western Civilization's starting-point being rejection, filled with the pain of this legacy's injustice. This was the beginning of the concept of confining religion and God to places of worship.

The Self, the Absence of Awareness, and the Resultant Attempts to 'Box In' the Almighty

With the appearance of the self-centered paradigm came a number of convictions and behaviors that produced what I have termed 'boxing in God', i.e. circumscribing the Almighty within a specific time and place. How? We have confined Him to a space – houses of worship – and sacred sites, such as Mecca, Medina, the Aqsa Mosque, the Vatican, and so on. We then confine Him to a time – for example, the five prayer-times, Friday prayers, and Ramadan in Islam – Lent and other fasting months, church on Sunday for Christians, Saturday and synagogue for Jews, and so on. We enter reverently and sincerely into houses of worship and other places designated as sacred; we conduct pilgrimages to our respective holy places; we fast and pray, each according to their creed. We then exit this designated time and place, to conduct our daily life in the rest of the spaces designated for work, friends, family and entertainment, under the overarching paradigm of self-centeredness, governed by lofty principles (assuming a civilized society) or base principles (assuming a degenerate society). The success or failure of society is nothing but a result of the success or failure of the Self's negotiations with other Selves within the community. In either case, the principles followed (in a virtuous society) or ignored (in a degenerate society) adopt the comfort of the members of the community as their moral compass, the community being the sum total of Selves, without any reference to Divine Will.

This schism led to such societies, in effect, worshipping two gods. The first, God, is worshipped via rituals and prayers; the second, Self, is worshipped via the systems governing daily life and interaction. The true name for this relationship is worshipping two gods: God, and the Self. We pray by rote, then worship ourselves. We pray to God in the narrow confines we have designated as His place, then go to the other god, the Self, and worship it via our day-to-day practices in its service. We withdraw all our human relationships – work, social, political, economic, family, and so on – from beneath the skies of God-centrism, and situate them beneath the skies of self-centeredness, leaving only one relationship under God-centrism, namely our prayers to Him. One of the symptoms of this 'boxing in' is the attempt to confine God to the concept of established religion, which in turn is circumscribed to mean only rite and ritual, thus confining our relationship to God only to ritual, leaving the practical application of everyday life to Self to do with as it will.

There are two types of society: Subject and Object. The first type, the Subject, are organic societies that have decided to render unto Caesar the things that are Caesar's, and render unto God the things that are God's. They agree to box God in by confining Him to a specific region of time and space, which makes religion not unlike folk tradition, far removed from everyday life. These societies do as they say, or they "walk the walk." These are the societies that wear the Subject's hat; these societies flourish beneath the standard of Western civilization.

The second, the Object, are confused societies that have not yet taken a stand: they wish to be like these authentic, organic societies, but then what to do with their old and profound traditional relationship with God? It is easier for these to deal with religion via the holders to its exclusive rights, i.e. clerics and theologians. They seek fatwas from such *Imams* that may allow them to conduct their lives in the manner that suits them, praising them if they produce such fatwas, and railing against them if their fatwas are not to their liking. In either case, God has no place in the equation; they deal with religion through its agents.

The Ultimate Question

After looking at the Three Main Questions, and their reflections on a number of paradigms, we now move to another level. I believe that there is an additional question to the Three Main Questions, a complex question – one that generates more questions in the attempt to answer it. Where does God's will lie?

I call this the Ultimate Question, the question posed to every person who believes in God, no matter their means of worshipping Him. The philosophy behind it can be found in every message God has sent us via His prophets:

"If you want to be with Me while you live and afterwards, you must belong to Me. My will (God's will) takes priority over yours. My purpose has priority over yours. My desires supersede yours."

The above is not a written text in any religion, but has a profound philosophical significance. It is conditional and complex: conditional because the correct answer comes with a number of conditions, and complex because the answer to it lies in the sum total of how you react to your experiences as long as you live. Because God is generous, He has given us a guide to what to do in every circumstance, great or small, yielding the correct answer as soon as we follow it: "God's will before yours." This guide is every religion's essence: religion is the guide that allows us to reach God in the way He demands.

This concept – "God's will above our own" – can be found in every message sent by God to us through his prophets, from Adam and Eve to Muhammad. Every one of the divine religions has two poles: worship, the direct relationship with God; and everyday dealings, in which you worship Him by treating another party the way God would want them to be treated. This shared meaning, found in every detail great and small, can be summarized as "God's will above our own."

An example of worship would be waking up in the cold to perform dawn prayers and asking God why. The answer is, "Because I will it: my will above yours." You fast in Ramadan, hunger and thirst, and ask God why; the answer is, "Because I will it: my will above yours." An example of everyday dealings: You form a partnership. Your partner robs you. You are presented with an opportunity to get your money back in an unprincipled manner. However, God forbids it. You ask why; the answer is that God has sent down the guide to how to behave in such circumstances. His will above yours. Your life partner mistreats you; you want to respond in kind, to get back at them. You search the guide; the answer you find is different. The response: His will above yours. And so on.

"But what good does it do?" We search industriously for benefits to God's various commands; we do find many, such as virtuous behavior, refinement of society, and so on. But this is not the cornerstone; we could live by lofty principles without seeking God's favor by so doing. The basis for all of this is, "God's will above yours." If there was no benefit to us or to society by implementing God's will, would that mean that we should disobey Him? If there were no benefit to fasting, would we fast? If there were no benefit to praying, does that mean we

31

would not pray? If there were no benefit to being truthful and honest, would we stop? The fact is that we must do what God wills because it is what God wills. Any temporal benefit we may or may not reap is a secondary matter, unrelated to the fulfilment of God's will.

Freewrite on what you think of the section on God's will. Do not attempt to censor or organize your thoughts; just set down what goes through your mind.

The Existential Question

Where can God's will be found in life's situations, and what is its priority? This is a question that may help us make a concrete start to practical applications which may constitute a response to the Ultimate Question, "Where is God's will?" A short question with a profound significance! It is a question that, in my opinion, we must keep close all our lives. It is the cornerstone of this book. There are two parts to this question. The first is, "Where is God's will in this situation?" This question is designed to help you practice the shift from obliviousness to awareness. The second is, "What is the priority of God's will in this situation?" This question is designed to alert you to the presence of a God and His will, in addition to your Self and its will. It is designed to show you that you have a choice: You can give priority to God's will over your Self and what it wills, or the reverse.

This is an essential question for your awareness as long as you exist in this world – that is why I have termed it 'existential.' It is a question whose existence, in itself, is more important than any answer there may be. Why? Because asking the question opens up and illuminates your path to God-centrism – and whether your answers are right, wrong, or incomplete, being in a God-centric place is the essential goal of your existence.

There is another meaning to 'existential questioning' of which we must be aware, because I believe it is of the utmost importance. Every holy book preaches the worship of One God, as though the only criterion for being religious (or not) were a positive response (or otherwise) to the call, "Believe in the Almighty." The question here is: Is belief in God alone an ironclad guarantee of God's approval? Let us examine how one of God's creatures earned God's wrath, despite his faith. The creature was Lucifer; the incident was his refusal to obey God's command to bow to Adam, and his subsequent fall from Eden.

A closer examination of this incident leads us to several important conclusions. First, the condition of belief in, and worship of, one God, and the absence of idolatry, was fulfilled; the devil never thought to doubt God, before, during or after his act of disobedience. Second, he was tempted by no-one. Since the condition of belief in God was fulfilled, and since no-one tempted Lucifer, who tempted him to damnation? His own Self. What did his Self tempt him to do? To give his own will priority over the will of God. "But he believed in God!

Isn't that enough?" The result of this incident shows clearly that it is not.

I believe that the expression, "necessary, but not sufficient" is relevant here. It shows that another element must accompany our belief in the One God. That condition is self-denial in the real world, subordinating the Self's desires to the Lord's. The moral of the above is simply this: living under self-centrism, subordinating God's will to ours, even if we believe in Him, exposes us to great danger. Placing God at the center, and subordinating our will to His, safeguards us.

Dear reader, Lucifer's story is done. Ours, luckily, is not. Your story is alive and continuing. The previous heading, "Existential Questioning", was meant to allow the reader to choose an existential philosophy to live by.

It may be useful to make a note of your questions and your own existential questioning that may have resulted from your reading of the past few pages. Note that the faster you write and the less you edit, the more questions may come to you. Go.

_____

_____

_____

_____

_____

_____

_____

_____

I _____

Who Is This Book For?

In the broadest sense, this is a book about civilization. It is for all stakeholders in civilization; since civilization is – for the first time in history – global, I believe that this book is addressed to the seven billion people on the planet, with the hope of making you think. It is particularly addressed to the members of the current dominant civilization, namely Western civilization, and members of the civilization now on the wane, Islamic civilization, to urge them to think and act.

I am trying to push you out of your comfort zone. I am trying to alert you to your responsibilities, and open your mind to think outside the box for solutions for us all, your fellow-humans. A place of responsibility is never a comfort zone.

To Believers

This book is about a civilizational framework based on God-centrism. This book centers on God Almighty. As long as you believe in God, no matter your religion, this book invites you to re-examine your awareness of God's place in your life. The following pages will explain to you what I mean.

To Atheists

There are a number of reasons for a person to choose not to believe in God, or choose to worship some image of God other than that revealed to us by the Almighty via His prophets. In the final analysis, you are free to choose, and bear the consequences of your choice. I have chosen differently, but I respect your choice.

You are also included in the audience for this book. I invite you to read it for several reasons: the first is that I am a believer, and my religion is Islam, which means that I believe you are my sibling and that we are descendants of Adam and Eve. I believe that you have within you a fragment of Divine Spirit, which God placed in all of us. This is the starting-point for my affection for you. Your disbelief in it does not affect my belief in it. Although I disagree with you, I am responsible for you before the God you don't believe in, as a brother is responsible for his brother. You are my brother in humanity; I am certain that God takes care of you as he cares for me, gives you your daily bread as he gives me mine, and protects you as he protects me. This certainty comes from my belief that God has told us so; I believe Him, and your disbelief in that has no effect on my own belief. The second reason is that, being a believer in one of the revealed religions, I am partially responsible for telling you something important: I shall briefly set it out here.

My atheist sibling, it is important to make a distinction between three things: God Almighty, revealed religions, and their followers. Why? Because there is a possibility, I strongly believe, that your rejection of God may be due to your rejection of some of the actions of His followers, perhaps imagining that it is He who commands or condones such actions. If this is the reason, I think you may need to reconsider. Start afresh with God; see where your heart and mind will take you in your search for God, away from noise and interference. You have nothing to lose, I think, by these attempts.

You may also have moved away from God because of a belief that progress and piety don't mix, as evidenced by Europe's Renaissance. After all, Europe left the Dark Ages and Christianity behind after what the common people had suffered under the unholy alliance of power, feudal lords and the Church. And look at the backwardness of all so-called Islamic countries, falling far behind in progress and civilization! In both cases, I invite you to read this book to see whether your diagnosis is accurate, and if you are calling things by their true names. Even if you decide to remain steadfast in your beliefs, we are all neighbors in civilization, regardless of religion, culture, country, ethnicity, nationality, or belief in God. In the end, each of us is responsible for their choices, and will bear the consequences before God – even if they don't believe in Him. This is the view of a fellow-human, the writer of this, who believes in God, His holy books, his angels, and all of his prophets, who loves them all equally, and you as well.

To Young People

Who will live in the future? Those who are young today. For this reason I speak to you. You stand to gain the most from a prosperous future; you stand to lose the most from a poor one. You are the main player. There is a claim that the progress we have achieved in the past two centuries exceeds the progress humanity has made in the rest of known human history. I would go further, and say that the progress we've made in the last thirty years outstrips the progress of those two centuries. The meaning of this, my dear young people, is that you are living in a time unparalleled in history. The world has never before been so completely connected in real time. When I say the world, I am not being strictly accurate: to be precise, never before in history have younger people been so completely connected in real time.

Why young people? Well, the tools of connectivity were invented by the young for their peers. The most cursory survey of the hundreds of millions of social media users will yield an overwhelming majority of younger people. Is the rapid development of computers, smartphones and tablets aimed at the elderly? The answer seems clear to me. They are not only focused on you younger people; they are, in effect, struggling to keep up.

A geographical breakdown of world demographics shows that the majority of the advanced countries have an inverted population pyramid, while in backwards countries the pyramid is right-side-up. What is the meaning of this? Namely, that the advanced countries will need young people from the backwards countries in the future, not only for reproduction but also to support the elderly sector of the population. Young people will be needed everywhere in future on the global level. If the foundation is laid for a single civilizational melting-pot that brings together people of all different cultures, it will facilitate this and lead to positive results; whereas if it is allowed to occur at random, cultural difference will lead to humanitarian catastrophes. Young people, this concerns you more than anyone: be alert to it.

Why This Book?

There were indications in September 2007 and 2008. The world was rocked by devastating economic shockwaves from which we have not yet recovered. This was followed by innumerable scientific studies and theories from economic foundations, all seeking to answer the following: 1) Why did this happen? 2) How can we stop it happening again?

Some wrote about historical parallels, starting with the Great Depression up to the present; they analyzed causes, lessons to be learnt, economic development, what went wrong, why we had not learned from experience, etc. The vast majority of these studies sought to uncover the economic reasons behind the collapse. However, only a tiny minority made the distinction between the symptom and the disease. A high fever in a patient is merely a symptom. A wise physician, while not neglecting to bring the fever down, will try to uncover the real reason behind it. This tiny minority whispered that the stock market crash of 1929 was not the disease; it was a symptom. The real reason behind this economic disaster was not an economic, but a moral failing. The cause can be expressed in a single phrase: greed.

Economic prescriptions for change were only treating the symptom, not the illness. The economists I talked to mostly nodded agreement when I posited this to them, but then took to prescribing economic remedies for short- and long-term relief. But I believe it runs deeper. Even greed is only a symptom. The true sickness is a cancer with a raft of symptoms: it runs deep. I believe it had lain dormant a long time, and started to signal its presence starting with the last century. World War I was a symptom, and so was the Great Depression, and then World War II, and the Cold War after that, and the War on Terror, and finally, the current economic crisis. All these were great symptoms; we should not underestimate them, even while searching for the real illness behind them.

The issue with cancer is that it is not a foreign body, but the body's own benign cells, which mutate and turn malign, eventually killing the patient and themselves into the bargain. They meet no resistance, being from within; the body's defenses do not recognize them as a threat or an enemy to be destroyed. A similar phenomenon is occurring in our civilization.

A civilizational cancer is growing. There are cells that are growing abnormally. I believe that the Self – an essential and benign part of civilization – has mutated and turned malign, starting to attack the body politic of civilization. A symptom of this disease is the loss of humanity's dearest possession: our humanity. The real disease, civilizational cancer, is the paradigm taking over the world today, pushing us into self-centeredness. All the tragedies and crises of previous centuries only confirm the symptom. If not diagnosed and treated, it will keep sending ever-worsening painful messages – symptoms – to the world. This book attempts to diagnose it: it offers some cures, but by no means all. It attempts to sound the alarm for this disease, civilizational cancer, and to mobilize the stakeholders in it, so that they may find a cure.

This book calls for a cure for our civilization – the dominant world civilization, Western civilization, which that has given the world gifts – and tragedies – like no other throughout history. Civilization is a complex, gigantic structure, bringing together all kinds of religions, cultures, populations, languages, ethnicities and nationalities, all of which comprise diverse elements and cultures. However, if we break each of these into their constituent components, we find that the main element – the condition for their existence – is the human being.

In my belief, the most influential element in the great machine of civilization, with all its religions, national entities, ethnicities, languages, and cultures, is the smallest unit, that miracle: The Human Being.

You, dear reader, are a human being. If you are convinced of this fact, and start your journey of questioning, and others with you, then we are surely on the way to creating such a civilization. This book will deal with civilization from the broader, more general aspect, to its smallest component unit, the main element that builds it and makes it flourish, that great creature, the Human Being. This book centers on God and our relationship with Him, and how this can be translated to daily life, which is the component of civilization.

This is not a book about religion. This may be confusing, as the current civilizational paradigm conflates God with religion: one of the main reasons for the civilizational disease mentioned above, and a main impetus for this book. I am a Muslim, proud of my religion. But this is not a book about Islam, nor any of the other religions – religion has its theologians to write about it, and I am no theologian. I only mention my religion because I use my own religious and cultural background to give a number of examples in this book; but this is not a book about Islam or Muslims. This is a book about civilization. Civilization, any civilization, comprises, as I have mentioned, diverse religions, creeds, cultures, ethnicities, languages and races. I also love every one of God's prophets, and learn from their actions. I love Jesus, Moses, Abraham, King David, and all of God's prophets and holy men; I respect them, learn from them, and seek their wisdom in many situations. Yet I repeat: This is not a book about religion. This book is about civilization and about people. God's holy prophets are the best of all people; it is only from this angle that I use their example.

Civilizational Cross-Pollination

Let us, dear reader, examine the term "cross-pollination" as it applies to civilizations. Every civilization inherits many things from the one that came before it: sciences, arts, culture, literature, inventions, and other human contributions. That civilization learns from these and adds its own touches, then eventually ages and passes on its own inheritance to the next, and so on. This was the case with Ancient Egypt, then Ancient Greece – with a comparatively short flourishing compared to other civilizations, only 200 years, although that did not prevent its profound and far-reaching influence on successive civilizations, even today – as we shall discuss – then Ancient Rome and Persia, then Islamic civilization and finally Western civilization.

It is worthy of note that previous civilizations were centered around the Mediterranean Sea, and therefore engaged in historical inheritance and cross-pollination. This was not the case with other great civilizations, such as China, excluded by geographical distance from taking part in this genetic chain, despite some exchange at geographical intersections.

Western civilization is the one under which humanity witnessed the most progress. The development in the past 200 years is many times greater than the sum total of the progress achieved since the dawn of history and up to the start of the 19th century. The development in the second half of the twentieth century and the first ten years of the twenty-first is many times greater than the progress achieved in those 200 years.

We are currently experiencing a period of accelerated progress unprecedented in history, thanks to and because of Western civilization. According to Huntingdon in *Clash of Civilizations*, this progress consists in a great number of contributions to humanity. Virtually all political and economic theories currently in use are generated by Western civilization; every labor-saving invention is created by Western civilization; the sciences, arts and popular music are likewise its products. There is a general consensus among humanity that we owe Western civilization most of what we enjoy today: in fact, in *The End of History,* Fukuyama calls upon us to consider post-USSR Western civilization the end product and the only choice for humanity. The most important point, in my opinion, is that it is the prime candidate for a position never granted to any previous civilization: namely, the status of global civilization. This may be a great boon to the world, or spell trouble for the planet. This book will explain why and how.

Civilizational Monopoly and Civilizational Contempt

There seems to be a global accord to fight monopoly in every field; anti-trust laws in Western countries, adopted by most countries, forbid any one company or its subsidiaries to corner the market. Having only one brand of, say, coffee, with no competition, ends up being unfavorable to the consumer. The same is true if there are four or five brands, all produced by the same company under different names. On the civilizational level, though, this seems to be absent, as the Western paradigm of self-centeredness currently monopolizes world civilization. It has been offered to every community in different forms, under different brand names, in the past 300 years: "European civilization," "Western civilization," "American civilization," and last but not least, "globalization." Different names, but ultimately, the same product, all built on self-centeredness. This in itself is a civilizational monopoly, breaking the anti-trust laws of that very civilization that preaches the evil effects of monopoly on the members of the community. It abrogates their right to choose between diverse products. We need diverse civilizational products to choose from: diversity is a global requirement, a natural alternative to monopoly that ultimately benefits all of us here on Planet Earth. The freedom to choose what suits one is an essential human right, part and parcel of the humanistic outlook of Western civilization.

The broad smiles and polished phrases of board members, businessmen and policymakers alike conceal a deep contempt for any civilization prior to their own. This tends to be reflected in their interactions with their counterparts from different parts of the world.

Objects, People and Ideas

In *Les Conditions de la Renaissance,* Algerian thinker Malik Bennabi sets out a profound concept, namely that everything in the world belongs to one of three realms: the realm of objects, the realm of people, and the realm of ideas. Since this book proposes a civilizational framework, we are sure to interact with these three realms. Before discussing how this book will interact with them, I would like to add something to the great philosopher's theory of the three realms. The three great prophets and their divine revelations all brought creeds belonging to the realm of ideas, speaking to their communities – the realm of people – to urge them to rethink, change and develop their thinking to reflect these divine methodologies.

The prophets never sought to modify or change all things; they merely planted the germ of an idea within people's hearts, and then left the change up to them. How refined, how profound! I detect in this two wonderful humanistic values: liberty, and creativity. The Almighty allowed people, humans, the freedom to shape the objects we live with into reflections and manifestations of the guidelines – the ideas – He sent to us. If God had willed it, He would have sent us detailed blueprints to live by, daily detailed instructions, but I think he has not. I believe that the Lord's liberation of humanity, to create our lives as we will, is the highest honor He confers upon humanity – and the greatest responsibility.

What is your opinion of this claim? If you agree, would you say you have lived up to this responsibility, the responsibility of freedom to create? If you have, in which direction have you worked? Have you worked to benefit you and yours only, or to benefit the Other in addition to you and yours?

This book discusses concepts; it is a book about ideas. This book speaks to its readers, knocking at the door of the realm of people, urging them to find their own questions, and urging them, once these are found and answered, to dream, create and innovate manifestations and applications of these answers. The above will, I hope, throw some light on what I mean by 'creativity.' Before we reach the stage of creation, everything is easy. Once we are at the point of creating, that is the challenge.

The Realm of Ideas

This is where we examine how things are right now, the reasons why, and how we got here – then offer new ideas and examine their social, economic and human effects. The first part of this book will explain this proposition in detail, as clearly as possible. That will be our interaction with the realm of ideas.

The Realm of People

An idea remains nothing but an idea, lying dormant in books – in the realm of ideas – unless it is adopted by people who believe in it and think it can contribute to the common good. This also applies to the ideas in this book.

The Realm of Objects

This will occur if the ideas in this book convince a number of people, who think them over, then feel inspired to seek out their own questions, then discuss these with their peers – if the idea becomes attractive enough for them to organize seminars and lectures around it. If the idea is not translated into real-life applications, it will remain mere theory, no matter how small or large its audience, confined to discussion, never moving beyond it to action. That goes for the people convinced of these ideas as well: if their conviction manifests only in discussion, it remains only talk. But this is not a book of ideas; it aims at establishing a civilization that is God-centric and not self-centric.

I am aware that those with the courage to start this initiative may not stay to see it through to the end. Beginnings are demanding, requiring creativity and courage. The courage to dream; the courage to move outside the confines of the past; the courage to break away from the herd; the courage to leave the safety of answers for the empty space of questions; the courage of attempting to transform dreams into reality; and the courage to fail, again and again and again. The creativity to come up with new questions; the creativity to find fresh answers to these new questions; the creativity to turn the fresh answers into fresh solutions; and the creativity to learn from repeated failures, and transform them into success.

Here is another space, dear reader, to write down your questions. What about you? What about the realms of ideas, people and objects? Make a note of your questions regarding these three realms. Do you think there is a fourth realm, unknown to us, or not? This is a space for your thoughts on the introduction and the preface.

I

SECTION ONE

Self-Centeredness

PART ONE
Life under Self-Centeredness

Which Skies Do You Live Under?

What kind of question is that? Many of us live without ever asking it. Some live without ever having chosen, following others all their lives, willingly giving up their right to choose – perhaps never knowing they have it. Still others live under one sky, laboring under the delusion that they live under another. I direct the above question to all of these. They are free to answer, accountable only to themselves – a great responsibility – and to God – an even greater one.

If you are one of those who have asked themselves this, and chosen which you shall live under, of your own free will, then you have my heartfelt respect: regardless of your choice, I respect you because you are one of the few people in this world who practice what they preach. That is an admirable way to live.

To choose life under God-centric skies, or self-centered skies, is a central choice in life. Being too busy to think and choose does not absolve you of that responsibility. The first goal of this book is to make you face your responsibilities.

An example may be useful to illustrate the concept of Self under the umbrella of self-centeredness.

Spousal Relationships

For our example, here are six people:

Ahmad, an Egyptian Muslim
Kareem, a Tunisian Christian
Yasmeen, a Moroccan Jew
Karin, a Danish Muslim
Richard, a British Christian
David, a French Jew

Let's imagine that these people live in a major European city, home to a multinational corporation. Let us further imagine they all work in high-ranking positions for this company, and are neighbors in an exclusive housing development. They are well-educated, in high-paying jobs, with happy families, rich social lives, and plenty of surplus income. Their children go to good schools, and the families mingle socially. Their lives outwardly look the same: they are all decent and polite, following a similar code of ethics based on truthfulness, honesty, cleanliness, respect, and generosity.

Let's look at their spousal relationships. There are two groups: the first, Ahmad, Kareem, and Yasmeen – the Egyptian Muslim, the Tunisian Christian, and the Moroccan Jew – are bound by marriage to their partners. The second, Karin, Richard and David – the Danish Muslim, the British Christian, and the French Jew – are living together but not married. If you ask the first group, "Why are you married to your life partners?" a chain of answers will arise, different at the start but reaching the same point at the end despite the difference in their religions: 'Because God commands us not to have sexual relationships outside marriage.' If you ask the second group, "Why are you not married to your life partners?" the answer will also be a chain of diverse answers that end in the same point: 'Because we – my partner and I – thought it most convenient for ourselves.'

If you add, "But what about God?" the answers will politely and respectfully cover the following: "What about Him? What has He to do with our living arrangements?" Karin, the Danish Muslim, might add, "I fast some days on Ramadan because it makes me feel better, and I go to the mosque on Eid and sometimes pray at home." Richard, the

British Christian, might say, "I go to church on Sunday." The Jewish Frenchman, David, might add, "And I go to synagogue on Saturday."

What is striking about this example is that one would expect the followers of the same religion to give similar answers: one would expect Ahmad and Karin, both Muslims, to give the same answer, and so on with Richard and Kareem, the Christians, and Yasmeen and David, the Jews. But the reverse is true. Why is this? Because Ahmad, Kareem and Yasmeen, despite their differences in religion, subscribe to a shared paradigm, based on God-centrism: 'God's will supersedes my own.' Karin, Richard and David, despite the difference in religion, also subscribe to a shared paradigm, based on self-centeredness: 'what I want supersedes what God wants me to do, even though I believe in Him.' This example demonstrates how the paradigm one follows affects not only one's life but even colors one's religion with the same brush. Many such examples abound, practical applications of self-centeredness vs. God-centrism in daily life.

When I say 'I choose self-centeredness as my paradigm', therefore, this by no means indicates that I don't believe in God; what it does mean is that I believe in Him, but that I have chosen to privilege the will and desire of my Self over the will and desire of the Almighty, and that I am aware of the consequences of my choice.

It may be useful, when discussing self-centeredness, to define the Self: but before moving on from the spousal example, I would like to pause for a moment and ask you to think of an example from your own experience similar to the above and make a note of it in this space. If you find one, make a note of any questions you may have about it.

I

You and Your Self: Not One and the Same

In some worldviews, we are made up of five component parts: the Spirit, the Self, the Body, the Mind, and the Heart. The leader of these, I think, is either the Spirit or the Self. The mind, heart and body follow the leader: their performance and status change depending on who is holding the reins. This explains what some of the wise folk of history and some twentieth-century philosophers and psychologists have said in their study of human behavior – that you are not the same thing as your Self. Deeper examination of this statement is reflected in the fact that there is more than one voice in your head when you find yourself in a given situation. One voice tells you to take a certain action, while another justifies acting differently. In the end, you choose how you want to act, after internal deliberation among these voices and others besides. We will now build upon this assumption: that you and your Self are not the same thing. You are one thing; your Self is another. Some experts say that the Self is actually the Ego; others say that the Ego is part of the Self, not the entire Self, but let's go on regardless.

Distinction and Difference

When we say someone has an "ego," negative associations spring to mind, to do with appearance, artificiality, vanity, and other unpleasant attributes. When we hear someone indirectly boasting of their wealth – for example, the odd allergy they have to the pure gold in their watchband, or how much better their new car is than last year's model because it has tinted turn signals, or how the golf course their house overlooks is much bigger than the other courses – or a lady bragging about her children's expensive school, or how superior her French au pair is to other nationalities – we intuit that the ultimate goal is to convey a message: "My wealth makes me better than you and others." Another person might hold forth on his family's noble and ancient aristocratic roots and their many important relations by marriage, explaining how such a rare pedigree is worth far more than the wealth of *nouveau riche* upstarts. This person's ultimate goal is to convey, "My lineage makes me better than you and others." A third might tell of their important job, or their family's prominent and powerful positions in government; this man's message is "My job, or my important connections, make me better than you and others."

Others brag about how many books they have read, their influence in high places, and so on.

There are many types of audiences for the above. Some will listen and learn, others will reply in kind, and a third type will disapprove of the uncalled-for boasting. The shared meaning in all the above is, "My money/family/power/position/culture/etc. make me better than others. I demand to be treated better than others because I have superior assets." Others disapprove of such bragging, and say that this person has an inflated ego, dragging irrelevant topics into the conversation. But what if we saw this person as constantly threatened and fearful, believing others perceive them as poorer, less powerful, less influential, or less cultured? What if all this boasting is a pre-emptive strike against an attack they feel is inevitable? What if there is an internal defense mechanism that strikes out pre-emptively against incoming threats – even imaginary ones – and seeks to face them constantly? And what if this defense mechanism is one's ego?

The Castle, the Guards, and the Walls

Here is another example. We all remember childhood images of impenetrable castles surrounded by drawbridges and moats. I would like to ask you to add something to the image: imagine that the drawbridge is not only at the gate, but that the entire castle fence is constructed of a number of adjacent drawbridges, descending to cover the moat at will, so that the wooden fence disappears completely, raised back into place if any danger should threaten the walled city. Naturally, there is a Captain of the Guard who decides when the drawbridge should be raised or lowered. When the Captain suspects a threat, he does not wait for it to attack: he orders that the drawbridge be raised.

Let us imagine that the castle is the Self, and that the Captain of the Guard is the Ego. The drawbridges are our defenses. What happens in real life? When our Ego – the Captain of the Guard – senses a threat to the Self – the castle – it immediately calls on defense mechanisms suited to the threat. "I am richer! Don't think me less!" or "I am of good stock! Don't think me less!" or "I am superior! Don't think me less!" or "I am important! Don't think me less!" or "I am more knowledgeable! Don't think me less!" Once the Ego realizes that there are no real threats to the Self, it commands the defense mechanisms to retreat. From a military standpoint, this is an extremely efficient mechanism. It leaves no room for danger: it never waits to check whether there is a real threat or not, it activates the defense mechanisms regardless.

A defense mechanism this efficient has got to be costly. In return for the superficial sense of security granted by the Ego's efficient defense mechanisms, there is a constant state of defensiveness and a continual readiness to engage, repeated in an endless loop. Life becomes a battlefield. "Constant vigilance!" becomes the battle-cry. Life becomes exhausting. This may lead to an even more dangerous stage.

At the next stage, the castle and the guard become one and the same: the Self and the Ego merge. More precisely, the Self comes to imagine that what it *is* is what it *does*.

But you are not what you do. You are not what you own. You are not your profession.

Why is this belief dangerous? This becomes clear when the Self acts as though losing its possessions means *actual* death or disappearance. In the previous examples, the self that uses money as a defense *actually believes* that it is nothing more than money, and that the loss of this money will mean the loss and disappearance of the Self. Gaining or losing money is, to such a Self, quite literally a matter of life and death. A Self that uses family lineage as a defense mechanism imagines that losing the pedigree is a matter of life and death. The same is true of position, power, education and so on.

Once we realize this, we can understand the savagery with which the Self fights to secure wealth, position, power, education, or social status. Competition over money or power or position becomes a fight for one's very existence: when it loses its wealth, Self thinks itself dead, nonexistent – such a feeling is almost impossible to live with, leading one to withdraw from life, figuratively or literally. Being dismissed from an important position is a threat to life: losing a job tells Self that it no longer exists, whereupon it hides in panic. In this state, we will do almost anything to keep our position, fighting to stay close to the centers of power. Losing power, to the Self, reduces it to nothing. The Self quite genuinely believes it has been reduced to nothing, and that others will treat it as such. This is a hard feeling to face. Some decide to withdraw from life figuratively, developing agoraphobia; some seek out new social circles and abandon their old ones. Others withdraw literally, committing suicide.

In this light, one can more easily understand why some people kill themselves in stock market crashes, and why some important politicians or celebrities disappear from public life entirely when they step down. The key to the Ego's use of defense mechanisms is the Self's assumptions – right or wrong – about how people see it. There may be a great many admirable qualities to the person, but the Self can only imagine others' appreciation on the basis of certain roles it plays, making light of, and even concealing, its other admirable qualities. The controlling Self cannot fathom that others could judge the whole person by any criterion other than what they do, and thus hides the person's good qualities and prevents others from seeing them. Unfortunately, this creates a shell of ice around the Self and the Ego that only grows as time passes.

In the above example, the Self sins doubly against the whole person: first by driving people away by mobilizing the Ego to defend against a possibly imaginary threat, and the second by making their life miserable, causing them to withdraw from life if they are defeated in the imaginary battle raging in their minds. All this because your Self decided that someone else was a threat, and used Ego to defend you!

Did the above touch a chord? Do you have questions about it? Perhaps it may have reminded you of some incident? Make a note.

_____

_____

_____

_____

_____

_____

_____

I

Possibly Controlling Self and Ego: An Exercise

If we look at the Ego as the Self's defense mechanism, we may be able to convince the Self not to use it, if we can just calm it down and convince it that it is not under threat. Try this suggestion in the following situation and make a note of your reaction:

Imagine meeting an acquaintance with an inflated ego, who starts to talk to you about the advantages of his new car. Instead of rolling your eyes, smile and let him know you approve of what he is saying. Express your admiration for his car, and ask him to let you test-drive it. Do so, and tell him yourself how wonderful the car is. What do you think the effect will be on him? I think there is a very strong possibility that your preening peacock will turn into a purring kitten. Don't you?

Why do you think this happens? I believe your actions will have convinced the Captain of the Guard, the Self – which mobilizes the Ego – that you pose no threat, and that there is no need to drag out the weapons and defend the fortifications, since no enemy is at the gates. What would you call your behavior? I would call it taking the initiative and acting wisely.

Have you met such wise people? You may not have; they are in the minority. These will behave very differently if they lose their position, wealth, etc. This minority is aware that these assets are like clothing – you know that your suit, even your favorite suit, must one day be changed, or taken off. They know that they are one thing, and the suit is another. These people are aware that there is a great difference between being and doing.

According to a famous psychiatrist, there are many entities inside us. Inside each of us is a child, a youth, a girl, a woman, a killer, a fool, and many, many more. There are many brains: you have a modern brain, a primitive brain, a reactive brain, a right brain, a left brain, etc. You have levels of consciousness: a conscious, an unconscious, a subconscious, a devout consciousness, and a polluted consciousness. And finally, you have a mind: a logical mind, an existential mind, a mathematical mind, a realistic mind, a contemplative mind, a critical mind, and a creative mind.

Similarly, in life, we play diverse roles: the father, the son, the brother, the friend, the boss, the employee, etc. I believe it is important to make a distinction between who we are, and the roles we play. I also believe that the roles we play, with varying degrees of success, are just one use of what we are. A good boss uses the aptitude they were born with; a successful leader uses the leadership aptitude they were born with, and so on. I must make a distinction between what I am, and how I use what I was born with. Who I am is not what I do. As I have said, the road to allowing Self to control you is to fall into the trap of believing you are what you do.

Have you had an experience where you felt that you are what you do? Make a note of it here.

I

Fear Under Self-Centeredness

We have a natural self-preservation instinct. When we speak of instinct, we speak of involuntary acts prompted by the subconscious mind. It is in our nature to snatch our hand away from a flame; there is no logical thought process where we analyze the fire and conclude that it poses a threat, then command our hand to move away. Our hand moves away from the flame unbidden. If you are on a bus or plane and the overhead bin pops open, sending bags hurtling down, you'll duck and cover. Was analysis involved where you concluded that raising your arm to protect your head was the correct option? Not really. Inside each of us is a reception center that controls our actions far quicker than the conscious mind can; it evaluates the situation and mobilizes a defense, commanding the body to assume a protective position instinctively. The muscles around the spine will go from completely relaxed to tense in a fraction of a second if there is a blow to the spine: even if we lose consciousness, the muscles will tense and remain in the protective position, as the body is instinctually aware of the danger to the spinal cord and the death or paralysis that may result.

From the above, we can see that the body reacts to perceived threats not only involuntarily, but without our conscious permission. The body, then, has an instinctive protective will, of a sort. At the bottom of this is *fear*. Fear, your body's fear for its safety is what automatically activates the self-preservation instinct and makes the body bypass your conscious will, acting without permission. Your body's fear for you is what sends it springing into action even when you are unconscious. Fear, then is the motivator for the body's unconscious defense mechanisms without our conscious will.

Are there, then, other resources within us mobilized by fear? I think so, and it may not be going too far to say that it is fear that mobilizes the Ego within us to activate the defense mechanisms within us, albeit unconsciously.

Fear: The Instinct that Mobilizes Ego

Do you recall the example of the castle with a drawbridge above? In that section, we mentioned that the Ego bristles when threatened. Before the threat, though, comes fear. Does every threat lead to fear, mobilize the ego, and set the entire chain of events in motion? Not necessarily; this depends on how finely tuned your consciousness and awareness are. When the body springs into action, bypassing the conscious mind, to neutralize a threat, it is always as a defensive reaction, a result of some accident, a bag falling from an overhead bin, a candle-flame burning your fingers, etc. The Ego similarly raises the drawbridge and loads the cannons of wealth, power, position, etc., bypassing your conscious will, upon sensing a threat or some fear: Ego, too, reacts to a threat, in this case a threat to its existence. However, unlike the body, this is not the Ego's only option. If we are alert enough, or if we reassert our conscious will after a temporary lapse, we regain the ability to deal with situations in a proactive, not a reactive manner. When we manage to do this, we can curb our ruffled ego.

Have you ever found yourself startled by a barking, growling dog? A comic-strip of our feelings might be as follows: Panel 1: A dog is barking menacingly at you. Panel 2: A feeling directly connected to this incident arises: fear and threat. Panel 3: There was no choice in the previous panels, but Panel 3 is subject to your choice. You can either give in to your fear and run away, in which case the dog will probably chase you down and attack, or curb your fears and stand still until help arrives or the dog leaves you alone. In Scenario 1, you were reactive; in Scenario 2, you were proactive. The Ego, though, is always reactive.

Ego and Reactive Motivation

When we are unaware and unconscious, we may slip into a vicious cycle where Ego repeatedly springs into action to neutralize what it sees as a threat to the Self, motivated by fear which is motivated by reactiveness which is motivated by lack of awareness – and so it goes. When we make a move to break the cycle by seeking to become more aware and conscious, we move into the realm of proactive motivation, neutralizing fear, thus calming the Ego and the Self in turn. Our choices are:

1- to allow the Ego to scare the Self due to an absence of conscious awareness, making us purely reactive;

2- to use our conscious awareness to control the Ego and relegate it to its proper place, preventing it from scaring the Self into reactive behavior.

We can – indeed, should – never completely be rid of our ego. We can, however, be aware of its existence and its role, and control its actions. The first step towards finding a cure is a correct diagnosis. The first step to conscious awareness is to ask yourself, whenever you feel threatened: "Am I being controlled by my ego right now? Is Ego in the driver's seat?" The very presence of this question indicates the start of conscious awareness.

Based on what you have read about Ego and Self, put this book down and think of recent events in your life. Try to find out when your actions were controlled by Ego and Self, and make a note of possible reasons for this.

_____

_____

_____

_____

_____

_____

_____

_____

_____

_____

_____

_____

_____

_____

I

Choice, Awareness, Perception, and Initiative

Life is choices. Taking the reins of your own life is a choice. Allowing others to choose for you is also a choice. To be a subject, to be an object, to choose – all these are choices.

The first condition for choosing is to know your choices. Only then can you choose what you want – even, by the way, if you choose not to make a choice, out of fear, confusion, apathy, etc. You remain conscious of your choices in any case. Even in the great choices, you have the right to choose. The Almighty has granted every human being the choice to believe in Him or not as they please, and tells them the consequences of their respective choices, then allowed them to live beneath His skies in the mode of their choosing, and bear the consequences of their choice. God does not deprive us of the right to life, nor our daily bread, if we decide not to believe in Him; He lets us live, and earn our living, and bear the consequences. Choice, then, is an essential part of what we are.

Being unaware of our choices, or confused, is surrendering an important part of what makes us human: our awareness. To be aware and know our choices is to be proactive and not reactive. What this means is that you have decided to map out your life according to your convictions, not to be part of someone else's plan for living. Applying this to the Ego allows you to remain in control of your own life, free to choose and follow the life path dictated by these choices, unfettered by the Ego that might block them.

Self-Centeredness

Since the Self controls every aspect of our life, it is easy for one's life to revolve around oneself, in other words to follow the self-centered paradigm. This life paradigm does not deny God's existence; it merely places Him in a lower priority than the Self, by choice or unconsciously, and may, as we have mentioned, lead to 'boxing in' the Almighty into a specific time and place.

In the "Free Your Will" experiment that I give at the Baladna Foundation, I ask, "Which of God's creations can you can never be apart from for more than a few moments, from birth until we give up the ghost?" I give the participants a minute to answer. 90% cannot find the answer in a minute.

Think a moment for yourself and try to find the answer before you keep reading.

Have you found it? If you haven't, the answer is Air, with its oxygen and attendant elements. We cannot be without air for more than a few moments, even underwater or in space. We must be connected to a source of air to stay alive. However, the overwhelming majority could not recall it when asked. Why? I believe that the response here is that it is taken for granted. We are so accustomed to its presence, and make so little effort to get it, that we forget how important it is.

That meaning was shaken when I stood near the top of Mount Kilimanjaro. At such heights, the air is thin. For the first time, I experienced breathing without taking in air. Merely standing there made me breathless and gasping. I can assure you that I did not take breathing for granted then; I couldn't stop thinking about oxygen until I came down from that peak.

Let us go on. Since a well-balanced life is necessary for comfortable living, science tells us not to allow one part of our life to take over the others: we should allot time for work, time for friends, time for family, hobbies, exercise, mental activity, etc. Can we add "time to breathe" then go back to doing what we were doing in whatever part of our lives? I doubt it; we breathe naturally, whatever else we are doing at the time. Air is the common denominator linking all parts of our lives: if our activities were set out in a table, it would be the shared row going across the top of every column.

With self-centeredness, we do to God what we cannot do to air. Rather than living with Him in mind 24/7, we do the reverse. With self-centeredness, we have 'tabulated' God, reducing Him to a column in the table of our activities. We treat the Creator as we cannot treat His creation, air. We have relegated the Almighty to a blank space in a schedule, visiting Him in a specific time and place, confining God, as I have called it.

There are two paths to self-centeredness:

First, there are those who consciously choose a self-centered paradigm, then use its concepts in their day-to-day living, tabulating their lives as I have explained, and relegating God to a box, with the courage to bear the consequences.

Second, what I call reverse engineering: choosing this way of living and then being affected by their underlying concepts, thus going down the slippery slope of self-centeredness. Some people on this earth – a proactive minority – have chosen the first path, freely and with the courage of their convictions. The vast majority of people on this planet, though, have never thought about things or made a decision, merely chosen the actions that lead them down into unwitting self-centeredness, becoming objects instead of subjects.

Both paths are fraught with responsibility. Even if you are a mindless follower, this does not absolve you of responsibility. The start of self-centeredness is not denying God's existence, but relegating him to a backseat. When this happens without our conscious choice, it is a result of abandoning our awareness and thus our ability to choose.

There are a number of factors that can cause the descent into self-centeredness.

Warning Signs for Descent into Self-Centeredness

There are many, but I shall focus here on a small number of these: 'boxing in' God, forgetting God, doubting God, competing with God, and blocking God.

'Boxing In' God

One of the leading factors in the descent into self-centeredness, as explaincd carlicr in this book. Make a note of what this subheading means to you and the thoughts it generates.

_____

_____

_____

_____

_____

_____

I

Forgetting God

The communications revolution has made most of the seven billion people on the planet aware that the world has a God, who has sent prophets to assist us and point out the path to Him. These paths, in my opinion, are revealed religions. I also think that most of us have decided where they stand on this: some have taken the initiative not to believe in a God, whereupon it is of course natural not to follow the God-centric paradigm. Some have arrived at a different conception of this God, and elected to worship Him in their own way; for these, it is natural to follow their own God-centric paradigm as they imagine it, and the values it represents. There are those who adopt one of the Abrahamic religions: the heading "forgetting God" is addressed to some of these, the people I shall dub The Forgetter.

The Forgetter believes in God's existence, but always forgets that He is there, and that He has created a methodology for us to follow in our day-to-day lives. The Forgetter follows a different, specific path, one he found ready-made and followed without thought or conscious choice. There are many forms of forgetting God: one of these is Success and Crisis.

Success, Crisis, and Forgetting God under Self-Centeredness

There are many examples of those who have succeeded in life. Some have succeeded in business, making a fortune through their skills. Some have succeeded professionally, such as doctors, engineers, CEO's and so on, and others have achieved success in the field of culture and the arts, such as musicians, authors and artists. Still others succeed in public life, such as politics, or the academic field, such as professors with valuable contributions to human knowledge. All the above is essential to human development; people such as these are ruled by a raft of values adopted by society, manifested as principles and laws. When any one of these people is in crisis, they immediately remember God, and scramble to meet Him in the ritual spaces designated for the purpose, praying for an end to their trouble, after which they forget Him once more. They deal with God as the Rescuer in times of crisis, and then rely on their own rescue when the crisis is averted. This manner of forgetting God is an element of self-centeredness.

Doubting God

Do we trust ourselves more than God? This question may sound shocking. Ignore it if it doesn't apply to you, but before deciding that it doesn't, please ask yourself: Why did you immediately deny it? What, in the language of business, are the KPI's you used to judge?

Some have the courage and honesty to admit that while they trust in God in matters of worship, they'd rather rely on their own abilities. Some people have faith in God and know that nothing happens unless He wills it, and work on this basis, trusting their own efforts secondary to their faith in God. These respective groups, despite the difference in attitude, share an important point: both are honest with themselves. Unfortunately, though, both these groups are in the minority. Who, then, are the majority? Those who say they trust in God's will to be done, but whose actions indicate the complete opposite. There are two levels to this: individual behavior, and collective behavior.

Studying collective behavior involves looking at the individual in society. In Western civilization, after centuries of bloody conflict, the individual has come to feel secure in the society that protects and supplies their needs, serving them better than their village. The social contract states that society is superior to family, clan or tribal affiliation. Governments replace the mother; political parties compete to show how, if elected, they will provide the greatest number of services to society. Law is the ultimate guarantor of the values these societies call for: justice, freedom, accuracy, honesty and so on. Individual respect – or lack thereof – for the law is the key indicator of the individual's relationship with society.

In backwards societies, it is still the tribe that affords security to its members. In such societies, there is only a bare minimum of public services: people grasp at what they can thanks to their tribe, whether it is a true tribe bonded by blood, or a tribe of convenience formed by mutual interest. Examples of such 'tribes' are trade unions, clubs, congregations, various institutions of the State, ethnic and racial groups, clubs, companies and other wealth-based communities, underprivileged groups, service organizations and political parties.

Tribes, whether based on blood or benefit, supersede society in terms of loyalty.

In both cases, whether the society is advanced or backwards, faith in elements of society is greater than faith in God Almighty; the rules set out by groups are willingly and gladly followed by individuals. If any of these rules contradict Divine Law, divine law is either ignored, or else valiant efforts are made to bend divine law to the occasion at hand. The painful truth here is that under God-centrism, conflicts between Divine Will and the Social Will would not arise; such conflicts arise only under self-centeredness.

So much for collective living. On the individual level, this dichotomy is clear when individuals diligently pursue religious ritual, yet ignore God's commands when it comes to daily life, and regard divine commands suspiciously as outdated principles formulated for another age. Such individuals seek out clerics to reinforce their beliefs, and present them with the divine seal of approval confirming that they are not violating the tenets of their respective religions. There is always a minority of clerics, then and now, who seek to profit by telling people what they want, easing such people's conscience and lining their own pockets. They indicate, implicitly or explicitly, a lack of faith in God and H is abilities.

If we look around us at the world, even so-called God-fearing societies, will show that most societies have more faith in their own abilities than in God's, but lack the necessary courage to call a spade a spade. It's just easier. An examination of day-to-day practice reveals that not only do people lack faith in God, they don't even give Him the benefit of the doubt. Shocking? Perhaps. The question is, is it true or isn't it? Does it happen or doesn't it? Make notes. Jot down your observations in this space.

———————————————————————————————————

———————————————————————————————————

———————————————————————————————————

———————————————————————————————————

I ⸺

Competing with God

Yes, competing with God. We may not be honest enough to admit it, or in denial, but competition with God is alive and well. Where and when it started is a mystery, but it may have its roots in the ancient writings of bygone civilizations. In these works, there is a marked contradiction between the gods' supposed omnipotence and their frailties – such as being jealous of humans and competing with them, now vanquishing them and now losing to them. These ancient works, bursting with tales of competition between gods and people, may have established the concept of competition between the Greek gods, at least, and humanity. The same can be found in the literature of Ancient Egypt, in the battles with evil gods, where the good gods came down on the side of humanity. Again, some of these were won, some were lost. There are other ancient civilizations with a similar heritage, speaking of conflicts between humans and gods.

The writings about such conflicts may or may not have influenced the collective consciousness during the Renaissance, and crept into recent centuries via Darwinian thinking. Theories were built upon this that stripped God of His godliness, and placed him in the position of a competitor. The concept of God being merely a choice among many reinforces the possibility of competing with Him. I am not against any theory, culture or concept: what I am against is not making a choice, and submitting blindly to things you have not chosen, simply out of confusion and unawareness. Collective concepts creep into our minds, forming our individual consciousness and, more importantly, our unconscious, without our knowing it.

Here is an example which illustrates the competition with God, and also how the concepts around us can form our consciousness without our knowing it.

Humanity vs. Divinity

When we meet someone who is generous, kind, compassionate, strong, giving, and helpful, we admire such a person. When we try to describe this person, we might say "So-and-so is a real *mensch,*" meaning, "So-and-so is truly human." Mightn't we?

Why do we say this? Well, because of all the good qualities we just mentioned. I will ask you again: Who do these good qualities come from, in essence? Think before you answer.

The fact is that these are all attributes of God. It is He who describes himself as such, He who taught them to us and urged us to act that way with others: God is described as "generous, merciful, loving, strong," and so on. There is no counting the attributes of the Almighty. These adjectives being divine, it might be more accurate to say "This person is truly divine," mightn't it?

Why, then, have we labeled these qualities as 'human'? The answer may lie in Renaissance literature. That age was characterized by a rejection of priests and of the Church, which resulted in people moving away from God. The writers and thinkers of the age needed to find a suitable conveyor of these values sent to us by God: there was nothing for it, they found, but to call them "humanist" values, exacerbating the competition with God. Another example of this is what happened with the term "conscience."

Conscience and the Divine Spirit

When we say someone has a "clear conscience", or an "attack of conscience," we tend to admire them for it. This means that a person knows right from wrong and is basically a good person, doesn't it? The time has come to question just what a "conscience" really is. What is a "conscience?" When did the term arise? What for? The term was commandeered into existence, to serve as a placeholder for the good that is already in us. Why? To avoid attributing it to God. Why? I think that this too may have its roots in the Renaissance writers, whether they were atheists, or believers who put God in second place – so a collection of words was pressed into service to express the good that lies within us, without, at the same time, bringing God into the equation at all.

This, too, reinforced the culture of competition with God. For why should I attribute good things to one I have decided – for reasons of my own – to oppose?

It is easier to invent new names and concepts to express the things I want to strip away from my opponent. Words like "humanity" and "conscience" were invented to praise human beings, and cut off these attributes from their main source, Almighty God. The Self's opposition to God takes the following stages:

1. To learn God's attributes as He commands us.

2. To disconnect them from their main source, Almighty God.

3. To corrupt them by attributing them to humans.

4. To forget their main source.

5. With the passage of time, to come to consider them part of our basic humanity.

The perfect con job! It's like someone borrowing a piece of clothing, then claiming it as his own, denying that its original owner has any rights to it.

Was this your conscious choice? If you did, you have my respect. I believe that the ones who need to be alerted to this are those who have accumulated these terms in their consciousness, not realizing that by accumulating them, they change their entire outlook on life, and descend into self-centeredness without knowing it. They need to be alerted that there *is* a choice, a choice that must be made consciously; that they are absolutely free to choose, as long as they are aware and conscious of the responsibilities of that choice.

This simple example is found everywhere in life. What matters now is not who did this, nor why; what matters is its effect on all of us, its effect on you, dear reader.

Make a note of what you think of the above. If you find any examples, make a note of them.

_____

_____

_____

_____

Blocking God

To say blocking God, we need three elements: a blocker – a blockee – the act of blocking itself.

The Act of Blocking: When we raise our hands up to block the sun from getting in our eyes, that does not make the sun disappear. The sun still exists; we have merely blocked its rays. The sun remains on high, sending its light and warmth into God's creation.

When I say "the act of blocking," what I mean is that we, intentionally or unintentionally, block our consciousness from basking in God's light; God remains God, with His power and glory.

The Blocker: The blocker is the Self, whether our own self does the blocking or calls in other selves to assist with the act of blocking. The Self places attributes upon these others that make them Godlike.

The Blockee: The self's continued confusion, its self-focusing and resultant distraction from God, blocks God from our awareness; the blockee is God.

I believe that there are a number of conditions for this blocked state. The first is abuse of patriarchy, and the guru/disciple relationship.

Abuse of Patriarchy: In most cultures everywhere in the world, there is some system that governs society: the state, the village, etc. Just and successful governance ensures a healthy society, and a satisfied populace. Unjust and unsuccessful governance results in dissatisfaction. A cursory look at unsuccessful governments, those that rule by fire and the sword, shows that most of them are oppressive systems that place all power in the hands of an individual. Individual oppressive rulers need to reinforce their power and suppress opposition. The reign of terror, the usual tool, tends to achieve dramatic success. Throughout history, such rulers have exploited a minority of spiritual leaders of dubious integrity: the village shaman, the priest, or the Imam, or others regarded by the common people as sacred, to confer legitimacy upon them. Throughout history, religions have urged us to obey our parents, especially to love and revere the father; this is seen as a key value in breeding obedient children and well-balanced families, the seed of a well-balanced society. However, some corrupt societies have exploited this benign exhortation to obey the father for their own nefarious ends. Oppressive and despotic regimes have found a virtual treasure in paternal obedience.

The first step here is to set up the ruler as a father, and his (virtually always 'his') subjects as his children. An admirable metaphor, supposedly based on compassion, but unfortunately false. In a healthy familial relationship, children are supposed to avoid angering or displeasing their father so as not to make God angry and arouse society's ire. This twisted transformation creates the concept of the Ruler-as-Father. Any decision by the Ruler-as-Father cannot be challenged or contradicted, so as not to anger the Father, and hence God. Every individual is thus under siege, censoring their own self.

This also results in a highly centralized hierarchy of power where all power lies in the hands of either an individual, or a small group of people for which the individual is only a front. The fate of large groups of people thus lies in the hands of a tiny elite, with supposed Divine Right on their side, supported by corrupt clerics. Over time, this minority becomes like a collection of demigods, or idols. They demand absolute obedience and loyalty to them, and only to them.

Why is this?

It may be because most people follow the patriarchal paradigm. Since we can biologically only belong to one father, most people find comfort in being loyal to a single extremely centralized, extremely hierarchical system, with our designated 'father' at its center and at its apex. This father is the source of all things wise, good and generous: he gives, he takes away, he is the seat of power and authority. The tyrant's position at the very top of the hierarchy grants him access to the mainstream of people's consciousness, to the point where God is blocked from people's awareness, replaced by the tyrant.

The Guru/Disciple Relationship: This is conceptually linked to the teacher/student and the mentor/follower relationship, at any stage of education or upbringing. The focus, I believe, is not the teachers or educators, but the knowledge or values they convey to their charges. I also believe that this relationship is temporary, only lasting for the duration of the educational process. (I also believe it is, for the most part, currently practiced in an extremely unhealthy manner, but that is a subject for another book.)

The 'guru' here merely means someone whom people seek out for a variety of reasons. The 'disciple' indicates the people who seek the Guru out. Throughout history, the worst disasters have been caused by the combination of the guru/disciple relationship with the abuse of patriarchy. Why? The guru places himself between God and his disciples, blocking God from them.

This is the result of a collaboration between two parties: the Guru and his inner circle, and the disciples themselves. Sometimes the leader and his inner circle begin to transform him into a Guru, impressing those around him who become disciples; sometimes the disciples themselves, in their search for a guru, turn him into one. In any case, the net result is the same. The Guru blocks God from the sight of the disciples. In religious cases, the Guru (or his inner circle), in his disciples' eyes, becomes God's earthly image, the representative of God on earth, sole sponsor of all things divine.

What happens as a result of this blocking? Usually, there is a kind of collaboration between a tyrannical "I", and an extremist "We." This unholy alliance is the result of the disciples worshipping their guru, and leads to the blocking of God.

Before giving more concrete examples, I would like to make an important point: The Almighty has chosen the best and noblest sons of Adam to be His prophets. None of these attempted to make himself a guru, obtain disciples, or block God; on the contrary, they tried to liberate their people from their mindless worship of some idol, allowing the light of God to fill their people's hearts and souls. By "people" here, I mean their disciples, freed from their unwitting worship of the intermediary or idol. That is only natural. People recently liberated from worshipping a false god would enjoy their newly acquired awareness, brought on by their prophets. In a word: The best and noblest sons of Adam never sought to make themselves into gurus. They were never the destination; they merely led the way to the worship of the Almighty.

It is their followers' followers' followers who exploit the words of the prophets to set themselves up as demi-gods. It is easy for an inspiring political leader to turn into a guru. It is easy for a just tyrant to turn into a guru. It is easy for a powerful king, a military savior, a great thinker, a popular artist, a wealthy celebrity, a famous athlete, to turn into a guru; and of course there are the clerics, the easiest of all to turn into gurus. Of course, not every one of these will become one; but how do we tell the difference? The method is simple. Look, dear reader, into every historical tragedy in the history of nations; most probably, you will find some idol, some person who turned into a guru. People relinquished their minds, and let him (almost invariably

79

'him') think for them; they relinquished their will, and let him want for them; and the result was always disastrous.

To exist, a guru, a tyrannical "I", surrounded by the extremist "us", has always needed a "them" against which to define the "I/us." Most often, there is a clash between "Us" and "Them." Bloodshed and ruin tend to be the result. Hundreds of millions of deaths throughout history have resulted from the guru/disciple relationship. Holy wars between European nations in the Middle Ages, that killed millions, were nothing but clashes between gurus and their disciples. The Second World War, where 60 million died, was the result of a nationalist guru and his disciples on one side, and his enemies on the other. The intra-Islamic conflicts that have claimed millions of lives are the same. On a smaller scale, there are celebrities, athletes and artists and intellectuals, that have turned into gurus with their own disciples, and these celebrities exercise more influence over their fans than the fans' families, their religions and their societies.

There are countless examples, but in sum, the presence of a guru who places himself between God and his disciples results in the blocking of God from the consciousness and awareness of these disciples; this leads to a speedy descent into self-centeredness.

What do you think of the above? Make a note of all your observations.

———————————————————————————————

———————————————————————————————

———————————————————————————————

———————————————————————————————

———————————————————————————————

———————————————————————————————

———————————————————————————————

Celebrity, Self-Centeredness, and Blocking God

In societies where there is no political misuse of patriarchy, we may find a simpler manifestation of the concept of the Guru. A survey of politicians' opinions of successive American administrations will be split between those who see America as the devil incarnate or not, depending on whether or not they believe in the American dream. At the same time, the majority of these will praise the values of American society, such as kindness, openness, honesty and fairness. In this society, described by many as a healthy society, there is a factor that leads to the blocking of God, the cult of personality, or celebrity.

American society, like many Western societies today, is accustomed to 'boxing in' God; it only speaks of God in houses of worship or specially designated religious meetings. The 'gods' that overwhelmingly occupy people's day-to-day attention are celebrities. The media report 24/7 on these celebrities' lives: what they did, what they were wearing, where they dined, where they partied, where they vacationed, whom they married, whom they divorced, their children, their moods, and on and on and on. These celebrities are an essential ingredient of the social consciousness of this good society; recreational spaces, such as beaches and restaurants, are measured by their popularity with these demi-gods, the glitterati. This has gone beyond recreation to schools, hospitals, libraries and other public services, all measured by their popularity with the rich and famous demi-gods. Real estate prices soar when populated by celebrities.

Perhaps this obsession with the cult of celebrity has to do with the early Renaissance writings' preoccupation with the Greek gods (and we can of course comfortably assert that this was replicated in most parts of the world). Society's obsession with every aspect, important or otherwise, of celebrities' lives detracts from the brainspace devoted to God.

This is paralleled in the sky: the sun's brightness overshadows the stars' relatively dim light, which can only be seen when the sun's light is blocked. These stars, or celebrities, dazzle us in the absence of our awareness of God.

Before we move on, make a note of the factors that lead to self-centeredness in your own life. Are there any other factors you have encountered in your life's journey?

Personal Relationships under self-centeredness

Two things affect our personal relationships in self-centeredness. One of these is the win/lose paradigm, the adversarial position: we want to win, even if our partner loses. Every man for himself! Secondly, one tends to be reactive, not proactive, in relationships. Our relationship with our partner is largely formed by playing follow-the-leader. If they are violent, we follow suit; if they are calm, so are we; if honest, so are we, if they cheat, we do too, and so on and on whether they are honest, dishonest, untrustworthy, etc. What follows is a number of examples of relationships, bearing in mind that these are all manifestations of a single paradigm, symptoms of a single the disease.

The disease is this: the question "Where is God in my relationship?" does not even arise, although it is a question that needs to be kept as close as your body and soul. The presence of the question, in itself, is way more important than finding an answer.

Make a note of your relationships: When you are in a car and another driver screams at you, do you yell back, or do you think "Where is God?" and act accordingly? When your neighbors fail to keep their area clean, do you follow suit, or think of God? What about if your spouse screams at you, if you are plotted against at work, if your employees are cheating you, if your political opponents are fighting dirty, if your workplace is running on bribery, do you follow suit? Do you do as others do, or ask "Where is God?" The examples are endless; the answers are all similar. One either asks "Where is God?" or fails to do so, by chance or choice. You may choose to do what everyone does, or seek a nonexistent answer. You can choose to be "smart" or what people pityingly term "idealistic."

Smart vs. Idealistic

Smartness is internationally understood to mean the ability to win no matter the obstacle, and no matter the prize. An idealist is one who chooses not to win, even though they have the chance to, but places moral and ethical obstacles in his own way, based on society or based on God. I believe that the smart man seeks always to win, while the idealist seeks success.

Winning vs. Success

There is, I believe, a difference between the concept of winning and succeeding in people's minds. The first-place podium is too small for everyone to fit on it, whereas the plateau of success has room for everybody. Winning is a state of bitter competition, a virtuoso solo performance dominated by "I" and "Us." Success is a symphony of players in a grand orchestra that is larger than the concept of an "Us," although it includes it.

It is easy to be seduced by winning and its bitter competition under self-centeredness. Success, and its broad plateau, makes it easier to choose God-centric living. If bitter competition drags us into self-centeredness, our faith in ourselves and our abilities (and in others and their abilities) may have risen above our faith in God and His abilities. The pinnacle of success in God-centrism must lie in achieving God's purpose for you: the measure of success, and the measure of learning from failure, must follow the North Star of God's purpose, regardless of those who pityingly dub you 'idealist'. The sweetness of success while fulfilling God's purpose can never be understood by the winners who practice self-centeredness.

Make a note of what is going through your head. Do you have any examples? Write them down.

_____

_____

_____

_____

_____

_____

_____

I

The Worst Kind of Idolatry: Praying to God while Worshipping the Self

The Self is a creative genius – in the service of itself. This is the source of what I am proposing. Do the people who have chosen God (regardless of their religion) truly worship Him as He wishes? There are shocking signs of the reverse. I believe that some have arrived at an odd equation: praying to God while worshipping themselves. The holy books speak of this, in the dialogues of the prophets with the idolaters. Often, the latter would respond, "Why not worship both our gods and yours?" People often did not reject the call of prophets out of a rejection of God; they were merely reacting to the prophets' insistence that they not be allowed to worship both, their gods and the God of the prophets.

I believe that now is a similar age, with a difference. The idolaters of old had the courage, truthfulness and honesty to say clearly what they wanted. Now, these traits are gone. We are not honest enough with ourselves, or some of us, to see what we do: worshipping the Self while praying to God. An entire framework facilitates this: we live under self-centeredness, where we have tabulated our lives into columns for work, family, recreation, health, friends, fitness, etc., and boxed God into one of these columns. This came about unconsciously, little by little:

1- Some members of the dominant civilization do this as a reaction to the Church's stranglehold in the Middle Ages.

2- For others, belonging to the vanquished civilization, it is part of belonging to the broken civilization (civilization, not religion). History tells us that the vanquished imitates the victor and seeks to be like him; also, the victor is no longer an enemy, but a role model whose lifestyle the vanquished seeks to emulate (honesty, sincerity, efficiency, cleanliness, etc.).

3- Every manifestation of the vanquished civilization is misery, and since every manifestation of the victorious civilization is luxury.

4- Every impressive civilizational framework comes from the victorious civilization.

5- The victorious civilization is the mecca of science, where the world sends its best and brightest to learn; the mecca of medicine, where the world comes to be treated; the mecca of invention and development, and so on.

6- The velvet glove of the victorious civilization – its culture, its arts, its films, its music – is a sincere product of its dominant paradigm (self-centeredness) – is eagerly absorbed by the world as-is, or translated wholesale with its attendant values and principles.

The members of the vanquished civilization feel the pressure on their values and principles. Most of them present the confused diagnosis that it is their religion (mostly Islam) and not their civilization which are under pressure. But there is a great difference. They then accuse the victorious civilization of attacking Islam, ignoring the fact that there are many non-Muslims in the vanquished civilization who are under just as much pressure as Muslims. They also ignore that it is we, with our vanquished civilization, who are chasing after the victorious civilization and seek to copy it unchanged. This is all much easier to face than the fact that we have created a graven image to worship alongside God: ourselves.

These selves have found what they sought in a different paradigm. It is easier to adopt conspiracy theories than to admit that we have deteriorated over the centuries, and lost faith in ourselves and our ability to create paradigms that reflect our God-centrism, and present them to the very Other that we are racing to emulate. Unfortunately, with such low self-esteem, we can hardly compete; we have adopted the Other's paradigm wholesale. To ease our consciences, we have found a brilliant solution, which is just to call things by different names. Instead of calling ourselves "apathetic," instead of saying we are a "vanquished civilization", instead of saying that our paradigm is broken and defeated, we say there is a "war on Islam," or "a war on our principles" and so on, accusing the Other of attacking us, and relieving our consciences of the burden of guilt at constantly playing the victim.

This is not the whole truth. Everyone on the planet seeks their own interests. If someone else's interests are at odds with mine, and I am unable to fight for my rights, they will not fight for my rights on my behalf. What we are facing is competition, not conspiracy. It makes no sense to demand that the Other seek my own benefit, and call him a "conspirator" if he fails to do so. That would be like a football match where one team tries to score goals and the other merely wails, "Help, save us! Can't you see the conspiracy? Can't you see they are trying to score goals?" We love to do this, I think, to play the victim. It requires no effort, after all: all we need to do is sit at the café and complain about the global conspiracy against us, and drink our coffee, and go home feeling that we have done our duty. At the same time, we stare longingly and resentfully at our so-called conspirators, secretly and not-so-secretly wanting them to take us along for the ride on their victorious journey, conspiracies against us and all.

What we are doing is not new; every vanquished party does the same. Some have recovered; some have disappeared without a trace. History tells us that those who disappeared are those who spent their lives complaining and drinking coffee waiting for death. Those who recover are those who analyze and diagnose the reasons, then take the initiative to search for means of recovery, proactively. They know that the world has no room for whiners and complainers, but makes way for those who find solutions and carry them out. Those who recover do not insist that the world is full of conspiracies; they rightly call it competition, even unfair competition; "my opponent," they say, "is doing what's best for them; they won't do what's best for me, especially if I don't work for what's best for me, or stand up for myself." They know that there is no place for the weak in this world, and that we need to find a place for ourselves. We need to shoulder others aside to find our own space; then, we may do what's best for the weakest, out of our own moral values. Lying helplessly, complaining, and living as a victim is the ultimate victory of the Ego, and of self-centeredness. It's a classic case of the Ego dragging you into reactive behavior, keeping you helpless to do anything but protest and scream, thinking that the louder you yell, the more things will improve. When nothing changes, we move to what I call "ceasing to fight, the Ego's delight; the sweetest of systems, playing the victim."

Dear reader, I suggest you reread the last paragraph and make a note of your observations.

I

Victimhood and the Self Under Self-Centeredness

There are two manifestations of the victim role in our lives: the Self's Victim Violin Solo, and the Us, or the Collective Ego's, string ensemble. Here, we will address the solo performance by the Ego, and the second, ensemble performance later.

There is doubtless a certain sweetness to the role of victim. Once you cast yourself in the victim role, you enjoy the following:

- Others will lavish support and sympathy upon you; you will be able to enjoy the apathy conferred by victimhood, as one of the attributes of a victim is not doing anything to change their situation.

- You will find moral justification for all the envy and resentment you feel towards the person or circumstances that made you a victim, warranted or not.

- You will be able to withdraw from the present and enjoy living in the past, at the moment of the occurrence that made you a victim.

- You will enjoy collateral damage, i.e. physical and mental ailments resulting from the atmosphere you have decided to live in, or the unexplained disasters that fall upon your head, unaware that it is the victim identity you have chosen that makes you a magnet for ill-fortune, or perhaps falling behind your peers as a result of your passive acceptance of the victim role.

This is only part of it; please add your own after the following question. Try to remember a time when you played the part of a victim. Were you actually enjoying it? It takes effort to change from victim to survivor. It takes willpower. But I think it's worth it to get out of the victim role.

Just as we can slip into victimhood, we can climb out if we want to. How to do this will be handled later.

Stop reading for a moment and jot down your previous victim experiences. Try to recall your feelings while being a victim, then ask yourself: Would you like to go back there? Take down your internal dialogue.

I _____

Specialness, Ego-Stroking, and Self-Centeredness

The bigger the ego, the more self-centered one becomes. What has being special to do with ego? In his wonderful *New Earth,* Eghart Toll specifies that the ego is built on separation and identification: what follows is based on this profound definition.

Based on the above, why are the best-known brands the most expensive? Because they make us special. This short question and answer are the basis for the fashion industry, on which a giant industrial complex is built. Most of us would prefer, if we can afford it, to buy the 'best' – i.e. best-known and most expensive – brands of car, clothing, watches, eyewear, shoes, perfumes, and shoes. When I buy an Armani shirt or my wife buys an Issey Miyake scarf, we do so to tell the world that we are special. If we can afford it, we buy new clothes not when the old ones wear out, but when fashions change. Being seen in the latest fashions affords me a sense of status and superiority over others in their old clothes, and so on.

The big tycoons, aware of this desire, pander to it. What they produce is not luxury goods but specialness. That is why there are new collections for every season, and new auto models every year, even if the only difference between this year's and last year's model is the color of the turn signals – but what matter? Won't whoever sees these turn signals know that this car is of the very latest model, and that its owner, by extension, is Special? And so on with luxury products of all kinds: we want to buy specialness, and the manufacturers oblige.

There are also varying degrees of specialness: some people want to be even more special than others, to show off their extreme wealth. So limited-edition, high-priced products were invented, to make their owner special among the special.

What about those of modest means? Not a problem. An industry has sprung up, built on creating knockoffs – affordable copies of luxury goods. The idea of specialness is everywhere: the gated community, with fences to keep out undesirables, special people's clubs, in the form of exclusive gyms, and on and on. These are all very popular because they sell their members something important: the security of knowing that they are different from the others outside these walls. They are Special.

But what is that part of us that thirsts for specialness? What is the other part that only cares about how it appears to others? The Self, and

93

its Captain of the Guard, the Ego. Why? Because the latter overpowers the Self and convinces it that this specialness is one of its best defenses against others. After all, there must be others to be more special *than*, and there must also be others to see how special I am, or else the whole process loses its meaning. If a couple are invited by wealthy friends to spend a holiday at an exclusive resort, the preparations for such an excursion will involve buying new clothes, perfumes, eyewear and so on, to live up to the company they will be keeping. Now imagine that the trip is cancelled, and the couple decides to spend a pleasant weekend alone together in the woods. Will there be this much concern for appearance? I doubt it; there is no-one there to show off *for*. Self and Ego need an Other to justify their defensiveness and activity; without an Other, such activity and such defenses become meaningless.

The activity of the global production machine, feeding my need to be better than others, hums along on a giant scale. Hundreds of millions of people earn a living in its factories; millions more make a living marketing what it sells, specialness. An important point needs to be made here. These manufacturers want to make money from consumers. Their ultimate aim was never to activate the Ego when seeking profits; it was a by-product. They mercilessly used all the tools at their disposal to empty our pockets: marketing, media, etc., to lead to a cornerstone of modern economy: consumption. These three words: marketing, media, and consumption – have had a malignant effect on the growth and expansion of the Self and the Ego within individuals, and in society.

Is there some way to be special that occurred to you as you read? Make a note of it here.

_____

_____

_____

_____

_____

Consumption, Marketing, and the Media: Effects on the Ego

The culture of consumption is a cornerstone of modern Western economy. The rise and continuation of this culture is justified as follows: a factory produces a certain product, and employs a certain number of workers. If we can increase sales, the owner of the factory makes more profit, and as profit accumulates, a new factory will be built, providing jobs to more workers. These workers will earn an income, in turn becoming consumers, buying this and other products, increasing the profits of the factory-owner and others like him; a third factory is built, giving jobs to another batch of workers, and so on. This is a model with proven success, if we ignore that it threatens to destroy the planet, but that is a matter for another book. Many praise its positive results. However, for the purposes of this book, a question arises: how does this model affect the ego? Indirectly, but powerfully.

Consumption's brigadier-general is marketing; this depends on the most influential power in modern history, the media, and its stepchild, advertising. "We must learn what products are on offer so as to have free choice," an apparently innocent statement that may lead to the destruction of the planet. The beginnings were humble: we needed a way to alert potential consumers that we had some product they needed, and might not know was available. It then developed into the right to find out about every product to make comparisons and buy the most suitable; means of communication proliferated, until the fatal blow: the invention of television.

Television, in and of itself, is a wonderful invention, but its misuse can lead to disaster. Its profound effects on our consciousness demonstrated almost unbelievable success in marketing products – commercial products, ideas, and ideologies. It was the marketing tool that marketers had never dreamed of.

The tools of marketing – media and advertising – rely on the subconscious as well as the conscious mind. A TV commercial, for instance, may urge you to buy a house or car, and tell you to "Call Now" the number on the screen for a visit or a test-drive. This is an example of addressing your conscious mind, the aim of which is to make you get up, go to the phone, and make a call to make an appointment to investigate the product. Here, the role of marketing ends; once you have made the call to their sales department, their job is done. The next step is for the sales department to close the sale; if they do, the salesperson disappears, giving way to a third party, the customer service agent. This is all addressed to the conscious mind of the consumer, a group effort of marketing, sales, and after-sales service; the effort, and the labor, is divided among the team members, each in their job.

There is another means, dealing with the subconscious. This is harder. Advertising a brand of coffee, liquor or clothing does not presuppose you jumping up from your screen and heading to the supermarket. The goal here is to stick in your head, so that when you find yourself in the supermarket to pick up a few necessities, and catch sight of the product in the commercial, the attractive commercial springs to mind, replete with the benefits of the product, making you buy it. Marketers discovered that memorable commercials make an impression on the subconscious, and mobilize an array of sounds and images that make it cling.

Let us say that a certain drink is endorsed by a beloved celebrity: the subconscious associates the image of this celebrity (in the case of an actor or athlete) or their voice (in the case of a singer) with the drink, reminding us of the drink whenever we see or hear that celebrity. This is the work of the subconscious. Well, what has that to do with the ego? What happens is that with the global growth of production, an urgent need for marketing channels has sprung up, to spur a consumption explosion to keep pace with this production explosion. This explosion has, I must admit, been created with admirable efficiency, despite its tragic consequences.

What I Want vs. What I Need

This explosion has been created by confusing two things in the minds of consumers: a desire for a product and a conviction that you need that product. Slow down and think a little about that last, and look at your own self from this perspective, then keep reading.

If you look around you, you will see that the message that most advertisements have in common around the world is, "You need this product." The concept of *wanting* is all but extinct. There is a great difference between what you need and what you want. What you want is more than what you have; you would like to have it, but you can certainly do without it. What you need is a lack of a necessary thing; you will suffer so long as you do not have it. To control your thoughts and transform your wants into needs, we focus on you. We focus on your Self and the improvement in your appearance if the product concerns appearance: clothing, accessories, perfume, makeup, slimming aids, and other things that will make you 'special'. We tell you that if you do not rush to buy the product, the Other will vanquish you; the Other will be more attractive, sweeter-smelling, thinner, in a word, more special. The same goes for your home: all sorts of ideas to improve your social position, your children's physical and emotional well-being, and to make your wife as beautiful and perpetually smiling as the model in the commercial! This miracle can only happen if you swap out your bathroom, your kitchen, your windows, plates, cups and so on, and preferably buy a whole new house. You will also be more refined, of a higher class… and Special! If you do not, well, you allow the Other to become better than you; not only that, but They will form a clique, in their gated communities, and look down on you and laugh. How much better, then, to join Them and become one of Us, and look down on some other Them from on high.

All these are subliminal messages, invisible and implicit. Most commercials now are based on these messages: different forms of pressure to become special, and threats of the Other becoming better than you if you do not give in and buy. Mission accomplished: "I want" has been turned into "I need." But again, what has Ego to do with this?

The fact is that Ego is at the heart of the matter. Deliberately or not, the buttons to activate Ego have been pushed. I/Others/Specialness/Threat. This has resulted in the consciousness-washing, and unconsciousness-washing, of the consumer, by activating the individual and collective ego. This in turn activates self-centeredness.

Make a note of what you want and what you need in your life, and the difference between them.

_____

_____

_____

_____

Media under Self-Centeredness

When the sport of boxing started out, decades ago, it had no clear rules. After a while, it became an organized sport, with clearly defined regulations. With the passage of time, people realized that a professional boxer could potentially fatally injure an opponent with his bare fists; some countries classified boxers' fists as deadly weapons.

Similarly, at the dawn of civilization, anyone who could was allowed to own weapons; later, this right was confined to the aristocracy, in a form of class distinction. Some theorists, such as Max Weber (1864-1920), laid out their conception of the modern state: only the state could legitimately use armed violence. This greatest of liberated thinkers saw no issue with confining the use of armed violence to the apparatuses of the state. Even in the most liberal countries, no citizen is allowed to own military aircraft, tanks or nuclear submarines. The ownership of these is confined to the state.

I believe that the media, like a boxer's fists, and like military armaments, cannot be allowed to remain in the hands of individuals indiscriminately, unregulated, in the name of freedom. Such a powerful instrument, I insist, is so dangerous and destructive in today's world that it must be classified as a weapon, and some new way found to regulate it. One incident, I believe, is a canary in the coal mine for the importance of media effects on the populace.

In February 1917, US president Woodrow Wilson was re-elected on a number of platforms, most important among which was keeping the US neutral and thus out of World War 1. In April of the same year – just three months later – Wilson asked Congress for war against Germany, and the motion passed overwhelmingly, 373 to 50, bolstered by tremendous pro-war public opinion. How did this happen? Simply, the media industry. The American media – only print in that era, before the advent of television – coordinated with the US administration to print truths and dubious documents such as the Zimmerman Telegram, in which Germany offered a military alliance to Mexico, and embarked on a concerted effort to brainwash the American people into wanting war – the same population who, three short months earlier, had elected Wilson on an anti-war platform!

The matter was hushed up. Another weapon was added to the deadly arsenal: the media. The bloody results of World War II came about partly because this deadly weapon was wielded by Hitler and Mussolini. It has been in the hands of those who use it for good or abuse it for evil ever since, from the propaganda of dictators to the publicity of multinational corporations. The victims are the billions of people on the face of this earth.

The media, I believe, reigns unchallenged as the world's most powerful weapon. Its dangers lie not only in its effectiveness but in the philosophy it is based on. The absolute majority of media establishments worldwide are merely copies of the media establishments in Europe at the dawn of the twentieth century, and in America at its close. These media establishments control, not to say brainwash, the collective consciousness of their citizens in their respective countries. They fill people's minds with whatever ideas or imaginings they wish, whether their own or as a front for another who uses them for their benefit. When I say 'media establishments', I am referring to complete empires in every sense: unofficial empires, starting with media schools, governmental institutions and private media organizations that control print, audio and visual media, as well as research centers and so on.

A discussion with a mogul of any of these worldwide empires into the content or philosophy of what they do will most probably yield the following answer: "I fulfil the viewer's right to know." A closer look will reveal that the media establishment rests on two main pillars: the viewer, and the information. Naturally, if you follow on the first question with a second, namely "Where is God in this system?" you will gain only a puzzled look, no matter where or when you ask it. The response – explicit or implicit – will be, "What's God got to do with it?" –an honest answer if you can get it. It is certainly true that the rabid, deadly media structure worldwide is based on self-centeredness, represented by viewers' rights, the interests of media moguls, etc., and that God is completely absent from it.

This is not an accusation, it is a diagnosis. Why? Because when the strongest and most savage influence in the world is built on self-centeredness, we must be aware that it influences the billions it addresses, luring them away from God-centrism and into self-centeredness. Whether this is intentional or unintentional is another story; my focus here is to alert the reader to the power of this influence upon us, exercised almost 24/7/365.

Dear reader, make a note of your personal experience with these three elements: marketing, media and consumption. Set down your feelings, questions and impressions regarding these experiences.

_____

_____

_____

_____

_____

_____

_____

_____

_____

_____

_____

_____

_____

_____

Beauty vs. Luxury

Beauty is a God-given value that nourishes the soul. As humans, we enjoy beauty and are nourished by it. Enjoyment occurs in the moment, while nourishment endures. A lovely view from, say, the window of a train, leads us to pause and feast our eyes before returning to our activities. This simple example of appreciation via vision has parallels with each of our other senses, auditory, olfactory and so on. Beautiful birdsong, a delicious fruit, a sweet-smelling flower, are all forms of beauty: nourishment means the persistence of beauty in your life, feeding your soul daily, for example if your home overlooks a lake or other natural source of beauty, or is surrounded by singing birds, or fragrant flowers, providing your soul with what it needs every day. Daily nourishment of the soul leads to a compassionate heart.

Since many of us have no access to such daily sources of beauty, this has provided an impetus for the global consumption engine to spring into action, offering products to nourish the senses to people of different income levels. We now have an incredible array of fashions, perfumes, arts, food, and music to satisfy every taste and nourish every soul. This has generated two paradigms for our relationship to beauty: a self-centered relationship, and a God-centric relationship.

Beauty Under Self-Centeredness

When the Self holds the reins, we run the risk of enjoyment and nourishment turning into gluttony. The Self is an insecure hoarder: fearing famine, it hoards nourishment for the body (food and drink) and the soul (things to enjoy with the senses). Since insecurity is always the main motivator under self-centeredness, the time spent in getting, hoarding, and storing this food for our souls is far greater than the time spent enjoying it. We have no time to enjoy the beautiful things we already own – clothing, homes, perfumes, et cetera – because our mad desire to accumulate more and more, and our fear of losing them, eats up the time and opportunity to enjoy them.

Try and observe how this manifests in yourself. Try not to use it to judge others; that will only activate Ego. Merely make a note of how Ego does what it does best, namely use all available resources to build a defensive wall of 'specialness' – how it takes beauty, food for the soul, and instead of allowing you to enjoy it, turns it into a tool for competition with others.

Observe how Ego turns beauty into luxury.

I

Luxury

With self-centeredness, food for the soul, such as beauty, can turn into competition tools for the Ego. The question here is, how do we know whether our appreciation of beauty is nourishing our soul, or providing a tool of competition for the Ego?

The answer? The Other.

Observe whether your relationship with beauty is directed at your own soul first, and at others second, or the reverse. In the former case, it is nourishment for the soul, and in the latter, it is a competitive tool for the Ego. If you want the best home, clothing, view, etc., that you can afford for yourself and those you love, in accordance with your own taste and what nourishes your soul regardless of what others think of it, you have probably departed from beneath the skies of self-centeredness. However, if your aesthetic choices are dictated by others' opinions, and you find yourself selecting the most expensive 'designer' items, you have probably moved from beauty to luxury.

Luxury items are beautiful things that are costly, expensive, and exclusive. Luxury is owning, or wearing, designer items even if they aren't comfortable and don't suit you, since all that matters is what others think. It is breaking the bank to fill your home with things to impress your guests, even if you never use them and don't really like them all that much. In short: You appreciate beauty for yourself, and assume luxury for others. When your goal is luxury, you are squarely in a place of self-centeredness.

Beauty turned into an industry when it began to manifest as "luxury items." The engines of production began to whirr, in service of the ego and not in the service of enjoyment. Luxury products sprang up everywhere: cars, tools, homes, makeup. One of the most prominent examples of beauty being transformed into luxury is the yachting world: these industries are based on the right of the rich to acquire the best, fastest and sleekest seagoing vehicles, and an entire industry of marinas, marine furnishings, and entertainment options surrounds it. If we count the hours, or days, per year that these yachts are used, it seems a waste of money – thousands, indeed millions, of dollars' expenditure on something that is only used a few hours per year; but that is not to say that these items have not fulfilled their purpose! They have advertised to others that So-and-So is rich enough to own a yacht, whether or not they actually use it.

Make a note of your observations of the sources of beauty and luxury in your life, then write down the questions you have about them.

Controlling Access to Beauty

Under self-centeredness, as a result of the overpowering culture of insecurity, a means to calm this fear – not get rid of it, for it never completely goes away – is controlling access to beauty. Instead of enjoying natural locations such as the seaside, parks and rivers, the Self works towards gaining exclusive access to them, motivated by the fear that it will one day be deprived of access to them. Instead of visiting them, it makes attempts to own them, or parts of them, to ensure its continued ability to enjoy such beauty. The rights of others to enjoy it are not taken into account. Every Self for himself!

As a result, we now have luxury real estate, offering us second homes overlooking natural beauty that nourishes our soul. When we tally up the time we spend in these places, it is probably about the same number of days that others spend in the same locations without going to the trouble and expense of buying homes and maintaining them – in hotels, renting empty homes, or camping.

"But", I hear you say, "it's an investment!" Well and good; but take a moment to check whether this isn't the voice of Ego, attempting to protect what it views as your protection, especially as it has an entire global real-estate complex behind it, worth millions of dollars and employing millions of workers, all laser-focused on the Ego within you and its need to defend your right to own a piece of beauty in the form of real estate.

Interestingly, your ownership of a piece of this beauty may prevent you from actually enjoying it. The Ego, competitive by nature, forces you into an exhausting competitive position by constantly asking, "Is what I have better than others'?" This ownership also deprives you of enjoying the beauty that exists in every corner of this beautiful planet. Once you have expended money and effort on acquiring a piece of beauty, this actually limits your freedom to visit numerous sites of beauty: you have, after all, the right and obligation to make use of your investment. You think you own beauty: in fact, it is this place that owns you, your freedom, your time, and your life.

Does this mean that anyone who seeks to buy a home in a beautiful location is a victim of the Self or the Ego? On the contrary. To check, go back to the basic rule: What is the weight of the Other in this decision of mine? The honest answer to this question will tell you what paradigm you are operating from when you decide.

_____

_____

_____

_____

_____

_____

_____

_____

_____

_____

_____

_____

_____

I

The Minimum and Maximum with God

Let's think about the following examples:

When grocery shopping, we get the best we can afford, not just any old thing. Why? Because we probably are not only thinking of the bare minimum when selecting food. When buying clothing, we buy the best we can afford, again because we aren't seeking the bare minimum. It's the same with choosing a home and a school for our children; even at school, many of us tried to get good grades so as to get into as good a university as possible. I could give endless examples of this, because most people try to improve their living situation as much as they can – a normal and healthy situation. Let us now approach the bare minimum as it applies to God. It is normal to find out how much fasting, praying, etc., is required of us; often we go to great pains to find out God's purpose for us, then compare ourselves with others, and feel secure in the knowledge that we are doing as much as others, or warm ourselves with the observation that there are many others around us who do even less than we do. In real terms, we discover the minimum that God asks of us and do our best to do as little as we can of it. Think a little: isn't this mostly what happens in our relationship with God? With ourselves, we find the maximum and try to achieve as much of it as we can; with God, we find the minimum and try to achieve as little of it as we can.

I merely mention this to draw your attention to it. If it doesn't apply to you, well and good; if it does, then let me further ask you: Must this be the way we interact with God? No; it is a sign of self-centeredness.

Make a note of your questions about the above, and set down your experiences with this.

_____

_____

_____

_____

_____

I

Despotic Regimes Under Self-Centeredness

In societies ruled by despotic regimes, a culture of fear prevails. This has two main effects, direct and indirect, both dragging us into a place of self-centeredness. Both of these are results of self-centeredness, while the presence of both indicates the presence of an environment suited to self-centeredness.

Direct Effects: As mentioned above, fear is the primary motivator for egotistical activity, and every despotic society's means of asserting its control is spreading a culture of fear. All day long, people in despotic societies are bombarded with messages telling them they are being watched, and that punishment for missteps will be swift and severe. Their days pass in fear; they work, play, socialize in fear; in short, moment by moment, fear saturates every moment of their daily lives, seeping into their cells and becoming an integral part of their constitution.

Indirect Effects: Such a culture of fear, manifested in practical applications in society, generates a general atmosphere where the Ego flourishes and self-centeredness is virtually assured. Despotic regimes operate on 'divide and rule,' and work against any sense of community that might potentially rise up against them. They also use different means to pit diverse groups against one another, which deepens the rift. If we look at the communal ego of divided and warring factions of society, we find the results, *par excellence,* of the collective Ego, or the Us. Every entity forms a tribe; each tribe divides the world into those who belong, and those who threaten it from outside. Fear reigns supreme: fear for the tribe and its members, and fear of the Other tribes and their members. Different groups seek to outdo one another and compete fiercely, a competition encouraged by the despot and his apparatchiks. If society is steeped in these two factors, the individual and collective ego reigns supreme – an unquestioned victory for self-centeredness.

Despotism and its Effects on our Relationship with God

It has been mentioned above that in despotic societies, fear is the primary value in society, and the main conduit for the relationship between the ruler and his subjects, the apparatuses of the state, are pressed into service to implement a reign of terror. Every despot seeks to make his subjects fear his power rather than his person; he surrounds himself with the trappings of power, placing many layers between himself and the common people, making himself virtually impossible to see, and creating more fear of his person and his power.

Any despot is careful not to allow any member of society to feel secure enough to start plotting against him, or organizing with their fellow-citizens to get rid of him and his tyranny. He places huge photographs of himself in public places, and appears constantly in the media as an undefeated and undefeatable superman, establishing the image in the mind of the populace that their ruler is a hunter and they the prey; a predator/prey relationship is established.

All unconsciously, we find ourselves treating God the way we treat the ruler: as part of the general culture of fear, insecurity, and predator/prey. Two things happen as a result of this:

- Fear turns into an unhealthy culture of defeat, which reflects on our relationship with God. People who know nothing but fear will unwittingly base their relationship with God on this; all too often, tyrants encourage it, and use it in their favor, either directly by propagating the image of themselves as God's proxy on earth, to be feared by any God-fearing person, or indirectly by planting the seeds of fear so deep in society that nothing else can take root. A distorted view of the Almighty is formed in the minds of the populace: a vindictive, predatory God lying in wait to torment them.

- It is human nature to shrink from what we fear. People in these defeated societies start to put distance between themselves and the predatory God. Separated from God by fear – broken fear – we lose contact with the divine attributes of love, compassion, kindness, gentleness and justice, the very attributes that the Divine Spirit within us uses to communicate with those around it. By allowing these attributes to atrophy, we diminish the divine presence within us, ceding the space to the individual and collective ego. Unhealthy fear of God replaces healthy love of God. If the love of God is absent from a society, it becomes cold and cruel; if you add fear to the mix, we can then comfortably predict misery and despair, coldness and cruelty.

Egotism Under Self-Centeredness

I would like to make it clear that a person living under self-centeredness is not necessarily selfish, egotistical or lacking in morals. Selfishness, in some definitions, is placing one's interests above those of others, while egotism is an inflated view or estimation of oneself. The difference between the two can be illustrated by a simple example. If you go into a room with a selfish person, and there are four oranges on a table, and you are both hungry, the selfish person knows perfectly well that your share is two oranges each; however, being selfish, his only concern, upon finishing his share, is how to take part or all your share away. If the same thing happens with a self-centered person, this person will *truly believe* that his share is four oranges, or three at the very least. A selfish person shares with others their awareness of his rights vis-à-vis theirs, and tries to take away what is theirs with malice aforethought. Egotists are not aware of, or in accordance with others about, their rights: when others demand their rights, they genuinely feel as if they have been subjected to an injustice, because they believe, with certainty, that it is their right.

I believe, further, that every selfish person as well as every egotistical person *must* be living under self-centeredness. The reverse is not true, though: not everyone who lives under self-centeredness is an egotist. How? It is entirely possible to live under self-centeredness, with people who share your choice, and develop, with your community, a wonderful value system: sharing, honesty, sincerity, efficiency, fairness, giving, and any number of positive values. You may have agreed upon a refined goal for yourselves, comfort and happiness, and realized that this system of values is the best path to achieving it.

"But what's so bad about that?" you may ask. The question isn't complete without asking, "Whom am I doing this for?" There are two parts to the answer, the first, "What is 'bad' and what is 'good'?" and the second, "Whom are we doing this for?"

There are two possible answers to the first question. The first occurs when your Self takes over, mobilizing your selfishness and egotism; this translates into a negative relationship with those around you. Most people would consider this bad. The second occurs when you and those around you believe in a virtuous moral code, and apply it so that you can all live happily. Most people would classify this as 'good.'

The second answer, in turn, bears two possibilities, being motivated by God-centrism, or being motivated by self-centeredness.

a. Motivated by God-centrism: You desire God's approval and love. You apply the aforementioned virtuous moral code, which is good for you and those around you, because God tells us that this is the path to His love and approval. You obey God by treating those around you according to a divinely-inspired moral code, seeing God in all His creatures, and treating them with kindness and friendliness accordingly, wishing the best for them, for yourself, and for those around you as part of an absolute moral code aimed at fulfilling God's purpose for you to treat those around you well.

b. Motivated by self-centeredness: You want the best for you and yours and those around you. You apply a moral code you all agree upon. These codes are changeable, by mutual consent from all concerned. You want the best for you and those around you as part of a relative moral code, whose ultimate goal is what your Self wants for you and yours. In any case, the recipients of your kindness will be grateful. Your motivation makes no difference to us; the difference concerns you alone. Are you applying a virtuous moral code of which you are the center, or of which God is the center?

"Well, what difference does it make? Isn't what matters helping people and having the right morals?"

To us – the recipients of your kindness – it makes no difference. To you, the giver, it makes all the difference in the world.

God-centrism, Charity-Centrism, and Self-Centeredness

God does not necessarily reside in Charity; but everything, including Charity, resides in God.

What does this mean? What's the difference?

An example may make this clearer. Medical charities that work in remote regions of the world devote their efforts to treating people in disaster-stricken regions, where war, conflicts, epidemics, and so on, pose a danger to all who go there. As a result of the high risks, regular rescue organizations will not send personnel there; but the members of these noble organizations do. Let us imagine, dear reader, that you and I are doctors on the staff of one of these rescue organizations, working in Africa; you in the arena of God-centrism, and I in the arena of self-centeredness. What would our conversation look like?

You: Why did you volunteer here?

Me: Because this region needed doctors. What about you?

You: The same reason. But you know this region is dangerous, don't you? Why risk your life?

Me: Because there are people here who need me. What about you?

You: Same reason. I don't think it's right to ignore people who need me. But tell me, why do you do what you do?

Me: Well, chivalry and altruism. I think those are the greatest human values. They make me feel that I've really done something good. I can face myself in the mirror. And you?

You: I'm just the same. The same values, really, make me feel I've done good. But why do you want to do good?

Me: I just told you. Just doing good makes me feel good about myself. What about you?

You: I feel good about myself when I do as God commanded, and God commands me to do good, and I need another person to do good. When I do good, I feel I've fulfilled God's commands and His will; that's what makes me feel good.

This dialogue could very well be repeated in various aspects of life. Some notes: The answers are virtually identical. The person under self-centeredness stops at doing good, while the God-centric person has an extra answer in addition to doing good, which is that he does good for others because of God, because God commands it, or because he loves God in His creatures.

This is what I mean by saying that charity need not contain God, although God contains charity. Not everyone who lives under self-centeredness is selfish, bad or disgusting. On the contrary – they may be good people, but they do good because it makes them feel good, not because God wills it. People who take charity as their center are in fact living under self-centeredness, although they have a noble spirit.

Do you have relevant experience or questions about charity-centric living? Take your time thinking, then make notes.

I _____

_____

_____

_____

_____

_____

_____

_____

_____

_____

_____

_____

_____

_____

_____

_____

_____

_____

_____

_____

Dying for God for the Self and for "Us"

To examine this subject, I'm going to ask you to imagine being a situation where you decide to give up your dear life for God. I'm going to claim that the most valuable resource God has given you to achieve what He wants of you is *you*. We can probably agree on the fact that you have only one life, and no second chance to get it back if there turns out to be some error in your assessment of the thing for which you sacrificed your life. A question thus presents itself: How can you be absolutely certain that this sacrifice is, in fact, for God?

Let's imagine two scenarios.

Scenario One: Your social, economic and political situation is abysmal. You are overcome with despair; you have given in to the victim role. You have decided – prompted by the thoughts of others, or independently – to put a dramatic end to your life, taking with you a large number of those whom you believe – possibly rightly – to be the reason for your misery. Does this count as dying for God? Think, then think again. Isn't there a possibility that Self here is the leader in this enterprise? The signs of Ego are everywhere, pressing you to achieve its own ends in defiance of, not in accordance with, what God wills.

Profiting at God's Expense: By "profit," I mean that your Self rejects the challenges you face in life as part of God's destiny, and tempts you with what seems like an offer you can't refuse: Why not get rid of all life's pain, suffering and difficulties, while receiving an ironclad contract to Paradise? And the price is cheap – a few seconds of suffering while dying! We allow our minds to be seduced and surrender completely to the Self's blandishments, rechristening our decision to withdraw from life and reject God's Destiny "dying for God." We accept the falsification practiced by the Self so as to believe this new nomenclature.

Scenario Two: Your social, economic and political situation is abysmal. You don't give up. You do everything within your power: you work hard, you struggle, you innovate, to change things for you and yours, and for those around you. You are creating a new paradigm: *living for God*. After years of unrelenting toil, you achieve it; alternatively, you work towards it all your life, but die before achieving it. Which of these two scenarios, in your opinion, is undertaken for God, and which is undertaken for the Self?

Let's think and examine both. Each of the above scenarios has its own form and content. The drama of Scenario 1 is certainly impressive and final, but the content is dubious. Scenario 2, while lacking an impressive blaze of glory, is actually closer to achieving what God intended for you. The first question I ask myself to make sense of my actions, and which I ask you to ask yourself as well, is, "Where is God in this? Where is God's purpose?"

Since God doesn't need anything, being the Owner of everything, and since He sent others to us so that we might love them and treat them well in Him, seeking and finding God's purpose through others, I shall add another question: "Where is the Other in this? Where is their best interest? Does the best interest of others supersede mine, or the reverse?"

If you ask yourself these questions in Scenario 1, requiring you to give up your life for God, it may help you make sense of the main motivator behind it. You do, though, need to strip your contemplation of all extraneous matter, so as to limit your question to two possibilities: the Almighty, and the Self. Then, seek your answer before Him, with Him and only Him. Imagine, analyze, think, enumerate, and strip away all noise – then seek your answer.

Before I leave you to think of the above, dear reader, I will leave you with two additional questions. Do you imagine that dying for God, doing your very best to withdraw from life with all haste and speed, out of desperation, rage or fear, is the same as dying (sooner or later, it makes no difference in my opinion) after a life spent in doing everything you possibly can to secure a life lived for God for you and yours and for those around you?

Do you think Scenario 1 is a genuine attempt to fulfil God's purpose for His sake, or an attempt to fulfil it for your own? And what's the difference? The difference is immense: the former is a use of your own self in the service of God, while the latter is a use of God in the service of yourself. What a difference!

The Self is slippery and tricky: beware its deceptions! Not only could it ruin your life, but it could ruin your afterlife – so beware! Remember, the Self can subvert the nobility of dying for God into dying for Self. Dying for God in the service of the Self, individual or collective, is the Ego's ultimate triumph. Dying for God, I believe, can only be achieved through your struggle to find a life for God for you and yours, and for others. Anything else is a rejection of God's Destiny, and a withdrawal from life.

The issue of death under self-centeredness is food for thought. Make a note of your impressions here.

I

Freedom under Self-Centeredness

An understanding of freedom under self-centeredness will help avoid much confusion; it will not solve everything, but it will assist in arriving at a correct diagnosis. There is a prevailing idea in the vanquished civilization – Islam – that Western societies, especially European societies, are in a state of moral decline. Evidence of this is usually trotted out in the form of sexual liberation, gay freedoms and the general state of undress that prevails, especially on beaches, plus the freedom to consume alcohol and, more recently, drugs. If you ask how this can be when most people, even the most ardent preachers of the theory of moral decline, turn to European societies as the best examples of hard work, cleanliness, respect for neighbors, environmental awareness, respect for diversity and minority rights, not to mention truthfulness, politeness, good manners, appreciation for art and culture, and so on, the answer is, "Well, they're afraid of the law. Without the law, they would turn into savages." If you respond that it is a high moral value in itself to have laws that are universally respected by their communities, the answer will be, "But they're a heartless society! If they saw someone lying in the street, they wouldn't lift a finger!" If you should then respond, "If a society's charity can be measured by the ratio of charities to citizens, how do you explain that this ratio is highest in the societies that you call "morally deficient?" and if you alert them to the fact that most international charity organizations that help every country worldwide – even theirs – are based in these "morally deficient" societies, they have a pat and ready response: "These charities are only a front, concealing other interests," then return to the original point, "Can any society be said to be moral, when it engages in such sexual debauchery?" Your interlocutor will then announce confidently that these are Godless societies. If you retort that they certainly do believe in God, and that places of worship for the Abrahamic religions are everywhere, not to mention that the constitutions of these nations guarantee freedom of worship, or if you alert them to the fact that self-dubbed "conservative" societies have the most hits on porn sites worldwide, and that the ratio of sexual repression and sex crimes is through the roof, you will be met with bewilderment and sometimes anger for not agreeing with their preconceived notions, or perhaps wry smiles as a front for confusion.

The issues will be the same if you enter into the same dialogue, only this time with a member of the aforementioned advanced societies. Here, too, you will find that they view these conservative societies, the Islamic communities mentioned earlier, are barbaric and savage groups of people driven by their primal urges whose only concern, and the only lens through which they see things, is their sexual desires. This, they say, is a type of animal instinct which only time can cure. You will further hear that conservative societies place no value on individual freedom within the law. If you ask one of these people, "How can you judge these societies as barbaric and driven by instinct when they complain of your own total freedom? They are only trying to preserve their traditions, values, habits and identity, which are incompatible with yours; it's only fair, as part of the freedoms you call for, is to respect diversity," your conversation will end with much the same wry smiles and perplexed stares.

Neither of the two camps is going to move an inch; neither will abandon their ideas. Each of them lies in wait for the other, watching the news with confirmation bias at the ready, waiting for reinforcement of their certainty about the other party. In my opinion, each party is looking at the other from their own side of the fence, unwilling to move from their own space to understand the Other. When we do so, we become more understanding, and hence more accepting, of our own differences – provided, of course, that we do want to understand them, regardless of who the Us is, and who the Them.

Another suggestion may be helpful in the attempt to understand. The issue is not morality or religion; it goes deeper. I believe that it is based on a paradigm. You may remember when, in the Introduction, I used the example of the solar system. Just as the sun is the center of the solar system, in the self-centered paradigm, we place the Self in the center, in the place of the sun, and God along with the planets, orbiting the sun. This manifests in day-to-day living when we prioritize our own desires and wants over God's, although he is present in our lives, only boxed into a time and place, as I have explained above. If we apply this paradigm to freedom under self-centeredness, we can find the key to the code that causes all this confusion.

Under self-centeredness, I have absolute freedom. I am free to do as I please with my mind, heart, and body. These elements take priority, despite my belief in God – I repeat, despite my belief in God.

For example, physical freedom might be described by someone living under self-centeredness as follows: "I have absolute freedom to do as I will with my body, because it's mine. If I want to sunbathe nude, I'm free to do so. If I want to put it on display, I can. I can have sex with whomever I please, whenever I please. I can have sex with someone of my own gender or someone else, change my gender from male to female, change my face and body as I please. I can fill it up with intoxicants, inject the drugs I want. I'm free to do as I please with my own body as long as I don't break the law I've pledged to obey. If I believe this law has become too narrow for my freedoms, I will seek to change it through legitimate channels to obtain more freedom within the law." For this reason, anything that was illegal years ago and is now legal forces those who objected to it and turned up their noses in disgust at it some years ago, to respect others' freedom to do whatever that thing is: they are, of course, free to do what they please with their bodies so long as they do not break the law. This is manifested in abortion laws, gay marriage, gay rights, relaxed drug laws in some countries, etc.

There is a great deal of honesty and sincerity on the part of people practicing what they see as their freedom, in all good faith. These are people who walk the walk. You can see this in how different societies treat nudity. In the self-centered civilization, wearing revealing clothing is a manifestation of freedom. Everyone on the beach in these societies, from young to old, wears revealing swimwear. Why is this? Because it is the costume best suited to practicing one's freedoms in that place, whether the freedom to enjoy the sun and surf, show off one's beach body, etc. The source here is the practice of freedom, not moral dissolution: for this reason, there is a sense of *rightness* about the place. Why is this? Because the beachgoers don't feel they're doing anything wrong; everyone is practicing their freedom as best they understand it. These same people wear heavy, warm clothing when skiing, again, because it is appropriate for the occasion; and the same people, again, will dress appropriately when visiting their place of worship. Why? Because they see this as the appropriate way to dress when visiting God, in the narrow confines of time and space allotted to their perception of Him.

What will happen if this is applied to so-called "conservative" societies, i.e. the societies (comprising diverse religions) that were part of Islamic civilization? These societies were living under God-centrism, then declined and fell, leading to a disturbance in their paradigms; they began to imitate other societies in form, while still confused as to content, unsure whether they live under self-centeredness or God-centrism. On the beaches of such societies, you will find the same revealing swimwear worn in the societies they imitate; however, you will immediately be struck by a sense of *wrongness*. Some, especially women, will feel uncomfortable undressing; the wrongness is in the air. Why? Because these societies have not yet made their final choice, since quite recently they, with all their religious diversity, were still God-centric; God was in the center, and the Self was subordinate. God's will superseded the Self's. One of its basic values was that the Self did not enjoy absolute freedom, but was free within the confines of its belonging to God, i.e., its paradigm was based on God-centrism, not on self-centeredness. Since it has not yet decided to remove or change this paradigm, it will keep imitating the form adopted by others, not the content; its inhabitants will keep on imitating the Other's freedoms without the attendant sense of rightness, always haunted by a feeling of doing something wrong, however much they rebel and defy it – which is why the beaches of these imitator societies are filled with a sense of *wrongness*, unlike the beaches of the societies they imitate.

There are thousands of examples like this beach example, where the freedom of the heart, mind and body differs from one society to the other, and the stress that builds up from what I believe to be an incorrect diagnosis of differences. I have chosen physical freedom and revealing clothing because we seem to have a positive obsession with this subject, surrounded by so much sound and fury that it cancels out any objective capacity for examination and analysis – leading to a failure of diagnosis, and the attendant failure of treatment.

Another simple example of freedom under self-centeredness is the right to die, or end one's life. Absolute freedom states that I am at liberty to decide whether or not I want to continue living. Since it's my body and my life, it's my decision; doesn't that make sense? To cut a long story short, self-centered societies of all faiths will practice their freedoms to the extent that their desires dictate, controlled only by the laws agreed upon by these societies that, by their very nature, change in accordance with the community's desires.

The practice of total freedom will naturally result in negative social values, in response to which new laws are made, and societies develop by trial and error. If you ask the existential question, "Where is God in this?" you will hear a lot of indirect talk, and a little direct talk, to the effect of the following, "God is there, in church, mosque and synagogue, where we visit Him at a certain time; otherwise, we decide what to do within the confines of the law."

Before I end this section, a question must be asked: Did conservative societies choose God-centrism as a paradigm under which to live their daily lives? To tell the truth, the answer is no. Societies – let's call them by their true names – societies, of whatever religion, that used to, and I repeat, used to, follow a God-centric paradigm – used to belong to a cultural framework that was defeated and broken hundreds of years ago, and have been confused and lost since then. They have adopted the outward forms of self-centered societies but never been able to adopt the content; at the same time, they have failed to revive their God-centric paradigm and create innovative ways to manifest that paradigm in their daily lives. I have said above, and will repeat, that this is due to a lack of confidence in themselves, and in their ability to innovate, invent and develop. The main reason, last but not least, is the inability to correctly diagnose the ailment: the issue is with the paradigm, not with culture, religion or sex.

Is there anything you would like to write down on this subject? Do any other examples of freedom under self-centeredness come to mind?

_____

_____

_____

_____

_____

_____

_____

I

The Formation of Consciousness under Self-Centeredness

Consciousness, choice and initiative have been discussed in previous chapters. Let's look at another side of consciousness. Was your consciousness formed haphazardly, or selectively? When you woke up this morning, did you enjoy a healthy, delicious breakfast? Nutritionists tell us that a good breakfast is the best start to a fruitful day. To have a good breakfast requires some time to plan something healthy and tasty that will support your body, mind and spirit in doing their tasks to your satisfaction, while not being too hard to digest. You probably have breakfast at a set time every day. Why do we do all the above? Because the more carefully we choose our ingredients, the better the result; the more regular our mealtimes, the better our health. This was a simple example of your awareness, initiative and selectivity in your breakfast, and its positive impact on the rest of the day. I doubt that we routinely wake up and eat whatever is handy in the kitchen or in the fridge, do we? Would you be comfortable filling your stomach with a random slice of pizza, some pasta, a bit of fish, some hot sauce and leftover Chinese, just because they happened to be in front of you? How would you feel the rest of the day? Imagine if this was your routine with all your meals, not just breakfast. How would this impact your life? Can you imagine how your stomach would suffer, and the medications you would need as a result of what you shovel into your mouth? What about your figure and the excess weight your poor body will have to handle, how your sleep will suffer, etc.? In such a case, you would be haphazard, unselective, and unaware when choosing your breakfast, and this would impact the rest of your life. In the first instance, you respect your body, mind and soul, and supply it with the nutrition it needs. In the second, you respect none of these, and treat your digestive system like a trashcan, throwing anything into it that you lay your hands on.

The above example shows that, at least when choosing our meals, we are aware of our choices, and bear their consequences. The same thing happens with forming our consciousness. First, what is consciousness? I believe it is the sum total of our concepts and thoughts (mind), feelings and emotions (heart), which affords us accurate perception of what goes on around us and how to deal with it correctly. I further think that consciousness is formed through two processes:

I

A selective process, via the information you glean from the society around you in a number of different ways, and the feelings and emotions generated in you via social interactions you choose, of your own free will, to engage in. This information and these feelings are stored in your conscious, and unconscious mind.

A haphazard process, in which you are subjected haphazardly to information and emotion from the surrounding society, via social interactions imposed upon you by those around you and what is happening around you, beyond your control; as a result, both your conscious and unconscious mind become saturated with the emotions of those around you – in a word, treating your consciousness like a trashcan, allowing those around you to throw what they want to into it.

In this age of the communication revolution, we interact with televisions, computers, smartphones, etc., and so are connected with what happens minute by minute, in a virtually unlimited media stream. Media operates on the premise that the viewer has the right to see the news item, the definition of "news" here being not news as such, but anything that may grab the viewer's (or listener's) attention. In the perennial example, "Dog Bites Man" is not news; "Man Bites Dog" is. Therefore, if you are not organized and selective in your dealings with what you see and hear, you fall into a vortex of hundreds of messages all saying "Man Bites Dog," hounding you with information you are never sure is true, with unknown impact on your emotional and spiritual state. Can you imagine how this may affect your mind, body and spirit? This is the haphazard method of forming your consciousness: turning yourself into a receptacle for the news others send, true or not. Or would you rather be selective, and control the Who, the What, and the When? What and Who to watch, listen to and read, and When to watch, listen, and read them? Timing is important: Some of us like spicy food, but most of us don't want it for breakfast. Dealing with your consciousness is no different. You need to be alert, and select a suitable time to deal with the news and other elements that shape your consciousness. It is hardly wise, I think, to have the first thing in the morning or the last thing at night be news of catastrophes and disasters.

What happens when we form our consciousness haphazardly is the following: We are in a negative mood most of the time; we see the world through dark glasses; we are constantly reacting to an Other(s) filling us with materials we did not choose, and would not, if given the choice; and most importantly, we lose control of the process of forming the very consciousness we use to make decisions in life, and live accordingly.

What has the above to do with our main issue, God-centrism and self-centeredness? A lot, in fact. Under God-centrism, you are not living aimlessly; you are living to fulfil God's purpose for you. This requires you to be selective in forming your consciousness, which will translate into goals. Achieving goals requires research and study; this requires setting educational targets and moving towards them, and devoting resources, including consciousness, to this path. In other words, you are a Subject: you are proactive. If the general climate is negative, you will take what steps you can to stop it from affecting you; if positive, you will do what you can to let it support you in your journey. In short, you will find your consciousness shaping itself around achieving your goals, and the further down the path you are to achieving them, the more tools are added to your consciousness-shaping toolbox, in a mutually beneficial relationship where you use your consciousness to fulfil God's purpose for you, and this in turn enriches your consciousness the further you go, and so on.

In other words, since consciousness and awareness are the first step to breaking Ego's vicious cycle within you, *how* these are formed is an essential indicator of their condition. While we are on the subject of Ego and its effect on the Self, have you noticed something? We have not yet encountered the existential question, "Where is God in this?" That is because, under self-centeredness, the Self is aggrandized, and blots out everything else, even our awareness of God's presence among us.

This is such an important point that I will venture to impose upon the reader with a request. Please set down, in detail, the elements that affect your consciousness daily, for a whole week. Remember: in detail! Make notes in this space.

_____

_____

_____

I

Forming Children's Consciousness Under Self-Centeredness

Before speaking of raising our children, we need to define our terms. Children, specifically, share a universal language, the language of children. Children understand each other after mere minutes together, no matter their differences. I believe that this merits our attention: anyone addressing children in the world is addressing the children of the world.

What, dear reader, do you think are the sources that form children's awareness? I think it is the school and their peers there, plus the home and its family and friends. Schools work towards raising children, a noble goal, but how many hours does a child spend at school daily? About seven hours a day, plus two to three hours for homework. Add to that 8-10 hours for sleeping, eating etc., and you have an average that differs very little from home to home around the world, regardless of whether the schools are cheap or expensive. Out of the 24 hours that make up the day, there are still three or four hours left. What happens in these hours? This is my focus.

Anywhere in the world, children spend their free time in front of a television, computer, tablet, or smartphone, depending on the family's financial resources. What do children watch? Mostly animation. What is the content of these works? This is the problem. The subject-matter of most of these works worldwide, in whatever language, revolve around the following: A bad guy oppresses a good guy. The bad guy wins at first, then the good guy defeats the bad guy in the end. This plot is repeated endlessly in all children's fare throughout the globe. Most of these plots do the following to our children's minds:

Reinforcing the concept of the Self/Us versus the Other/Them.

Reinforcing the concept that violence is the rule and not the exception.

Reinforcing the concept of eternal competition: Us or Them, with no compromise.

Reinforcing the concept that a victory for the Self/Us is the only way to win in life.

Reinforcing the concept that We must win, while the Other must lose.

Reinforcing the concept of tribalism, in its unhealthiest sense.

This can be found in most films and games mass-produced worldwide; these generate fantastic profits for their makers, who then get even more creative in building more movies and games around the same concepts. And so it goes. I invite you to play whatever games you want online, or watch whatever movies you can, and see for yourself whether there are any other concepts filling the minds of our children. You don't need to speak any foreign languages to make sense of what goes on in these works: the overwhelming majority revolves around similar concepts. Doubtless, there are others working towards creating healthy content for children; however, they are a negligible minority facing fierce competition.

"What's wrong with that?" you may say. Well, what is wrong with that is that we are addressing children, who by nature and by dint of their young age, have no ego, and we are filling them with not only individual and collective Ego, but with a competitive, exterminatory instinct. The meanings of these works are confined to the Other versus Us. Those who attack us are Other, those who protect us are Us. But there is no mention of divine intervention. Deus ex Machina is a tired plot twist, no matter the religion of the societies that show these films.

What happens as a result? I believe the universal model is geared towards saturating the consciousness of the world's children with the individual and collective Ego, preparing them for boxing God into specific times and places. This occurs automatically under self-centeredness, presented as the only natural way of life. I cannot tell whether this is deliberate, or a by-product of a commercial setup where, when a certain product is selling well, huge amounts of money are invested into it, and huge profits reaped as a result. The distortion of consciousness is, in my view, a by-product. No matter the reason behind it, the question is: If you agree with this diagnosis, what are you going to do? Our children – the world's children – are being raised from birth before our very eyes, with our full consent at that, on a steady diet engineered to build an individual and collective Ego. With our full consent, or our full ignorance, they are encouraged to view the Almighty as having no role in what happens in our lives, or at best a marginal and ineffectual one. Our children today are the youth of tomorrow: they are the future.

What concerns our children's awareness is no less crucial than what concerns our awareness as adults. Therefore, I will ask of you the same difficult thing I asked earlier: Please set down, in detail, the elements that affect your children's consciousness: your own, or your friends' and relatives', daily, for an entire week.

At the end of Part One, I would like to remind the reader of the main goals of the book: to urge you to ask the following kind of thing. Who is running my life, me or my Self? Is my Ego under my control or does it control me? Am I a subject or an object? and other questions. But I remind you of the golden rule: Ask these questions of yourself, don't use them to find fault with others!

Here is a space for you to set down your thoughts about the previous part of the book.

_____

_____

_____

_____

_____

_____

_____

_____

_____

_____

_____

_____

_____

PART TWO
Us under Self-Centeredness

"Us" is an expression, no more and no less than a greater or lesser number of "Selves." When a large number of Selves come together to form an Us, we get a whole that is not only the sum of the parts of the Selves, but comprises additional attributes of this new "Us." For instance, if you are a football fan attending a match alone, and the referee is so unfair that your team loses, you will exit the stadium filled with resentment at the defeat and at the injustice. As a general rule, you are unlikely to attack a supporter of the opposing team, try to smash their car, or vandalize neighboring buildings if you are on your own as you leave the stadium. However, if all of the above occurred with you as a member of a throng of football fans, enraged at the unfair defeat, it becomes very easy for this group to get into fights with the opposing team's supporters, and commit acts of violence and hooliganism.

Most non-extremists will go home and feel shocked at their own actions as part of a mob. What happened? What happened is that the "Self" became an "Us." It became more than the sum of its parts, each Self contributing a little, and a new thing formed: a mob mentality. It's like baking: a cake is a separate entity, more than the sum of flour, eggs, sugar and so on. Experts tell us that a mob has a life of its own, and its own characteristics, which is why demonstrations are ended by dispersing them, reducing them once again to component parts and making its members act individually as opposed to collectively.

Humans, as we often read, are social animals. We seem hard-wired to communicate with others and form groups and communities for warmth, company and safety. The relationship of an individual to a group of which they feel a part may be termed *belonging*. One feels at ease in one's similarities with the rest of the group's members, and feels strong and secure in their company. There are entities all over the world composed of people with a common inclination, benefit, or goal. Small groups of "Us" come together to form a larger "Us." Agricultural groups came together in the Middle Ages to form fiefdoms, provinces and duchies. They came together once more in the past two centuries to form larger collective entities – states – the basis for modern European nations. These in turn began to come together to form the European Economic Community, which may eventually result in a unified Europe. Similarly, we have ASEAN (the Association of Southeast Asian Nations) in Southeastern Asia, the BRISK union, Central Asian Union, the African Union and Asian Union, and the Union of South American nations. On a smaller scale, those with similar political leanings come together in political parties, business owners form groups that express their collective interests, workers form unions, and so forth.

Societies that afford their citizens a socially and psychologically healthy lifestyle, foremost among which are the Scandinavian nations, have gone through several stages of belonging. First, the nuclear family, the smallest unit of belonging, with well-defined members – father, mother, siblings – and a defined dwelling-place. Second, the nuclear families expand into an extended family, its units a number of nuclear families, such as the families of aunts and uncles. The family elder, not necessarily the breadwinner, is a grandparent. Third comes the clan: a large number of families connected by blood, with a family elder. Fourth, the tribe: a collection of clans, loosely connected – or not – by blood. A tribe may number tens, occasionally hundreds, of thousands. The tribe is the kernel of the state as we currently understand it: it has its laws governing the relationship between its people, its customs and values, its judges and wise folk, and a tribal leader.

The next step along from the tribe is the state. This contains a number of tribes inhabiting the land where the state arose. In some societies, tribes and clans have melted into the state, as in Central and Eastern Europe and Scandinavia; in others they have not, as in Iraq, Syria and the majority of sub-Saharan Africa. It is my belief that every society on the face of the earth has gone through the above stages, stages that belong to the Old World of Africa, Asia and Europe. In the

New World – the Americas and Australia – these components were part of the original inhabitants' civilization, but after the European colonization of these continents, and the defeat and attrition of the native population, the concept of the State had started to take shape, precluding a new tribal civilization: the new civilization was built on a large collection of nuclear families. All of this is an expression of the human need to build entities to belong to.

Most mature entities that have acquired some wisdom and are a healthy expression of their component parts have generally gone through a number of long-term stages, some unhealthy and claiming lives and property, before arriving at a degree of social maturity. Some societies managed to get over these violent patches and get to safety; others self-destructed. In general, there are two types of human community that reflect the concept of an "Us." I shall give each of them a name.

The first is the Inclusive Tribe, the healthiest manifestation of the individual who has not fallen prey to the Self or to egocentrism, with a healthy need for belonging. Such an individual forms a healthy Us, manifested in a tribe that opens channels and builds bridges and reaches out with the Others around it, in the forms of other communities, other Us'es, other tribes, with the aim of meeting and mingling, getting to know each other, and initiating exchanges of culture, experience, and mutual relationships and ties of friendship and affection, reflected in a large measure of security and familiarity.

The second is the Exclusive Tribe. This is the result of an unhealthy manifestation of the Self, one that falls prey to Ego, and centers around itself. Such a Self feels the need to create an unhealthily insular Us, thereby activating the curse of prejudice. This tribe is a fortress, surrounded by moats and drawbridges; if forced by circumstance to have dealings with the Other, it does so with fear and trepidation, reflected in suspicion, wariness and distrust. This section, titled "Us under Self-Centeredness", will examine this second, unhealthy type of tribe, where Self holds the reins of Us.

Abuse of Patriarchy and its Role in Creating Us/Them

Do you recall when we spoke about the abuse of patriarchy, and how this unhealthy paradigm allowed us to place our virtual 'father' in the center, and at the top of the hierarchy? One result of this was the emergence of a strong 'Us' orbiting this Father, and seeing only him. He is the source from whom blessings flow: wisdom, goodness and charity – and also has the power to withhold them. He is also the seat of power and authority.

Every strong and united Us needs a strong and obvious Them. The latter needs to present a clear and present threat to the Us, to reinforce our sense of its value, as well as the importance – and inevitability – of the patriarch's presence. Some struggle or war must be present, and no dissent is permissible while we are at war: we are, of course, at war, for the good of the camp of Us, from our political interests and supremacy to our economic interests. If the Them is absent, with its attendant threat, a Them must be created: its absence and the absence of a threat weakens our need for an Us, and works against the interests of an ill-intentioned minority.

There are many examples of creating a Them: every despotic dictatorship in the world has a Them to strike fear into its subjects. Not only dictatorships use this; Western civilization searched diligently for a Them after the fall of communism (a Them *par excellence*) towards the end of the 20th century, and found it in the Muslims. "We" here represents the collective ego: every ego, communal or individual, needs to define itself in relation to something different in order to survive. There must be a clear difference between Us and Them, in thoughts, beliefs, race, ethnicity, etc. Also, these differences must be emphasized and publicized. We need slogans to point out these differences. In the Age of Empires, from the 16th to the 19th centuries, the dominant slogan was the myth of white racial superiority, in contrast with the Wild Indian in America, the Childlike Savage in Africa, the Yellow Peril in Asia, the Primitive Aborigines in Australia, and the Barbaric Arabs all throughout the Arabian Peninsula and Northern Africa.

These reductive and unjust classifications paved the way for people's consciences to accept the necessity of exterminating all Others: they are, after all, different from the collective Us, and stand against the values we represent, in our superiority and intelligence. Sometimes this is cloaked in glittering phrases such as "the White Man's Burden," outwardly signifying the duty of white men to spread civilization to the corners of the earth, in reality justifying the appropriation of others' resources. Unforgettable examples are Hitler's notion of the Master Race, the Central African tribal conflicts, not to mention every massacre in the name of religion since the dawn of time.

The collective Ego, in its search for differences to create an Us and a Them, has been there since humanity started, and will be there as long as it exists. It is the main motivation behind every war and conflict since the dawn of creation. And since the collective ego always seeks to make itself special, it has devised flags and banners and signs, as well as special costumes and a different collective appearance. As a result of the constant flag-waving to emphasize how different we are from others (in thought, race, creed and so on), these symbols have come to acquire a special significance for us.

With the constant brandishing of signs and slogans, as the concepts of abusive patriarchy percolated into the collective consciousness, these individuals and their ideas and slogans begin begun to morph into (for example, national) symbols in themselves, a symbol of the collective ego. Defending these individuals and groups becomes high-stakes. Any criticism of these personages becomes an attack on inviolable, sacred principles: any threat to them is a threat to my very existence. It is only human nature to use every means possible to defend oneself: survival instinct is natural, isn't it?

I'm not sure what you will think of the above: what I think is that it is the stuff that idolatry is made of. Before I start speaking of graven images, let me make some points about belonging.

Belonging and Prejudice

There are two types of twins: identical and fraternal. Fraternal twins are when there are two embryos in the mother's womb due to the presence of two fertilized eggs, producing babies that can differ in sex, appearance, temperament and so on. Identical twins occur when two embryos originated in the same ovary/sperm pair. Although it is hard to tell them apart, their characters may differ, resulting in much innocent fun based on the resemblance, more so the more different they are in temperament.

I think we may use identical twins as a metaphor for belonging and prejudice. These, too, originate from a single embryo, the basically benign trait of belonging; they look the same, but are different in reality, which can generate confusion – not innocent fun, but tragedy.

On the outside, each of these traits is a manifestation of our instinct to belong to something larger than ourselves. However, belonging does this in a healthy manner, while its twin, prejudice, is malignant.

Belonging and prejudice are states of mind; we move between them consciously or unconsciously. We can choose to transition from one to the other. But feelings and behaviors are colored by our emotions. Since the two *look* identical, we may imagine that we are asserting our belonging, whereas we are actually being prejudiced, and the reverse.

Let us compare our state when belonging to our state when prejudiced.

1. The malignant state of belonging – prejudice – makes us belong to entities out of a need to do so. We feel protected and confident when within them; not belonging makes us feel alone and afraid, insecure and incomplete. When I meet a strange Other, I immediately search for his banner. If it is unclear, I start to form conspiracy theories and look for his hidden agenda. I can't imagine that a person – a Self – can live alone without belonging to a group; I am weak, in need of protection and belonging, and I am prejudiced in favor of it. I can't imagine a strong person living alone without protection.

2. The main motivator here is fear and wariness. Every moment of my life, I fear for myself and the entity to which I belong. I fear for Us, and I fear Them. They want to destroy Us.

3. My feeling of belonging tells me I exist. I also have a constant sense that They are waiting to ambush Us. This fear threatens my very sense of existence; therefore, I must be in constant readiness for the Other's attacks. Constant vigilance! This places us under constant stress.

4. I belong *only* to X group, Y group or Z group; I cannot belong to more than one, and when I join a group, I quickly become part of an Us against the rest.

5. Abuse of patriarchy prevails. This entity is my father, my family and everything, but I don't see that as a bad thing. I think it's necessary. Without my Father/Hero/Elder/Saint, I am lost.

6. There are immense differences between Us and Them that make it necessary to isolate ourselves from them.

7. We are always in search of differences with the Other.

8. We are usually reactive to what the Other does.

9. There is no room for compromise.

10. I am only a part of the big picture: I prefer 'us' to 'we' when speaking; it makes me feel stronger.

11. What We think is the truth; anything else is lies.

12. What I belong to is sacred and infallible. It is not to be questioned; there is no room for improvement. It is right personified.

13. There is to be no criticism. If you do not accept what we say uncritically, you are attacking us and want to destroy us; therefore, you must be pre-emptively destroyed.

14. "This town isn't big enough for both of us!" There is not enough room for everyone. Only one can survive: Us, or Them.

15. My allegiances are clearly and narrowly defined; the thought of multiple allegiances makes me confused and suspicious.

If one, or all, of the items on the above list pertain to you, I will ask you to be honest with yourself, and replace 'belonging' and 'allegiance' above with 'prejudice.'

In a healthy state of belonging, however,

1. We belong to things or entities because we want to, not because we need to. This is because we don't need an Other to feel an intrinsic sense of completeness.

2. When I meet a strange Other, I am eager to learn from them, and offer what I know. I am strong and integrated, and I see strength and integration in others. I don't feel threatened at others' allegiances, or lack thereof.

3. My main motivator and essential value is love: love for what I belong to, and love for the Other.

4. My allegiance reflects my inner peace, calm and assurance.

5. Your relationship with the groups to which you belong is non-exclusive: "and" supersedes "or." I belong to X, Y *and* Z. No-one and no entity monopolizes me.

6. There is no room for abuse of patriarchy.

7. I am open to the Other; I am prepared to accept them and have them accept me.

8. We seek common ground with the Other who belongs to other entities, and try to build on this shared space.

9. I am usually proactive, both with those I belong to and with those I don't.

10. In negotiations with the Other, there is always room for compromise.

11. I have an independent existence, and opinions of my own; I may differ from the other members of the entity I belong to.

12. In the words of the late Imam Shafei, "what we all think is right may be wrong; what others think is wrong may be right."

13. What I belong to is not sacred; it may prove right or wrong.

14. I value criticism, and attack on occasion, of what I belong to: I can see the flaws in my chosen allegiance, and work towards developing it and correcting its flaws.

15. There is room for everyone. We can all coexist.

16 I am prepared to belong to multiple entities; this gives me balance.

I would like to reiterate what I said above, about confusing identical twins because they look alike. Confusing belonging with prejudice happens often: we act with prejudice, thinking we are acting out of loyalty to our group. Sometimes we use misnomers, and then believe them, which only confuses us more. Most of us hate to be called prejudiced or racist, but sometimes we practice these traits under the banner of belonging, which allows us to be prejudiced in comfort.

Misdiagnosis renders even the best remedy ineffective. Prejudice and belonging are primarily *states of mind,* not a type or race; moving between the two, therefore, is a decision which rests in our hands. We can do it if we decide. But with a bad diagnosis, we won't feel any need to change: why fix what isn't broken, am I right?

Let me remind you of the main rule in this book: I am not pushing you to judge or find fault with others, but to question yourself. Are you practicing prejudice, or belonging? I ask because the state you are in is a good indicator of the skies beneath which you situate yourself, self-centeredness or God-centrism.

Make a note in this space of the experiences you feel you can describe as prejudiced, and the ones you would classify as 'belonging.' Try to make a note of your feelings and impressions in each state. What questions are in your mind?

I

Prejudice under Self-centeredness

Prejudice is a relationship with others – in my opinion, an unhealthy one. This unhealthy relationship can only end tragically if religion is brought into the mix. History tells us that there have always been those who used the name of God to justify bloody conflicts, for money or power. History tells us that there are vast chasms between thought and deed, what we believe and what we do. Out of prejudice, we labor under the delusion that we belong to God, and are doing God's work; the reality is that we are dealing with the Other as though God belonged to us, and to us alone. When prejudiced, we call ourselves God's faithful servants: but in our dealings with the Other, our belief becomes clear that we, and we alone, hold the sole right to represent God on earth. We think, and say, that we are preaching the Way to God; but our actions show that we deal with the Other as though we are the path to God. We say that we are explaining to people how their actions anger God; but our actions show that we are the sole sponsor of God on Earth, and on occasion, history shows, that we take upon ourselves the burden of securing people's entry into Heaven by selling Indulgences. We think, and say, that we are preaching the path to heaven, but our actions show that we sometimes help others on their way there with a little push!

When I say that we "think and say," what I mean is that we are acting out of conviction, not pretense. We are unaware of how we actually see, and relate to, God, in the sad place of prejudice. History shows that the name of God is all too often used in the service of the collective Ego and of Us versus Them, usually not consciously. Under self-centeredness, our prejudice in favor of Us outweighs our allegiance to God; our relationship with Him is a monopoly, in the service of what we are prejudiced in favor of. Most of the blood spilt, the worst tragedies in history, can be laid at the door of Us-versus-Them. These words express the dominant ideology in most of human history, a result of surrendering to the collective Ego under self-centeredness.

There is another word that conceals a deeper meaning: "Victims." It has flourished and still does; it is a clear manifestation of the collective Ego.

Never Forget! Victims and Sages

We have spoken above of victimhood and ego under self-centeredness. As the concept of victimhood is connected to the individual ego, the concept of collective victimhood is connected to the collective ego. History tells us that when a given group, united by tribe, race, religion, etc., is subjected to oppression (justly or unjustly), resulting in painful incidents, one of the following occurs: either they fall into the trap of reaction, starting to create a collective ego manifested in the emergence of a powerful Us feeling victimized by the barbarism of a savage Them (truth and justice aside), resulting in a State Of Victimhood, or some sage appears, asking an important question, "Why did this happen?", in an attempt to understand and avoid a future occurrence. In the latter state, the path is clear to social integration, reducing the probability of an Us/Them scenario, resulting in a State of Sagacity. Unfortunately, history is all too full of states of victimhood, while there are far too few states of wisdom.

Victimhood

One of the main attributes of a State of Victimhood is that those who have surrendered to it only see the world through the rigid framework of their own view, which only accommodates an Us-versus-Them view of what has befallen them, and do everything they can to stay in it. Historically, collective and collaborative scripts take shape in the consciousness of those who have fallen prey to such a situation: "We have been unjustly treated. We have been treated badly, even massacred, and no-one lifted a finger to save us. We are always at risk of being oppressed."

These scripts are a not-inaccurate expression of what happened, so what's wrong with them? Nothing is *wrong* as such, but let's look deeper and feel our way from victimhood to wisdom. Historically, in most cases of mass oppression, the oppressed group takes a reactive stance, their conviction colored by the collective Ego and the Us/Them dichotomy. This leads to a very powerful state of "We the Victims." Such a state of "We the Victims" must necessarily be accompanied by "Never Forget," which keeps the flame of We the Victims burning. Everything possible is done to make the acts of decades or centuries ago alive as though they happened yesterday, celebrated whenever possible, preserved by whatever means whenever possible.

"Never Forget"

To tell the truth, it must be said that when the collective Ego adopts "Never Forget," it is motivated by completely justifiable fear of what happened to them being repeated. We must also admit that adopting this stance leads to short-term gains. Adding to the confusion is that a constant state of "Never Forget" is actually essential to securing justice. However, a distinction must be made between using "Never Forget" as a means, and "Never Forget" as an end.

"Never Forget" as a Means

In this case, "Never Forget" is a means, and achieving justice the end. After justice is achieved, I believe it might benefit not only that specific group, but society at large, to abandon "Never Forget." I want to emphasize here the need for justice *before* leaving "Never Forget;" calling for people to forget an injustice done to a certain group before this group has fully reclaimed *all* of its rights is, in itself, gross injustice. For example, it would not do to ask apartheid victims in South Africa, or the victims of ethnic cleansing in Central Africa and Eastern Europe, to forgive and forget, without justice being first served upon those who caused these horrors and the victims adequately compensated and granted *full* status in society. Would it benefit these unjustly-treated groups, and the societies they belong to, to cling to "Never Forget" afterwards? I doubt it.

After justice is served, it may be merciful to allow those who have suffered injustice to forget, so that wounds may heal and hearts recover. The Almighty has made it so that time heals all wounds, if the wound is first cleaned before it closes. Justice cleans the wound. Should we not be wise enough to utilize this wonderful capacity for healing?

"Never Forget" as an End

"Never Forget" as an end is clinging to the memory of past injustices, even after justice is served. Such a state arises when a group has suffered atrocities, as a reaction to terrible pain. This reaction manifests in a state of surrender to the Self, forming a collective Ego of "We the Victims"; this functions as a barrier against what happened, and a confused idea that such a shibboleth will prevent the injustice from occurring again. Unfortunately, this confusion increased, and still increases, the probability of similar injustices befalling the victims. The reason for this is that it separates them from the collective "Us," and blocks their integration, leaving them unaware that integration is the true guarantee that what happened will not be repeated. Retreating into a shell of Self is only a prelude to the repetition of such atrocities in the future.

It would seem prudent to confront this state of "We the Victims" spawned by the collective ego, by means of getting rid of the strong "Us," as victim or otherwise; this will automatically dismiss the sense that there is a "Them" lying in wait to ambush "Us." This will grant mutual security to them and to those around them, wherever they are and whoever is around them. I believe that those who give in to the state of victimhood are held hostage by their own selves that trap them in a reactive space. Their Self does everything it can to keep them trapped in the past and take it with them wherever they go. They are hostage to the past, and to the Other who oppressed and tormented them, unaware that this Other is still dominating them after all these years, controlling their reactions, and driving them towards the same fate in the same manner, unaware that with this submission, they have surrendered not only their past, but their present and future, to this Other, who, in the ultimate irony, may be long dead, but still controls their lives from beyond the grave, in the form of reactions to what was done long ago.

You will notice that any attempt to move the victims from the corner they have confined themselves to will be met with strong resistance: this corner feels safe, affording them a sense of order and purpose, and an ability to go on. Finally, I would say to those who have given in to the corner of victimhood: Have you thought of moving from the area of inescapable historical burden to the area of "there are other choices?" And that the prerequisite for these other choices is abandoning "Never Forget" as an end? If you take this hard step, it will simplify other hard steps, such as leaving the area of the Victim, the Us, and the collective Ego; to abandon reactivity for proactivity; and to relinquish victimhood and the false sense of security it provides in favor of getting to the root of the problem.

Dear willing victims of victimhood: I believe that "Never Forget" is the illness that requires diagnosis, and that the rest of its consequences are the symptom. The start of recovery is to get rid of this mental state, after, of course, justice is served. Only when you can get past it will you dissolve the deep and clear boundaries between yourselves and the Other, and start the journey to healing. The journey to getting rid of victimhood, and moving towards wisdom. Have you considered that the start of real healing, and ridding yourselves of all these historical and geographical tragedies, lies in asking yourselves and the world: "Why did this happen, and how can we stop it happening again?" instead of, "Why us?"

Wise Folk

One of the main attributes of wisdom is the ability, courage and willingness on the part of these wise folk to abandon their own view, their own estimation of the crises they suffer, and the estimation of others' views of what happened, with the goal of understanding the Other's outlook. After the tragic events of September 11, 2001, and the attempts of the US administration to confront what had happened, the foolish slogan they presented to the world was, "You are either with us or against us." This created a classic case of the collective Ego, which claimed many victims – not submissive but vengeful victims. We all know the dramatic end to this episode of collective ego: the destruction of two states, the death of hundreds of thousands, with millions more driven from their homes, for no reason but the fulfilment of the vengeful collective Ego.

Despite the pain and rage, though, a number of wise folk kept their heads, and managed to ask the relevant question: "Why did this happen? Why do they hate us?" This question was rooted in a genuine attempt to understand why the incident had occurred, to find the real disease and deal with it, so as not to repeat it. They made attempts, and are still trying, to find the reasons behind it. These, although circumstances were ripe for a takeover of Collective Ego, resisted temptation and kept it at bay, rejecting the seductive role of the Vengeful Victim.

A more merciful and wonderful example of Sages was in South Africa after the end of apartheid. Nelson Mandela rejected the trap of the Vengeful Victim, and guided his country to Wisdom. This choice required courage, the ability to push through pain, and resistance to the temptation of vengeance – although vengeance was in their grasp – and transitional justice. You may notice that this example holds within it the ability to get over the "We the Victim" temptation of the Ego, and emerge into Wisdom. When the oppressed African, Asian and Black majority of South Africa agreed to follow the wise example of their leader, and resist the urge to exact vengeance on their white fellow-citizens, it was a rebirth. That wonderful African nation became an exemplar to be followed, geographically and historically. They could have fallen into the Vengeful Victim trap, but chose not to.

Historically, all those who have chosen healing by moving from a place of victimhood to a place of wisdom have had to pay a price. This price was a conscious choice to conquer their pain; to suppress their anger. They rejected shortsightedness, and short-term satisfaction; they looked further, knowing from their experience that so as to avoid a repeat of what happened, they had to pursue the interests of every party in the conflict and seek out what angered each of them, and avoid it in the future, seeking the interests of the entire community, not only the collective Ego of the victimized We. What they did wasn't easy; it was hard. To do it, they had to resist what came naturally; it was an uphill climb. But the hill they climbed was that of Wisdom. When we can overcome our baser urges, we actually give ourselves a choice: the choice to call upon divine assistance under God-centrism. When it comes to healing from deep wounds, such as those that afflict victims on their journey to wisdom, it only makes sense to call upon the assistance of Him who controls our sense of pain, and ask Him to ease it and help us to overcome it and not fall prey to it.

It may be wise to bring this existential question into play: "Where is God in this?" and the secondary question, what priority have we given His will? This is a choice; there are others, based on "the common good" and so forth, but I believe these to be a type of fragile ceasefire or alliance between a collection of "Us" entities. It is fragile because the Self and its Captain of the Guard, individual and collective Ego, are cunning: they can easily push us back down the slippery slope to victimhood. It is fragile because alliances of "Us" calls the collective Ego into play, biding its time and waiting its chance. Under God-centrism, when we decide to forgive and forget and pardon the Other for God, we strike deep roots into the soil of wisdom.

What do you think of the above? Make a note. Make a note of the victim-states and wisdom-states you may have fallen into in the past.

Competition Under Self-Centeredness

It is a sad fact of life that once we form a mental image of a certain thing, we tend to think that this is, has always been, and will only ever be, the only meaning. I think this is the case with the concept of 'competition.' As we use it now, it means exterminatory competition. I don't expect everyone to agree with me, but I believe it is. I also believe it is not the only form of competition.

Exterminatory Competition

In exterminatory competition, my victory is predicated on the Other's defeat. The fiercer the competition, the greater my victory and the greater his defeat: the greatest victory of all is to exterminate the Other and wipe them off the face of the earth. If this type of competition had a slogan, it would be, "Us or Them!"

To be fair, we must note that the concept of extermination – legal or otherwise – has always been implicit in competition since the dawn of history, but it was always limited to geographical clashes between nations. For the first time in human history, as a result of the communications revolution, there are concepts that reach into every corner of the known world, agreed upon by almost everyone on the planet. The concept of what we may call 'exterminatory competition' has become understood by all, so much so that it has become part of the financial health of businesses, a kind of economic Survival of the Fittest. Unfortunately, this Darwinian phrase has been used as an excuse for exterminatory competition, under a false claim that this is best for humanity, 'new blood' and the extinction of those unfit to keep up – socially, economically, militarily, etc. If a competitor can't take care of themselves, they reason, do they expect us to care for them?

Where is God in this? What is His priority? This world needs strong people. The weak must make way for the strong, and then quietly disappear. Where is God and what is his priority? It is normal in most businesses to seduce competitors' top talent, take over supply channels, and corner markets; if they can't fight back, it means they're not efficient. They deserve to go out of business, don't they?

Where is God in this? What's His priority? We can even use our political privilege as powerful nations to pressure weaker nations to open up new markets for our products, wiping out (or taking over) their small industries. We're big enough to swallow up anything that stands in our way: that's just competition, isn't it? We can even brainwash the people of those countries with the media juggernaut, convincing them that our products are the best, even if this changes the fabric of their societies: theirs are the past, and ours are the future, after all. You want to be like us, don't you? Just consume what we do, and you will.

"What has God to do with all of this? What's God got to do with economic and political competition? God belongs in His churches, His mosques and His synagogues. Stop bothering us and let us work in peace."

Does the above sound familiar to you, dear reader? Not the phrasing, but the philosophy behind it, and the significance. Whatever answers we receive will not be much different from the above. Whatever happened? Nothing: we are merely under the familiar skies of self-centeredness. If you look at the central tenets of exterminatory competition, it is based on the concept of Us *par excellence:* our interests, our prosperity, our success. There is always a Them with whom we must compete and annihilate, all of which feeds, activates and energizes our collective Ego.

Similarly, the culture of consumption also feeds, activates and energizes the individual Ego, as explained in the section on Self-Centeredness. What happens if both the individual and collective Egos are activated simultaneously? Simply, a shift from God-centrism to self-centeredness, a decisive and permanent one. Darwinism and exterminatory competition.

I would like to use Darwin's theory of evolution as an example of the above. My focus here is not on its content, but on Darwinism as an Event, and its attendant effect on humanity, which Darwin himself could not have predicted. Charles Darwin was concerned with the origin of species. The effects of some of his theories were as follows:

1. His statement that man and apes had a common ancestor resulted in an association among many that we are descended from apes. His research into the origin of creation established the popular idea that some Event jumpstarted the start of creation.

2. This theory spawned what was known as "Darwinists," believers in his theory who built extreme structures upon it: "Darwinism" entered into fierce competition with the opposing theory, the story of Adam and creation.

3. This led to an exterminatory competition.

4. This in turn led to the assumption that God – any god – could not exist. The concepts of Nature, great powers, and so on, resulted.

5. The theory of racial superiority arose: Since this occurred at the dawn of European civilization, White Man was established as the superior example of humanity (and later as the Master Race).

6. Racial superiority, specifically white people's, was used to colonize the rest of the world on the pretext of white superiority, and that these backwards, savage society were fortunate to be 'civilized' by that special race. (A painful irony is that ex-colonized African nations paid 'colonial tax' for years after independence to 'repay' France for the so-called benefits of French colonization!)

7. As a result, countries were crushed and indigenous populations destroyed in Africa, Australia, and North and South America.

Darwinian groups established the premise of competition with God. They further presented evolution as an alternative to God: a clear application of the concept of exterminatory competition, as though the success of this theory was predicated on the destruction of God and the story of creation. Now that the premise of competing with God was established, the premise of competing with His creatures was as well: for the white race to rise and flourish, other races must be exterminated. This was actually implemented in many parts of the world. All of this I see as part of the literature of "Us under Self-Centeredness," which still casts a bloody shadow over the world we live in today. It has legitimized the concept of exterminatory competition.

Another example of life under self-centeredness is worshipping graven images.

Have you encountered exterminatory competition in your life experiences? Make notes in this space.

Graven Images

The Lord tells us in His holy books of people in times gone by who used to worship graven images. A prophet is sent to guide the people; some accept him; some are devout, and become role models for others in life and after death. Someone comes up with the bright idea of making statues to them, to remind their descendants of these holy servants of God, the goal being, "If only we were like them!" Some exceptionally bad examples also have statues erected to them, less often, a kind of What Not To Do. After generations, people start to become confused as to what these statues represent, and begin to labor under the delusion that these good people have had statues made to them because they are either gods themselves, or intermediary gods that can intercede for people at God's seat; people start to worship them alongside, or instead of, God. Then God sends new prophets to correct these misapprehensions and remind them that the One True God has no intermediaries between Him and His creatures.

The biographies of the prophets tell us that all of them share one thing: a strong resistance on the part of the people to the Prophet's call to stop worshipping their gods and worship the One True God. Let us analyze this historically repeated scenario and its underpinnings from the perspective of the collective ego. Some points are repeated, such as the following:

1. These peoples were not wicked. Most were upright, moral folk following an established code of ethics.

2. Most refused to abandon their old gods, not out of a deep-seated belief in their Godliness as we understand it today, but as a rejection of the assault on the collective We, or Us: any assault on the community's beliefs was an assault on the tribe, and on the community's very existence. Each tribe had its own gods and banners, its gods' greatness and strength competing with the gods of other tribes. A tribe was only as powerful as its gods – or vice versa – enjoying high status, and political and economic privileges. The rejecters were primarily acting in defense of their social and political privileges that set them above others and granted them prestige. In my terms, they were defending 'Us' – a complete collective Ego.

3. Most of them tried to find a compromise, trying to worship the new God as well as their old gods, with the collective Ego and its privileges these gods represented. This is significant: for most of them it was not a matter of conviction, but of self-interest.

4. There were two kinds of people who followed the new prophets and what they preached: those who were convinced – the strong of heart – and others who believed what their leaders and elders believed – faint of heart, who might even believe in the new prophets but found it too hard to lose sight of the shore, represented by the collective ego, the Us, and would only follow their leaders.

Note that in matters related to an Us – a collective ego – the above is not confined to Abrahamic religions. It occurs in every time and place, in many aspects of life, when something new is preached. Our relationship to the collective Ego is one of mutual benefit: we feel secure in it, and defend its existence. These faint-hearted majorities who follow their leaders anywhere are fertile ground for the rise of graven images, always in search of a leader to whom they can subordinate their will and hand over the reins of their fate. The faint of heart are always in search of a leader to idolize. Some examples follow:

Sports

Football hooliganism, rioting, looting and destruction in Europe, and similarly all over the world, to the point of war breaking out in Latin America – a healthy expression of sportsmanship? I think not. The concept of collective ego will help clarify matters: to its fanatics (not members or supporters), the football club represents their very existence. Once I have acquired a symbol of my existence, any attack on, or threat to, this symbol is a threat to my very life, and I will defend it as I defend my life and property; often I will defend it more fiercely than my family, as it represents my continued existence.

When we are in a state of self-defense, fighting for life and limb, our defenses are instinctual, with no room for logic or reason. The football team, in this instance, is the manifestation of the true graven image worshipped instead of God or alongside Him: the collective ego.

Is this confined to football? Not at all – apply this to political parties, religious and ethnic organizations and race-based affiliations of different sorts, tribal groupings, national alliances and so on, and you will find that the collective ego is essentially the same, with some differing details.

The graven image – the collective Ego – Us – the tribe – may be explicit or implicit, depending on the degree of hypocrisy in a given society. One of the most striking examples is the tacit racism in many civilized societies, where the laws speak of equality, fraternity and equal rights for all, but are entirely different on the ground. The tacit feeling tends to be, "These rights belong to Us, not Them."

When Entities Become Graven Images

In the above examples, to examine the reasons behind this bloody combat is to find an Us behind it all. Every Us – as explained above – needs a Them to define itself against, and is at its best with tribalism. Anyone not of our tribe constitutes a threat. Tribal thinking under self-centeredness can destroy any healthy affiliation: the family itself, based on warmth and compassion, can turn into an Us, into a Tribe, under self-centeredness, making an Other of anyone not related to Us. In any altercation between one of our tribe and one of Them, we prioritize the interests of the tribe over truth, justice and fairness. Family businesses – conceived originally to profit the family and the community – can become tribes if they turn into an Us-versus-Them group, which explains why so much tax evasion goes on: it is an attempt to privilege the company's interests over those of the community and the state.

Political parties and organizations, originally conceived to serve the community and the nation, can turn into tribal affiliations, fighting fiercely for supremacy while excluding all others and doing everything they can to exterminate the Other, and privileging membership of the Party over membership in the State. Country – a place bringing together all its inhabitants under one flag, supposedly cooperating with open arms with others to improve trade, transportation, etc. – can, under self-centeredness, become a tribe: countries can then go to war with others to secure as many resources as they can for their "Us," their citizens, at the expense of other countries or of the planet. Even civilization – a broad framework bringing together diverse cultures, peoples and ethnicities – can be transformed by self-centeredness into a despotic, confrontational civilization, rejecting any Other: the choices are 'assimilate or die.' The common thread in all the above is that under self-centeredness, "Us" turns into a graven image, worshipped alongside God.

I would like to digress with regard to country, religion and civilization. What is the effect of what you have read so far? Are there graven images around you? Make a note of these, then of its effect on you, and any questions this may raise.

_____

_____

_____

_____

_____

_____

_____

_____

_____

_____

_____

_____

_____

_____

I

Country, Religion and Civilization under Self-Centeredness: The Tyranny of Ego
Country under Self-Centeredness: The Tyranny of Ego

Precision and sensitivity are required when speaking of patriotism and defining country. In the world today, there are written or unwritten agreements treated as self-evident: Country First! Espionage, plots, and wars claim millions of victims: the cruel irony is that *both* parties to these conflicts are in *total agreement* on the *same* principle, the victim's only weakness that they weren't strong enough to enforce their will on the aggressor. This begs the question: "But is there any other way to imagine how a country should be?" I think so, and I will start with our old familiar existential question: "Where is God in the issue of country, and what is His priority?"

If we were to choose any country on the planet right now, and ask its citizens the above, their answer – in word and in deed – will be: "What's God got to do with it? Religion is for God, and country is for all! Render unto Caesar the things that are Caesar's, and the things that are God's unto God!" Naturally, what is Caesar's is country; what is God's is the church, mosque or synagogue, nothing more. I repeat: Is there another answer? "Egypt is not a country we live in, but a country that lives in us," said the late Pope Shenouda, Head of the Egyptian Orthodox Church. Yes, our country lives within us, but that is hardly a reason to distort it into a collective ego or a graven image to be worshipped alongside God.

Allow me to give you an example. In my homeland, Egypt, I have many friends who were the first generation to leave their village for the big city, their grades securing them a place in university. They went on to become doctors, professors, and businessmen, doing a great deal for the country. "If your parents had refused to leave their village," I often ask their children, "would they have done as much for their country?" I think not. The natural thing is for that person to use what they learned to do as much for their village as possible, but also to enrich everyone around. This, I believe, may be called belonging to the larger homeland: your gifts reach all of God's creatures in all His creation. This, I believe, is a God-centric definition of country: loving your country in God. An archery target has concentric circles, each bearing a progressively larger number from the outside to the center: I believe that healthy belonging, without prejudice, resembles that target: concentric circles where you stand at the center. Your country is one of the first circles where you can fulfil God's commands; since it is closest to the center, you belong to it before your company, family, political party, trade union, etc., which means that there are progressively widening circles of affiliation, ending with your fellow-human beings, and your pride in this affiliation and your effective contributions to it.

When you are at the center of concentric circles, *Or* is replaced with *And;* there is no contradiction, and any difference is only one of degree. Succession replaces contradiction. When our belonging is less than healthy, it becomes something like volleyball: no part of an opponent can exist in your territory, a classic "Or" situation based on bias not on belonging.

When the first concept prevails – circles of belonging – our country is the stage from which we conduct our dealings with others, and the others take their respective stages, each according to their country, as we work towards the common good. Even if there is competition – fair or otherwise – it will not matter, because the benefit to the public far outweighs the harm. When the volleyball paradigm prevails, our countries become a collective Ego, represented by a strong "I" in opposition to "Them", and the harm brought about by "us vs. them" is far greater than any good it can do. Our relationships with our country become a main factor in our slide into self-centeredness.

Make a note of your thoughts and questions.

———————————————————————————

———————————————————————————

———————————————————————————

———————————————————————————

———————————————————————————

———————————————————————————

Religion under Self-Centeredness: The Tyranny of Us

Most holy men are men of integrity, thoroughly committed to their task of guiding people to God: throughout history, though, a minority has been overtaken by Self, leading them to use their position for their own benefits, not for God. These have made their mark on history – generally in blood. This will keep happening as long as self-centeredness persists. A moment of distraction and the collective Ego/Us/Tribe drags us into a place of self-centeredness, distorting a great many divine concepts, and affecting religion's status as a path to God.

Religion has been distorted and muddied under self-centeredness; why reduce God to religion, and reduce religion to clerics? The cleric, once established as a representative of God on earth, becomes the one who gives and takes away, and holds the keys to Paradise. Under self-centeredness, as time went by, people found that it was a good thing to have a cleric holding the reins of power: anyone, therefore, who sought power over the common people dressed in holy garb and used his influence – or employed the type of holy men who place themselves above God. Under self-centeredness, people's consciousness is primed for confusion and distortion. Self and Us are established in everyone's minds in a construct where it is well-nigh impossible for God to penetrate.

Followers and Leaders

This takes more than one form, but always has two parties: leader and follower. In some cases, the leader is aware while the follower is not; in others, rarely, both parties are. An example where both are unaware can be found in some types of mass hysteria: a few years ago, a comet passed by Earth, and some followers were convinced by their leader that the comet had been sent to harvest their souls if they killed themselves, whereupon they did. In this example, neither party had any awareness of reality: both chose destruction, which they perceived as a happy ending.

In the scenario of the aware leader and unaware followers, a holy man seeks his own interests, and uses his knowledge and position to achieve this end, directly or indirectly – indirectly via taking some position of political of military power where he does all he can to subjugate the members of his community, and is paid in money, power and/or position; directly by presenting himself as the seat of religious knowledge, in which case he does all he possibly can to make the community members submit to his influence. In either case, these are the unhealthy symptoms of primitive tribalism.

1. The Tribal Leader

A prerequisite for being clan leader is power, whether in the form of people posing a physical threat, or media (later in history) threatening unseen dangers.

2. Members of the Tribe

A given society becomes a tribe(s) – an Us – revolving around a leader who is feared and flattered. The leader's ego is the fulcrum of that society. In the presence of a sufficiently tyrannical "I", an appropriately submissive corresponding "we" is formed. A "Them" to reinforce the "us" and its need for the controlling "I" of the leader is indispensable: if one is present, its threat to "Us" must be emphasized, the "Them" demonized. If there is none, it must be created, and the populace convinced that it poses a clear and present threat.

3. The Witch Doctor

This part is played by the hypocritical cleric, who works to justify the actions of the controlling "I" and brainwash the submissive "we," to demonize the "Them" and establish it as a threat, and entrench the unity of Leader/Religion/God in the popular consciousness. If the Tribal Leader and the Witch Doctor are separate entities – for instance, in princedoms, kingdoms, states, businesses, etc. – the religious influence of the Witch Doctor/Cleric is used in the service of the Tribal Leader, i.e. the holder of political, economic and/or military power. The Tribal Leader and the Witch Doctor can also be one and the same: history is full of examples of this in sects, cults and religious groups.

When people become confused enough to confuse clerics with God, they start to believe Myths that "just ain't so":

1. God is religion.

2. Religion is represented by the cleric.

3. You cannot find God on your own, but need supervision from those closer to Him than yourself. Of course, such a guide must be a cleric.

4. Clerics are infallible.

5. The only path to God's approval is the cleric's approval.

This, in turn, distorts the concept of religion under self-centeredness. *Religion becomes an end in itself, not a path to God.*

Such a misperception poses its own set of challenges. Religion in itself can be a source of many useful things, which can seduce the Self with these benefits: instead of offering a path to God, religion becomes a source of other things that may well distance us from Him. This confusion also confers a false aura of holiness upon clerics that makes them infallible in the eyes of their followers, who race to confer attributes upon him that vie with those of the prophets, and make him virtually godlike.

This is how sects, splinter groups, cults, and sundry religious groups form: a closer look will reveal that each of these creates its own god and graven image, which it worships alongside God without knowledge or awareness. Religious wars throughout history are not really wars of ideas or schools of thought: they are conflicts between gods and their followers, all of whom are willing to give their lives for their leader.

The above is Stage One of eliminating consciousness and awareness. Stage Two, the ultimate catastrophe in my view, is taking God out of the equation altogether and worshipping religion instead of God.

Worshipping religion instead of God? Yes, unfortunately, this is largely the case. This is, in my view, the worst use possible of the concept of religion: instead of a path to God, it is treated as a collective Ego – a controlling Us – a tribe.

Religion and Tribalism

If religion becomes a tribe, all that applies to a tribe applies to religion: it becomes a collective ego *par excellence*, to which all the points mentioned above in "Belonging and Prejudice" apply. Prejudice, unfortunately, prevails. A powerful "Us" appears, seeking a Them against which to define itself, to serve as an enemy, and thus to reaffirm its presence. The tribe of Religion is now a source of security and prejudice to those who belong to it. The Self uses it for its own interests, or to drive away threats. Religion becomes the tribe that shelters us and gives us sustenance: we defend our existence when we defend it. Individual and collective Ego runs high when defending the Tribe of Religion. Instead of a means to an end – finding God – religion becomes an end in itself. The result? God is reduced to a footnote in the consciousness of those who imagine they follow Him, replaced by the Tribe of Religion, taking center stage.

The Self spills rivers of blood in its defense of the Tribe of Religion, its gains, its existence. In appearance, this is a defense of God; in reality, it is a defense of the Tribe of Religion, of Us, of the Collective Ego – self-defense. History is full, and the present is bursting, with examples of people dying for what they think is God, and in fact is religion. History shows us that the tribe is a source of belonging, pride, and strength. In the time of the prophets, the strongest force against new religions was not the individual, but tribal chauvinism. As soon as the tribal elder became a believer, the rest of the tribe followed. Why? Simply, because tribal chauvinism is the example *par excellence* of a collective ego – a classic case of abuse of patriarchy.

In tribal chauvinism, there is a clear Us; the sons and daughters of the tribe marry from among Us, not Them. In any conflict between one of our tribe (Us) and another (Them), tribal chauvinism supports its members. In tribal chauvinism, the customs of the tribe govern its interactions more than the laws of society. In tribal chauvinism, inviolable boundaries – social and/or geographical – are drawn, and none may cross without our permission. Historically, there is a strong tradition of marauding tribes attacking neighboring ones for spoils, killing the men and enslaving the women and children. In a tribal structure based on chauvinism, this is well-known and widely accepted. But in our dealings with religion, things are quite different. If we remained unaware, we might treat our religion like a tribe. What would happen? We might start dealing with our religion as a collective Ego, in flagrant violation of God's commands, and do everything we can to sustain this collective Ego, then say that our religion commands us to – and, worse, believe it!

Let us look at the conflicts between Muslims and Christians, or between dozens of sects of Islam. Are these chauvinistic struggles for God? I invite you, before answering, to do two things: to do a blind taste-test, like a television commercial, inviting a comparison between Brand Y and Brand X. Second: I would like you to add "football supporters" and "ethnic chauvinists worldwide" – such as white supremacists – to the list, as well as such conflicts as the Hutu/Totse conflict in Africa, and the Serb/Croat conflict in Europe. I believe you will find it hard to tell the difference between the practices of extremists under the banner of religion, extremists under the banner of race and ethnicity, the banners of various football clubs, and so on. All of the above are a representation of collective ego *par excellence,* only each flies a different flag. For accuracy's sake, I will say that those who fly the banners of color, race, ethnicity, and football clubs are more sincere and truthful, and more aware of what they are actually advocating (in form and content) than those who fly the flag of religion and creed. And now, let's examine the behaviors exhibited by the above groups. All of them seek to exterminate the other; there is no common ground, but a focus on differences. Although winning is our ultimate goal, if a scenario presented itself where we and the Other might both win, then we'd rather lose. The torch of resentment burns eternal; anyone who tries to put it out is a traitor.

If you apply these practices to the current religious and sectarian conflicts raging day and night in God's name – while He has nothing to do with them – the collective Ego emerges, overpowering and controlling. The collective ego sets up the tribe as a graven image, competing for position with God in the consciousness of its members. The end result of muddled thinking and distorted practices is a focus on the Tribe of Religion instead of God. The above symptoms are indicative of a serious illness: *worshipping religion instead of God.*

Is this shocking? No doubt. But is it true? Look around you and think before trotting out pat answers. Remember, the best medicines do no good with an incorrect diagnosis. Take your sweet time diagnosing. Let me offer you a few diagnostic tools. Some symptoms indicate the use of the collective Ego in the service of the Tribe of Religion, not as a tool to find God. One of these is only caring for those who share your religion. It is a danger sign to find Muslims only caring for Muslims, Christians only for Christians, and Jews for Jews. I am not talking about the specifics of each creed, but the greater good. I believe that every individual's desire to help others despite difference in creed and faith is a good sign, a sign that their relationship with their religion is taking a healthy path. Serving God's creatures in all their diversity and difference is part and parcel of all religions. Differences in faith should not prevent us working together for the common good. God and His prophets urge us to do so.

We may fall into the Tribe of Religion trap unknowingly if we don't heed the warning signs. One such symptom is if you find yourself always looking for differences, not common ground. "Shouldn't an Egyptian Muslim be closer to a Japanese Muslim," one may ask, "than to an Egyptian Christian?" Or, "An Orthodox Egyptian ought to be closer to an Orthodox from Ethiopia than a Muslim from Egypt." And so on: the examples are endless, Shia and Sunni, Catholic and Evangelical, Sufi, Salafi, Muslim Brotherhood, and on and on. This *type* of questioning is indicative of dealing with one's religion as a Tribe, not as a means of coming closer to God. Following others, malicious or well-meaning, into this kind of questioning is to fall into their trap.

Asking that question moves you into a place of "or": You are a Muslim *or* an Egyptian, a Christian *or* an Ethiopian, and so on. I believe that the correct way to deal with such questions, should they arise, is to guide them into a place of "and": I am an Egyptian *and* a Christian. Religion binds me to my sibling in Japan, while history and homeland bind me to my sibling in Egypt. The same holds for the Egyptian Christian, bound by religion to the Christian in Ethiopia, and history and homeland to the Egyptian Muslim. These areas of convergence are keys to coexistence: but, like any key, there are worthless unless they are used to open a door.

Religion as a path to God vs. a tribe becomes very clear in the method used by each group in preaching their religion. The question is: Under which metaphorical skies do you stand when calling upon others to adopt your religion? You can be doing it for them or you can be doing it for yourself. The first is closer to calling them for God, while the second is closer to calling them for Self. In the first case, you want the best for the other person, but you don't hate them for their choice: ultimately, everyone has a God-given freedom to choose what they want. Since you are calling them *to* God, you understand this right and respect your differences. In the second, you want the best for yourself. If they adopt your religion, you are happy for yourself. You are happy that you have added to the sum total of your good works against the Judgment Day. You are happy for Us; you are happy for the Ego, individual and collective, and for tribal chauvinism. If they don't accept your creed, you shower them with curses: they have deprived your Self of its profits, and you hate them – and may fight them – for it. You don't admit that they have the freedom to choose, nor do you accept your differences. To you, they are nothing but an opportunity, and you curse them if they deprive you of it.

Another symptom of the Tribe of Religion is the attempt to confine a certain religion to certain races, or certain geographic locations. You see this clearly when someone screams that "the Christian West" is out to get "the Muslim East!" If you ask innocently, "But what about the millions of Christians in the so-called East?" you won't get a good answer. The same goes for those who claim that the "Muslim East" is a threat to the "Christian West." If you ask innocently, "But what about the millions of Muslims in the so-called West?" you won't get any better answer.

But is there another, healthier, conception of religion? Naturally. It is religion as a path to God, as called for by the prophets, the concept of religion under God-centrism. This will be discussed more fully in the section on God-centrism.

Set down your thoughts and questions in this space.

_____

_____

_____

_____

_____

_____

Civilization under Self-Centeredness: The Tyranny of Us

The concept of civilization under self-centeredness is an attempt on the part of an "Us" to wrest civilization away from "Them" for the benefit of an "Us." In spite of the fact that civilization is built on diversity, some of these attempts have succeeded. History is filled with tales of conflict and struggle between nations and empires; wars broke out to claim or defend land, power, or strategic trade locations. However, about a century ago, there have been (and still are) empires trying to take over, not rival empires, neighboring countries, areas of influence, or trade locations, but *civilization*. Naturally, we mean victorious civilization, the center of modern world, Western civilization.

What Makes Western Civilization Special?

Western civilization, and its predecessors, are wonderful global civilizations. All of them have many bright spots and a few dark ones. This victorious global civilization has brought unprecedented good to the world, and has also been the source of the worst suffering in the world since it was created. As well as doing good for humanity, it also contains much that is inhuman: this civilization that now comprises the USA, the European Union, Canada and Australia, is a tribe of about 20% of the world's population, and controls about 80% of the planet's resources. Most importantly, the world is experiencing something unprecedented in history: since Adam's time, people throughout the globe have never been so connected to one another.

This is truly unprecedented. Even in the fifteenth century, there were civilizations on the planet that had no idea that other civilizations existed: even then, just knowing about them was the most one could hope for. When we speak of Ancient Egypt, Greece, or Rome, these are civilizations that sprang up around the Mediterranean Basin, whose circles of influence never came into contact with China, for example. Its citizens never knew that there were people living in three continents: the Americas and Australia. This historical moment is unique: I cannot claim that all the world's inhabitants are in contact with one of the others, but I can comfortably claim that a sufficient number of the world's 195 countries (the number of independent members of the UN) are in contact with a sufficient number of people in other countries for communication to be complete. Moreover, this communication is in real time – and *that* is happening for the first time in history, a kind of holistic awareness of what is happening on this planet: this is a kind of development for humans, that has created something new: a kind of direct impact. When you are directly connecting, and directly connected, to such a degree, there are unprecedented consequences. It is only natural for the stronger to affect the weaker, and the victor, the vanquished. The Victorious Civilization right now is Western civilization. It has an immediate and global effect on everyone on the planet – again, a unique and unprecedented occurrence. This also places an existential responsibility on that civilization, a responsibility never borne by any previous human civilization.

Historical Overview

A quick look at past centuries from the perspective of Collective Ego will yield an important conclusion. Let us examine the map of what is now unified Germany in 1648. Why that date? Because that was the signing of the treaties that comprised the Peace of Westphalia, ending dozens of years of war in Europe, and considered by many to be the first step in a 400-year journey culminating in the creation of the EU. Why do I say "what is now unified Germany?" Because it is a good example of a great many splinters – hundreds – of entities: in the language of this book, these entities great and small each clung to their own Us'ness, and viewed their neighbors with prejudice, and themselves – their Tribe – with a bloated ego. Long wars, claiming lives and property, resulted from the clashes between the different "Us" entities, each with its own bloated ego. The leaders of each "Us" were obliged to come together and sign the treaties that comprised the Peace of Westphalia.

After the signing of the treaties, the small entities in what is now unified Germany began to unite, forming comparatively larger units. In the language of this book, the multiple "Us" entities were obliged to expand their understanding of the collective Ego to form a smaller number of larger units of "Us." The tribe had to expand their conception of the collective Ego in order to accommodate some Others; the price of this expansion was the tens of thousands of lives lost in war, and hundreds of thousands lost in war-related diseases.

Germany, 1848

These tiny German entities had to come together into only 38, to confront the challenge posed by Napoleon Bonaparte's armies: again, in the language of this book, the multiple "Us" had to expand its conception of the collective Ego in order to form fewer entities, with a broader definition of "Us"; the tribe was again obliged to expand in order to accommodate some Others. This, again, came at the price of hundreds of thousands of lives.

Germany, 1871

Germany had come together into more or less the country as we know it today: in the language of this book, the multiple "Us" had to rein in its conception of the collective Ego in order to form a single "Us," which came at the price of hundreds of thousands of lives. The European model comes next: this required two world wars, WWI and WWII, dragging Europe, Asia and most of the world's countries into a bloody war, claiming tens of millions of lives, after which the European Union was formed, with close ties and trade between all the previous enemies, and Japan as well. The United Nations was also formed: again, the Us expands its conception of the collective ego and its definition of Us, and the tribe needed to expand to accommodate those who were once its enemies. After two world wars, the leadership hierarchy of the European empires changed; the empires themselves were dissolved, and the map of Europe itself redrawn to accommodate the influence of two rising empires with a new historical form: the USSR and the USA.

After the Cold War, the conflict was resolved in favor of the American Empire; its rival, the USSR, finally dissolved in 1980. Large parts of its sphere of influence are currently being annexed to the victorious empire's junior partner.

The above is nothing new: it's history. Why am I telling you this? Well, because I believe that the events of the past century has led – with or without attendant awareness – to the distortion of Western civilization, with all its healthy connotations, into "the Tribe of Western Civilization," with all its unhealthiest connotations: individual and collective ego, a despotic "Us" seeking a threatening "Them", and so on. How did this happen?

The Rise of the Tribe

I don't know whether the formation of the tribe over 150 years was the result of long-term planning, successive planning, or even chance, but in any case, I do know it took place over two stages: firstly, the Empire annexing Western civilization; secondly, the Corporation annexed both the Empire and civilization.

First: The Empire Annexes Western Civilization

One of the indicators of the decline of a civilization is the erosion of the empires that flourished within it. They then get swallowed up by the last empire standing, along with the rest of the nations that belonged to that civilization; the empire then begins to acquire a gigantic stature, dwarfing the civilization, at which point the situation is reversed: civilization follows empire. This was the case with Islamic civilization, which became the property of the powerful Ottoman Empire; it is now, I believe, occurring with Western civilization, which is gradually becoming the property of the powerful American Empire. In these cases, the fate of a civilization is dependent on the fate of the empire that annexed it; the decline of empire is a strong indicator of a historical end to that civilization.

The above was an introduction to this: When the giants were empires, "Us" under self-centeredness tended to be the Tribe of the White Race, or the Empire of the White Race. The British empire was formed on a truly remarkable and astonishing insistence by individuals whose only concern was annexing the largest quantity of territory possible to the Empire; they thought nothing of risking their lives for it, venturing to what, to them, was the ends of the earth for many reasons: to discover new countries (John Cecil Rhodes (1853 - 1902) – South Africa), to create new opportunities in new places (John Stuart Mill (1806 - 1873) – India), for international exploration with the Royal Geographical Society like Sir Richard Burton (1821 - 1890) and John Speke (1827 - 1864), or simply as wealthy adventurers like Samuel Baker (1821 - 1893), who discovered the sources of the River Nile. All of this opened the Empire's eyes to – and whetted their appetite for – the new lands that had been discovered.

"Discovered" is a telling term. Its very use is evidence of the inflated Western ego. There is no clearer indication of these explorers' complete disregard for these countries' thousands of years of history and geography, or for their inhabitants. For them, the history of these places began when they "discovered" them: they even went so far as to give them new names, as though they were only born the moment the "discoverers" set eyes on them.

There are other examples, of course, and other empires other than the British Empire. Some ambitious leaders employed a number of European discoverers and adventurers to annex large swathes of territory to their empires, most famously Henry Morton Stanley's (1841 - 1904) discovery of the Congo for Leopold II of Belgium,

179

transforming a tiny European country into a sprawling Afro-Belgian empire many times its original size. (The Egyptian Khedive Ismail similarly commissioned Charles Gordon (1833 - 1885) to discover new lands.) The main motivation, other than personal glory and financial gain, was these explorers' inner sense of being prophets, bearing to the world their message of the 3 C's: Christianity, Civilization and Commerce.

This feeling of being heaven-sent prophets of civilization to humanity at large was accompanied by a conviction of being racially superior to, and generally better and more refined than, the natives of the countries they visited. This was a by-product of philosophy, Darwinism, etc., i.e. the intellectual framework of Europe, especially Western Europe, at the time, which was flourishing in a manner unparalleled before or since. This created a deep-seated conviction in Europeans that they were superior to every other race, stemming not only from whiteness but from the discoveries during the Renaissance, the age of Steam, and the Industrial Revolution. This helped firmly establish their certainty that they were the superior race: it was easy to ignore civilizational cross-pollination, the fact that civilizations rise and fall, that there are always those who must be more advanced, as a result of circumstances and environment, not race or ethnicity. The inhabitants of this small area of the world acquired a sense of superiority, followed by a clear sense of individual and collective Ego: "We, the White European Race, are fully human; other races are incomplete, not like us, members of the Tribe of Western Civilization."

Due to the power differential at the time, the entrenched conviction of superiority, and the certainty of an exclusive monopoly on truth and right, this sense of superiority found explicit and direct expression in all the works of the time. Therefore, if there was any conflict of interest between the children of Western Civilization and any other race, the other race was simply exterminated, just like that, with ready moral justification: "the good of human civilization", which they felt at the time to be exclusively theirs. Native Americans were slaughtered by European immigrants in North America and Canada; the Aztecs, Mayans and Incas in South America were slaughtered by the Spanish. In southern Africa, the Boers and the British slaughtered the native population; in North Africa, the same thing happened with the French colonizers, and in the Congo with Belgians. In Australia, British, European and other settlers decimated the Aboriginal population.

I would like to alert the reader that in the era of empires, the zero-sum competitive model prevailed: I win everything, the other loses everything. In that era, when the New World had bowed to the powerful empires of Western Europe, hundreds of millions in several continents submitting to their power and military might, the practical application of racial discrimination began, a result of the prevalence of Darwinism in the minds of the powers controlling Western civilization. Since the Other was the Enemy, all that the makers of Empire cared about was getting rid of the other. There were military, colonial, and economic reasons for this. However, the Other – now subjugated into a citizen of the Empire – became a target for racial discrimination. Many of the countries and nations that had submitted to Empire had a rich heritage, culture and civilization. The Empire therefore had two choices: to consider the defeated Other a partner, view their civilizational and cultural heritage as a diversity to be respected, add to it and build on its science and culture, and thereby produce a heterogeneous civilization belonging to both victor and vanquished; or, alternatively, to consider the Other a prisoner of war, and his heritage as the spoils: a resource to be appropriated, with no obligation to respect its difference or diversity, and poured into the melting-pot of the victorious civilization, with the right to take what they want and discard and despise the rest. The result would be a Western civilization of hcterogeneous sources, belonging only to the victor. This is what is meant by Imperial takeover of civilizations, and the Tribe of Western Civilization.

It is noteworthy that the total takeover of other civilizations was delayed by competition between different Imperial powers: at the dawn of the twentieth century, two powers, the British and the French, were head and shoulders ahead of any other. Competition between these was the first priority, and its continuation slowed the Empire from swallowing European civilization entirely. The roots of the greatest tribe in human history were in the 20th century, specifically in 1904, with the signing of the Entente Cordiale between England and France, with its direct aim of facilitating France's takeover of Morocco in return for legitimizing the British Empire's hold on Egypt. It was especially directed at the ambitions of the new, rising power calling for its own international empire-building right: Germany. I believe that one of this agreement's direct results was the calming of the decades-old competition between the two empires. For centuries, these empires had butted heads, despite hailing from the same intellectual and cultural background; their desires always prevented them from collaborating. It took a threat from Germany for them to take this step. What happened in April 1904 started a countdown: the empires tasted the fruits of alliance, beginning a wave of alliances and unions that is still going on. From a civilizational standpoint, the alliance formed a weighty center of Western civilizational influence, soon joined by other countries in Western Europe, which in turn laid the groundwork for their alliance in WWI. From the tribal formation standpoint, this alliance paved the way for the formation of the Tribe of Western Civilization.

Do you recall the sociological definition of a tribe and its components? The desire for a group, and specific origins or provenance. These were at first shared by Britain and France, followed by the USA; the membership was completed in WWII, made up of the same countries/origins, bearing different weights. The end of the war was tacit permission for a shift of roles, the strongest member becoming the USA, while Britain and France took a back seat. Starting from 1904 to 1945, a clear definition of the Western empire appeared: "Us." This is our empire, this is our tribe, the tribe of Western civilization.

Second: The Corporation Annexes the Empire and Western Civilization

After World War Two, the triumph of the United States had wide-ranging and far-reaching effects on the world. What I would like to focus on here is the culture of multinational corporations. With the rise of the American Age came new concepts: for instance, the direct annexation of foreign territory fell out of vogue. Such an enterprise was prohibitively costly, in terms of money and human resources; besides, the countries of the world, crippled by two world wars, had taken steps and put mechanisms in place to prevent it happening again: the United Nations and the Security Council, which posed obstacles to any nation attempting to acquire colonies outside its own borders. This necessitated a change in tactics, not in strategy. The new empire sought world hegemony and control, only more cheaply. It succeeded. In place of the vast armies required by the empires of yore, the young empire used – or was used by – skilled players in the limelight and behind the scenes.

The players who took center stage were (1) a high-class diplomatic apparatus and (2) the leaders of giant multinational corporations; those behind the scenes were (3) intelligence and security apparatuses. Note the strong links and intersectionality between the three players. This becomes even clearer when we note that high-ranking diplomatic and intelligence personnel moved gradually to leadership positions in multinationals. This three-pronged apparatus largely succeeded in getting most of the countries of the world to work for the Empire's interests, without any official declaration of empire.

The circumstances were more than favorable for a young, energetic business empire to take over an exhausted and depleted world. The two world wars that had decimated the world had directly benefited the American economy, and transformed the USA from a state with middling economic and military capacity (at the start of the twentieth century) into a veritable international economic and military giant in less than fifty years. The USA had become the official representative of Western culture in the post-WWII world, and the American Dream, hitherto confined to that country's people, had become the world's. These corporations did business as official representatives of the Future.

The term "multinational corporations" emerged early on in their career. At the start the giants that took over the world were exclusively American, gathering the post-war plunder – plunder in a new form, markets, companies, sources of energy and of water. This was accomplished through honest and not-so-honest agreements and alliances with the administrations of the countries it had interests in. These corporations quickly became so gigantic that the operating budget of some of them was larger than the GDP of many countries. For the first time in human history, the world had come to know a form of powerful giant other than the old familiar form of empire. The eyes of the world were on these giant multinationals, their interests, their employees, their administration, management and literature. A fun fact is that some of their products became worldwide economic benchmarks: for example, the "Big Mac Index" is used by economists to measure the value of a given currency based on how much a Big Mac costs in that country's currency of origin – measuring purchasing power in countries with a McDonald's. The journey to gianthood has its own culture and literature, which rapidly affected world civilization as a whole. These corporations' unprecedented success set the rest of the world's businesses running to follow in their footsteps. Their literature, business models, management systems, and speedy growth were taught at business schools throughout the world. Whatever these companies did, wanted and advocated became what the "world" wanted and aspired to.

This was a blank check for the corporations to take over the Empire, and civilization: to take over history's largest tribe. And so went the second takeover of the Tribe of Western Civilization.

A look at the literature of this new tribe will seem like a digression, but I think it is of the utmost importance to examine how this literature has affected the collective consciousness of the world's people.

When a country was overtaken by an empire in the past, it survived with its heritage and culture mostly intact, its 'form', if you will, with a few changes to preserve its interests as best it could. In fact, conquering empires often found it best to leave the existing structures of government and administration in place in vanquished countries, with the addition of some sort of High Commissioner controlling the puppet leader of what was then known as a "colony." The leadership *appeared* to remain in the hands of the *ancien regime*, which completely surrendered to the new empire; but most people, and most of the land, remained as they were. (I say most, not all, because some of the people would have been exterminated, to persuade the rest of the people to surrender.)

However, when the world's giants became companies and not countries, swallowing up smaller companies and putting them out of business on the road to gianthood, there was a new type of 'takeover'. When a company goes out of business or is bought by another, it is a matter of course that some employees will be downsized or replaced; the old company will lose its name, 'cut up' and sold, or dissolve into the new entity. "The people" and "the land" do not survive. This helped establish a new model: your opponent will *actually* disappear.

A new meaning was added to the concept of 'extermination': disappearance. Your opponent vanishes; his component parts vanish. Most people accepted this idea at first; then, they adopted it. Over time, admiring this giant growth, they adopted its literature and terminology. There became only one definition of competition; "legal extermination." Most people developed a conviction that this had been the only definition in every time and place. Some of this literature also had a profound effect on the world. There have always been essential differences between states and corporations, size being the first of course. But with corporations annexing civilizations, the differences are eroding. In the literature of a company, any company, is based on a basic premise: profit. The management and the workers are merely tools to make and increase profits; if there is any conflict of interest between those who take the money (such as shareholders) and those who make the money, the latter are immediately fired and new management and workers hired. Profit is the only criterion for success. In the literature of business, anything is for sale, even the company itself if its owners are offered enough. This does not apply to nations. Nations have no owners or shareholders; being fired for not making enough profit does not apply.

Business principles not applying to nations was a principle that was deeply shaken when corporations annexed Western civilization. The situation was exacerbated when some companies became larger than some nations. As a result, the owners of some giant corporations began to treat some resource-rich and awareness-poor countries like companies: this signaled the second wave of attrition, after the dissolution of the colonies, this time at the hands of high-ranking state officials/corporations. The state/corporation changes its laws for the benefit of the corporation, the Tribe of Western Civilization, aided and abetted by the state's corrupt elite, at the behest of the companies.

To market a pharmaceutical drug, weapons or some food or consumer item, or to monopolize some natural resource, laws are leveled, to legalize exploitation; high-ranking officials of the state/ corporation are contained via complex politico-financial formulas. Companies make billions through modifying a given country's laws to accommodate its business practices. Companies pay comparatively insignificant bribes of money or guarantees of political support. This equation is paid for by hundreds of millions of people who live in such countries, via direct threats to life and limb, or to their mental health; or by depriving them of the right to use the resources of their own country. Worse is when the practices and literature of these corporations infect the laws of a country: corrupt officials become convinced that they own the country/company, and that their citizens are their subjects/ employees. Any objection to the practices of the country/company, for the benefit of the Tribe of Western Civilization, are fired for violation of the terms of service: they are either literally 'terminated' from life, or physically removed from the country/company as a kind of actual dismissal. The true tragedy is that the victims themselves sometimes assimilate these values: hundreds of the citizens of such states believe they don't own their own countries, but are like guests or employees, who risk being fired if they break the rules. Hundreds of millions of these unhappy people live out their lives in these countries/companies as though in a labor camp… or a battery farm.

In battery farms, a pair of animals, usually rabbits or chickens, are kept in adjacent tiny cages, for nothing but breeding and eventual slaughter. Hundreds of millions of citizens have become like these animals: they live in tiny boxes, only allowed to eat, breed, and wait to die. If anyone objects, they are terminated: an example for the rest. My point here is the way the owners and leaders of the Tribe of Western Civilization view and value these people. This tiny minority controlling the corporations now also controls dozens of country/companies, and by extension millions of battery-dwelling citizens. They know exactly what's happening to them, being the main reason – if not the direct reason – behind it. But what for? The answer immediately comes to mind, "Greed: the desire to make the greatest possible profit for the Tribe of Western Civilization." Is this the only reason? I believe that the underlying reason is greed. The remnants of Darwinian thought remain at the back of the minds of the controllers of Western Civilization & Co.. They have – I believe – never jettisoned the idea that the Other is an inferior being, undeserving of their riches, more befitting the superior members of the Western Civilization & Co. They still retain the sense of racial superiority: no matter how cultured, the Other is still undeserving of equal status in their eyes. That is why, deep down, they despise the Other. Looking down on the Other was explicit in the old, empire-building days: they were far more advanced and powerful. The Empire existed on the ground, with real holdings in colonized nations; there was hence no need to hide this disdain. Unfortunately, history tells us that many of the literary figures of the colonies shared this sense of being inferior to the members of the Empire. They really and truly believed themselves fortunate to be colonized by the Others, out of a conviction that this was the only road to progress, to resembling their masters.

This deep-seated disdain for the Other is now hidden under a thick layer of hypocrisy, which the tiny controlling minority feels compelled to adopt. They certainly don't want to pay the price of the return of the colonies: the experiment of the last century made it clear that the human and financial cost was too high, whereas the current experiment shows them that they can make far more profit from the colonies for next to no human cost, and incomparably lower financial expenditure. The only price is the thick layer of contempt concealing their disdain for the Other.

These words may be painful and shocking: what matters is how close they are to the truth. This is my opinion; I may be wrong. The main point is that the reason underlying corporations' annexation of civilization is the one mentioned above, a paradigm belonging to a particular era: "This civilization is ours. To join us, you must abandon all your history, all your culture, all your heritage, and become just like us. Even when you have done all we ask, we will view you as a freak, and treat you as a second-class citizen within our civilization." I believe that a great deal of confusion will be averted if we replace the term 'civilization' with 'tribe.'

Set down any thoughts and questions you may have.

_____

_____

_____

_____

_____

_____

_____

_____

_____

_____

I

The Foolish Conflict

Let me refresh your memory: Above, we said that the tribe was the largest social group in history before the rise of nations; it is originally a beautiful concept, offering its members safety, security and stability. A tribe is a group of people distantly related through ancestry. Sociologists tell us that the existence of every group depends on two factors: a place and a sense of community; both factors are present in the tribe, in the extended family, distant relationships, allies and so forth. Historically, the tribe, to its members, was a more primitive form what the state currently represents to its citizens. Tribal justice was based on tribal beliefs: every tribe had a collection of internal laws, applied strictly to its members. It had a collection of external laws to govern its dealings with other tribes. The tribe rose up as one man to defend one of its members from aggression, even at the cost of waging war.

When the concept of state gained power, this led to a weakening of the old tribal bonds, for example in the tribes of Germania and Scandinavia in Central and Northern Europe, and similarly in Southeast Asia. It is all too easy for the tribal bond to transform into a collective Ego, powerfully mobilizing the "Us." Some tribes were powerfully self-centered; they usually chose their own god, reinforcing their "Us" of collective ego. These tribes were known as idolaters. They were completely satisfied with their lot: they were sincere, if idolatrous. In the modern age, I believe there are groups to which the conditions for defining an idolatrous tribe apply, even though they are hardly as honest with themselves as their ancient counterparts.

The modern idolaters worships Us alongside God, even though they don't necessarily admit it. A tribe of idolaters is one that pays lip service to God, but in their dealings, worship the Tribe alongside Him. An idolatrous tribe is one that converges around a powerful collective Ego, a controlling "Us": its organizers are fanatically loyal to it.

The Foolish Game of Tribes: The Tribe of Western Civilization vs. Islam

Maybe it's a conspiracy; maybe it's a deviation, on the heels of our mutual collective egos. In any case, there is something illogical going on here that should not be underestimated. One of the definitions of being foolish is not knowing that you don't know, and I believe that a bitter struggle is being waged now in the world, best described as foolish. I believe it is a conflict between mental images more than any actual conflict. The result of these inaccurate mental images regarding this conflict is that hundreds of millions have swallowed the idea of a conflict between the Islamic religion and Western civilization; but I think the correct definition would be a conflict between the Tribe of Islamic Religion and the Tribe of Western Civilization. What a difference between Western Civilization and the Tribe of Western Civilization, what a difference between Islam as a religion and the Tribe of Islamic Religion!

In the following pages, I shall present what may be termed "The Game of Idolatrous Tribes." It is a game: it is practiced like war games on some console. They are tribes: the truth has been twisted, and enough people brainwashed, to generate false mental images that represent "civilization" and "religion" as tribes. These tribes I call idolatrous for the reasons discussed above.

Two concepts will make this clear: 1) The best cure, as I have said, is useless without a correct diagnosis. The world is suffering from a great, big incorrect diagnosis, in which immense things are incorrectly named, and the world's people believe this false nomenclature. There is something profoundly wrong when we come to the size and number of the combatants.

There *is* a conflict. But it is between a tiny minority on each side: a minority that has usurped the name of the majority, and speaks in its name. It operates on fear, and makes the majority so afraid that they continue to let it speak in its name, and create conflict in its name.

2) Perception Is Reality: Once an idea is established in our minds, we think it is true, whether or not it exists in reality. This is the first tool in the conman's arsenal: without force, they sell us illusions, and we hand over our money in all good faith. The conman's trick doesn't last for long, just long enough for him to make off with the money of his unfortunate dupes. History tells us of 'long cons' that take years to set up, with tremendous sums at stake. I believe that what is going on in the global arena is something not unlike this.

We have two entities, ironically similar in size: these have been turned – distorted, I should say – into two warring idolatrous tribes. We have a civilization that has been distorted into an idolatrous tribe, and a religion that has suffered the same fate. These entities are

Western Civilization and Islam, now turned into the Tribe of Western Civilization and the Tribe of Islamic Religion. Attempts are made to convince Muslims that the wicked West is at war with their religion, while efforts are made to convince the West that Islam urges its followers to violence and that they are its first intended victims. Have both these wonderful entities been distorted deliberately, or have we come to this pass via overreactions that have escalated over hundreds of years? Or both? I neither know nor care in the current situation: what matters is what we are going to do about it. How can we make the truth clear? How can we deal with the situation with wisdom and prudence?

To be fair, there are visible manifestations that might make it seem as though there is a grain of truth in this perception: each of them is filled with fear, enmity, anger and hatred of enemies belonging to the other camp, and to "Them." Each of them numbers about 1.5 billion, a little over 20% of the people on the planet. The cruel irony is that, in practice, it is invalid to have a conflict between a religion and a civilization! It would make as much sense as a company pitting its profits against the number of goals scored by a football team. There is no basis for comparison: profits vs. matches won. There is no basis for comparison, let alone competition. The same is true for civilization and religion: there is no basis for comparison, never mind competition. More importantly, the relationship between a civilization and a religion is one of inclusiveness: as we know, civilizations hold many religions, and diverse populations. This is part and parcel of the definition of civilization. It is the nature of religion to enrich civilizations intellectually and spiritually; besides, a religion can be adopted by anyone – or everyone – regardless of their civilization, race or ethnicity.

Most religions have been and always will be like this, by definition. However, if a religion is distorted into an idolatrous tribe, and the tiny minority is able to convince the majority that there is an Other completely different from 'I', and that this other belongs to a Them that threatens Us, it follows that we need our tribe to protect us from theirs. I believe that stoking the flames of hatred and fear is the result of a handful (a few hundred) of cultural and religious extremists, manifested in the actions of a few thousand people, maybe tens of thousands, which in turn has tarred hundreds of millions with an unjust brush, nothing like what they really are. The few hundred speak as if they represent hundreds of millions, and are commissioned by them to act in their name. This applies to both parties: Western Civilization and the Islamic religion.

The Tribe of Western Civilization

A tiny minority of people in Western Civilization treat it as an idolatrous tribe. This minority, though small, is vocal and influential: they are the ones who communicate with the Other, while most people in Western civilization are busy with their lives and families. The silence of hundreds of millions looks to the minority – and, importantly, to the people on the other side of the rift – like a license to speak in their name.

It is the same on the other side. Out of hundreds of millions of Muslims, groups have sprung up, no more than a few hundred in number, and begun to deal with Islam as though it is the Tribe of Islamic Religion – these, too, act as though they represent the rest of the hundreds of millions, whose silence tempts the minority to believe that they *do* represent them – a belief that has spread to millions on the other side of the divide.

In my opinion, both are false. The majority is merely silent, slumbering. Using this silence as a license to act in their name is a con – a long con, but a con nonetheless. But what about the silent majority, without whose silence none of this would have happened? I would like to remind these: *Ignorantia juris non excusat.* There is not much difference in our case between the ignorant and the foolish. This unique global influence has been horrifically abused by a few: by those who wish to transform Western Civilization into the Tribe of Western civilization. This minority has attempted to hijack the noble and lofty concept of civilization and turn it into a monstrous freak; it has, unfortunately, largely succeeded. This minority of people from Western civilization insist on a dark side that accompanied the rise and development of this civilization: the 'specialness' and exclusivity of the races of Western Europe, the world's most advanced race. At the time, this was explicit, with literature explaining it and roots in Darwinist thought. Europe and the colonies were inundated with this trend: but that was 150 years ago, and any attempt to view humanity through this lens, even in secret, is laughable. Some of the people in this civilization do their best to turn the rest of the world into copies of themselves, working diligently to exhort the rest of the globe to abandon all their cultural and civilizational heritage. Meticulous tests have been devised to screen for how well someone from another civilization has "changed his spots" and metamorphosed submissively into a creature they can approve as worthy of Western Civilization.

Such criteria are set out in international trade agreements, with the tacit understanding that the nonconformists are a kind of lunatic fringe who will soon learn to do what's right. The criteria can be found in international cultural, scientific and artistic awards, engineered to attract the world's best and brightest – changing, as we have said, their spots, in the form of clothing, culture and values, in the process. The same goes for sporting contests, entertainment, et cetera. The power of Western Civilization has been used – in conjunction with the power of real-time communication – to sell these criteria as "universal criteria," under the umbrella of that great term, globalization.

But what of those who don't want to join the club? These are destroyed. The powerful minority that seeks to turn Western civilization into a savage tribe – a confrontational civilization *par excellence* – makes its first rule: *Those who are different from us are a threat to us, and must be crushed.* This is a perfect example of a collective Ego, a controlling "Us." But, is the above only confined to Western civilization? I think not; the thing is, though, that no civilization before Western Civilization has ever had the capability to affect the entire world simultaneously, which explains its unprecedented influence, not to say dominance. This minority's way of thinking reflects their actions as a tribe with an overpowering collective ego, an overpowering "Us," that views others as the enemy, lying in wait for us as we lie in wait for them. If there is no "Them," it invents one, the way they invented the Tribe of Islamic Religion in the wake of the fall of the last enemy standing, the USSR.

The controllers of this tribe try their hardest to make its members believe that the world resents them, is plotting against them, hating their freedoms, and wants nothing more than to steal their present riches and future prosperity. The Tribe of Western Civilization, I believe, is an illusory construct: I have never seen hundreds of millions of people supporting it as an ideological leaning. The overwhelming majority who let themselves be threatened are, I believe, unaware, and uncaring: they are too busy with their daily lives. This does not relieve them of responsibility, since what is being done is done in their name, and the influential minority that seeks to turn civilization into a tribe has succeeded in creating a global assumption that they do represent the hundreds of millions of members of Western civilization. Its greatest success has been creating this assumption in the minds of those whom it has chosen for its enemies.

The minority controlling the civilization managed to bring about the dissolution of the USSR, and broke the back of the nascent economic power in Japan, clipped the claws of the Asian tiger, and is gearing up to face down the Chinese industrial giant: still, it was in need of a new enemy, so it came up with the Tribe of Islam. It was not, it must be admitted, the only maker of this tribe; it was assisted by others, either through practical assistance on the ground of through ignorance and apathy. Again, I neither know nor care whether the propagators of this illusion do it because they really believe it or whether they are profiting from it; the point is that under self-centeredness, these people enjoy an inflated individual and collective ego. The entire world has suffered from its manifestations.

The Tribe of Islamic Religion

There is a difference between Islam as a religion and Islam as a tribe. Islam is the valuable religion sent down by God as the last and most perfect of all religions. The Tribe of Islam is a collection of practices motivated by the collective ego of some of the believers in this religion, leading to a distorted image of this wonderful religion, making it into a parody of an idolatrous tribe, with all that that means. Unfortunately, this image has succeeded so far, and is gaining popularity. These attempts to spread it have been served by minorities on both sides (within and without Islam), and believed by the majorities on both sides.

I believe that to understand how the mental image was formed that managed to distort the perception of a lofty religion into a tribe, we need a great deal of disambiguation. At the start, I believe there is a great deal of confusion between four terms: 1-Islam, the religion; 2-Muslims; 3-Empires and states that flourished in Islamic times; 4-Islamic civilization. I imagine that this confusion prevails almost worldwide, including among a great many Muslims. Dispelling it is an essential step towards any diagnosis.

1. Islam, the Religion

A religion sent by God through the prophet Muhammad, peace be upon him, to guide humans on how to worship Him, like all religions before it.

2. Muslims

People who chose to adopt this religion. What they do is motivated by who they are, not by the religion they believe in.

There is a principle in law in some countries that forbids praising or criticizing a judge's decisions; this, the principle goes, has a negative effect on the judge's status and may prevent litigants in particular, and citizens in general, from feeling secure in the application of justice, which is contrary to the public good. Religion deserves, no less, to be dealt with similarly.

What has occurred is that a minority, not exceeding a few thousands, has decided that violence is its best means of expression, and the result has been a global perception of millions of peaceable Muslims as belonging to that minority that has chosen violence. That unjust mental image has prevailed worldwide, via the rule "perception is reality," and millions of innocents pay the price.

1. Empires and states that flourished in Islamic times

Examples are the Umayyad Dynasty, the Abbasid Dynasty, the Seljuk Dynasty, the Mamelukes, the Moghuls in India, Andalusian civilization, etc.

2. Islamic Civilization

It has been clarified in the introduction to this book that, like any civilization, it constitutes an umbrella comprising numerous and diverse religions, cultures, races and ethnicities. A question I had in mind when thinking about the distortion of the Islamic religion into the Tribe of Islam: When did Islamic civilization acquire that name? Who called it that?

Islamic civilization was an inclusive, worldwide civilization – as far as the 'world' meant in that era – a melting-pot where many civilizations came together. Why is this point important? Why might it have a negative impact on the perception of Islam in the consciousness of many?

Why call it "Islamic Civilization?"

Why even ask? Well, because in my opinion, there are two uses of that name.

1.   The healthy and fair usage of "Islamic Civilization" describes its universal nature, its inclusiveness of other civilizations and religions in its heyday.

2.   The unfair and misleading usage of "Islamic Civilization" in an attempt at distorting its history, creating the illusion that it was confined to one religion and one group, i.e. Muslims. This is a deliberate attempt at misrepresenting this civilization, belittling its past, present and future: it gives a false impression that it was confined to only Muslims, stripping it of its most important characteristic, its universality and inclusiveness. If this had been correct, it would not have become a civilization. It comprised many languages, races, civilizations and ethnicities; since it was a global civilization *par excellence*, it cross-pollinated with previous civilizations, intermingled with its contemporaries, and handed its achievements to the next civilization down the line, Western Civilization.

The same goes for Islam: confining it to the members of a single civilization detracts from its universal nature. Why, then, this confusion? There are some theories:

Option 1: This name was devised by some members of Western Civilization. It makes sense to call their own civilization that, as explained in the section on Darwinism: Some would like to claim it for their own race, and monopolize its resources exclusively. "This civilization belongs to *us*, and no-one can share," the name seems to say. Might some members of Western civilization then have come up with the name "Islamic civilization" so as to keep their own gains for themselves, and draw a dividing line between Us and Them? "Our" flourishing civilization must be clearly demarcated, and separated from the less-prosperous "Them." In my opinion, this is the work of a bloated collective Western ego, welcomed by Muslims, which generated an equivalent egotistical tendency in the so-called "Islamic world."

Option 2: This name was devised by the world's 1.2 billion Muslims as a result of the abysmal living conditions for most of them. Most Muslims live in countries that are at or near the bottom of the global index for nearly every category. Economic, scientific and social development; innovation; arts and sciences; liberty, justice and dignity, all are at rock bottom. This situation has made some feel inferior to the rest of humanity; they use the term as a sort of escape from a painful present to a flourishing past. In an attempt to feel special, they tried to convince everyone – and themselves above all – that this civilization was confined to themselves and their ancestors. Escape into the past and confining oneself to a specific framework creates favorable conditions for a collective ego.

Option 3: The concepts of Islamic religion and Islamic civilization were conflated when this civilization rose quickly on the heels of the rising new religion, making it seem that religion was the direct source of this civilization. This, I believe, is true, but not the whole truth: let's look for the missing pieces.

Religious scholars tell us that Islam is a methodology for living, and a path to God; this methodology is divided into *worship,* governing humans' relationship with God, and *conduct,* governing humans' indirect relationship with God through their relationship with other humans. Neither of these methodologies makes it clear how this civilization was formed, nor the speed with which it sprang up. What happened?

Allow me to remind you of the words of Algerian thinker Malik Bennabi on thought, things and persons. I believe that the world of culture and the arts belongs to the world of thought; the utilization of culture to invent things that will benefit humanity belongs to the world of things; I believe that those who have the ability to turn thought from theory/culture into these useful inventions are people, the world of persons. The degree of success in this depends in the quality of person; but what has all this to do with civilizational advancement? I believe that the great development that followed the spread of Islam had to do with the caliber of person who adopted Islam in its early years. It started in the Arabian Peninsula, then spread to the Levant, Persia. Egypt, India, Southern, Western and Southeast Asia, and other countries with deep cultural and civilizational roots. In Egypt was the Ptolemaic Dynasty, who had submitted to the Romans, and were deeply immersed in the knowledge of both Ancient Egyptian and Greek civilizations. The Levant was an integral part of the cultural heritage of the Roman empire. Iraq and Persia enjoyed ancient Persian heritage, and also ancient Babylon and Sumeria. In India, there was the ancient cultural tradition around the Sindh River, the Ganges, and many others.

Historically, those civilizations had waged war against one another, keeping their heritage for their members and using it against their opponents. What happened when some of the members of these civilizations adopted Islam? I believe that its methodology may have opened their eyes to what God truly wants, what He sent to them in this religion: that they are His property, and that their rich cultural heritage was the property of God, not of their monarchs, their empires, or their civilizations. It followed that it belonged to all humanity, and it was their duty to grant free access to it to God's creatures. And they did. The members of these civilizations offered their knowledge freely, and collaborated to develop it; because that part of the world had held the most advanced civilizations of the ancient world, its members' enthusiasm to benefit God's children led to unprecedented cultural cross-pollination. The change from warring entities to collaborative groups beneath a single civilizational umbrella made the geographical, political and psychological barriers between them more permeable; this led to an even greater cultural and scientific exchange, and rapid development. This change also gave rise to a fast-growing, young and energetic civilization built on the diverse and rich heritage of the era's greatest civilizations on the planet.

Let us imagine a contrasting scenario: What if this young religion, in the same era, had spread among primitive tribes with no culture or civilization to speak of. Would we have had the same magnificent civilization? I doubt it. The rapid flourishing of Islamic civilization was not only a function of Islam, but of those who adopted it. We must not forget that there were many non-Muslims among those who worked to build these civilizations, as well as non-Abrahamic religions. In fact, Muslims made up no more than 5% of the total population of the countries to which Islam spread; however, they were part of a tolerant and inclusive world civilization that welcomed scientists, intellectuals and artists of every race, creed and country, who remained free to practice their diverse faiths in whatever manner they chose. Liberty is the most fertile soil for the tree of innovation and invention.

The above was an attempt to explain two contrasting things 'Islamic civilization' could mean: a narrow, tribal, insecure one, based on collective ego, xenophobia, and isolation, riddled with oppression and inferiority, where religion is conflated with its adherents, and another meaning: global, inclusive, tolerant, based on self-esteem, civilized in the truest sense of the word, where there is a very real difference between a religion and those who believe in it. Which of these, dear reader, do you think currently prevails? The tribal one, I'm very sorry to say.

Muddled thinking and lack of awareness on the one hand, and apathy and suspicion on the other, are behind this misperception. They are the reason why tribal Islam comes to mind whenever we mention this glorious religion.

Now that I have explained what I think about the process of creating a misleading mental image of a brilliant concept, Western civilization, and distorting it into the Tribe of Western Civilization, and the distortion of a noble religion, Islam, into the Tribe of Islam, and the reasons for it in my opinion – a controlling Ego leading to a controlling Us, flourishing under self-centeredness – I repeat, in the minds of a small but vocal and influential minority, each falsely claiming to speak for millions (and setting aside the illogic of pitting a *civilization* against a *religion)* – these concepts need to be exchanged for others that can be placed into conflict: The Tribe of Civilization vs. The Tribe of Religion.

Now that I have given you my view of the conflict that captures the attention of most of the world's population, I'd like to ask you to reexamine the global situation – as a whole, or in day-to-day occurrences – and then answer the following. From the standpoint of "Us" under self-centeredness, can you crack the code of what's going on? If you can, then here's another question: What are you going to do about it?

Wait! Before you go looking for conspiracy theories – whether or not you find them – I urge you not to fall into that trap. I invite you to move beyond "Who caused this?" to "What are we going to do about this?" or rather, what are you going to do about it? What steps are you going to take towards creating a real reality instead of this virtual reality caused by your tacit acceptance of a mental image that grows day by day, creating a bitter tribal struggle? A struggle, not between a civilization and a religion, but between two creatures of fantasy: the Tribe of Western Civilization vs. the Tribe of Islam.

It takes time and effort to find solutions for such a serious and complex issue. But beware of silence. Your silence in this situation is tacit permission for the few thousand extremists – Western civilization or Islam – to pretend to represent you, and tacit approval of what is happening. Your silence brands you as a member of the idolatrous tribe declared by these extremists on both sides, and as a member of the inflated "Us" formed as a result of an overpowering collective Ego. Your silence, in sum, is a retreat from God-centrism and a choice to live with these extremists, Western and Islamic, under self-centeredness.

"But I don't know what to do!" you say. Well, if your choice is that you don't know what to do, but you reject this bitter tribal struggle; refuse to belong to an idolatrous tribe; refuse to be part of a bloated "Us"; refuse to be part of an overpowering collective Ego; to live under self-centeredness; then why not come out and say that? Why not come out and say that you don't know what to do now, and that you need time to find it, and until you find something, you proclaim the above?

"But what's the use if I don't have the answers?" The use is that you take away the legitimacy of those who take it by virtue of your silence. The use is that you deprive them of your voice, and the use of it, as long as you are silence. The use is that you show the world their true size, not the size they project. The use is that you destroy the false mental image; that, by destroying it, you pave the way for the truth you will take part in making. There is no room for neutrality in this. Your acquiescence is a choice, your silence is acquiescence. Your silence means that you have chosen. If you are with them, then all you need to do is remain silent; if you aren't, then don't. What choice will you make?

In this space, I entreat you, write down your feelings, impressions, and questions about The Tribe.

_____

_____

_____

PART TWO

God-Centrism

PART ONE
Living Under God-centrism

The Serengeti Question:

Why did God create all this? For whom? Where do we stand in this?

As I stood in the Serengeti, captivated by the natural beauty that surrounded me as far as the eye could see, I could not stop asking these questions. This was in the Serengeti Plains, in eastern Africa. In the language of the Masai, this means "the plains that have no end," an appropriate description for the scene that held me in its thrall.

Like an endless blue sea, this was an endless plain of savanna, unbroken but for a tree here and there, or a cluster of rocks they call Kobji. The difference between the blue and green scenes was just this: life. The Serengeti plains are home to millions of animals, reptiles and birds, and tens of millions of insects. Each of these creatures has a form, has a voice, has a life. This life invades your senses, filling them with its sound, its sight, its scent, without so much as a by-your-leave.

So much life! So many living things! True, you could see the same endless expanse in the ocean, and know that as much, if not more, life teems beneath the surface, but not see it or hear it or smell it. This was the first time I had experienced both together: the limitless vista, and the sensory awareness that every square inch was bursting with life.

Do I have your attention? I hope so. Now I want to share my mystery. In the city or the countryside, most of us live a life that revolves round human needs. In the former, everything revolves around your needs: homes, schools, hospitals, factories, roads, parks, shops and so on; in the latter, all around you, although there may be less variety, is geared towards your benefit: crops, cattle, etc. I believe that this has created a notion in us that everything around us has to do with us and our needs, and is made to serve us. This idea forms unintentionally without our knowledge, and settles into our unconscious.

My mystery in the Serengeti Plains was that this gigantic system, that had existed for millions of years and would continue to exist – god willing – for millions more, this system more packed with life than anywhere I'd been before, had no role for humans. It forms no part of our lives. We didn't make it. It doesn't serve us. It lives on independently of us; whether we're there or not makes no difference to it. In a word, it doesn't revolve around us.

Death was also something that occurred to me. To humans, death is associated with feelings – fear and panic, awe and grief – and actions – from crying silently to screaming. But in this immense ecosystem, death is part of the daily routine, part of the natural order: animals eat and catch each other, causing some panic at the moment of hunting; afterwards, the predator calmly dines on his prey, and everything settles back into calm contentment – even the herd one of whom is currently being eaten. There is no crying or screaming: even emotionally, we humans are set apart from this wonderful ecosystem.

It was an eye-opener. Questions came thick and fast: What is humans' role in this? Why do we have no central role? Why will this majestic ecosystem sail on regardless of whether we're there or not (apart from a few destructive episodes in history)? This was what I came to call the Serengeti Question:

What's our part in all this?

This question showed me the difference between two things: (1) that we, as humans, are stewards of the earth; and (2)being stewards of the earth does not mean that we're the center of the universe, or of all life. We are merely one of millions. Some were there before we ever came on the scene; some live with us, and may live far longer than us. Our existence, beginning and end mean nothing to them.

The Serengeti made me feel it, not merely understand, what I had known all my life. After this experience, I truly felt it inside me: *We are not the center of the universe.* But most of us, all unconsciously, believe we are; we live accordingly, without meaning to. This is due to a system of life practices geared towards fulfilling the desires of the Self, confusing us and leading the Self to place its wants and desires ahead of what God requires. To make matters worse, the Self created misnomers to get rid of any guilt, creating – and settling into – a deceptive comfort zone.

If we aren't the center of the universe, then who is?

I am certain that the center of the universe is God.

This is why I believe we all need to rethink our assumptions, fundamental beliefs, and convictions. If we do, we will find one of the following:

1. We have prioritized God's will over ours, and live God-centrically, which is a choice;

2. That we have consciously and willingly prioritized our will over God's, and chosen to live self-centeredly, which is also a choice.

3. That we are living thoughtlessly, without choosing a paradigm and without prioritizing. This may not be a choice: but knowing that you've been living thoughtlessly, like a boat tossed about by the winds, and *consenting to keep doing it, now that you know*– makes it a choice.

Choice begins with the existential question: "Where is God in this? What's the priority of His will?" The simple act of asking is as important, if not more so, than your answer. Asking the question is a shift from the darkness of obliviousness to the light of awareness.

The main question is, "Does God's will have priority over mine, or vice versa?" Your answer is all-important. There is a great difference between *saying* it, and *living* it. Choosing one of the above means that you have chosen a paradigm to live by: a self-centered paradigm, and a God-centric paradigm.

Once you've chosen a paradigm, it colors everything. Our relationship with God, ourselves, and the Other; our science, our culture, and our literature; every aspect of our daily life; our religions; in a word, our civilization.

Do you remember the first time your parent parked downstairs, held you in their lap and let you "drive" the family car? Or seen someone play this game? The child holds the wheel in all seriousness, pushing their parent's hands away; as an ultimate proof of their own control over the vehicle, they sound the horn. With great excitement, they run to tell their friends that "I drove the car! I held the wheel and sounded the horn!" Their parent, of course, backs up their story, making the child fit to burst with joy.

In truth, though, you could never let your child *actually* drive. Your legs are long enough to reach the pedals; you can see behind you in the mirror; you know the rules of the road; there is no way you could let a small child drive. What you do is keep your child safe and sound in your lap, while giving them the illusion that *they* are driving. Why? Because it will give them pleasure, and be good for their confidence.

Why? Because you love them.

The above is a metaphor for our relationship with God. God is limitless in His power and knowledge – so that while we are orders of magnitude higher than our child, He is incomprehensibly greater than us. Our minds are too modest to even begin to imagine His ability. Still, our awareness of Him sometimes resembles the child's awareness of the parent in the above example: we imagine that we are steering. Naturally, our relationship with God is far more complex.

Allow me to refresh your memory: How many times have you thought that your happiness lay in one direction, only to be thwarted, and have to take a different path, only to find that your true contentment lay in this second path, and that the first would have been fraught with difficulty? How many times has this happened? Take your time thinking. Make a note of your experiences.

_____

_____

_____

_____

_____

_____

_____

In the situations you remembered – I don't know what you have written down, but for me, it was everything in life – who steered you gently away from trouble? Who lovingly steered you towards what you hated, but which was good for you?

Another example. Think of your life's successes. Do you remember when you just happened to be in the right place at the right time? Has anything like this happened to you? Make a note.

_____

_____

_____

_____

_____

_____

_____

_____

_____

_____

_____

_____

_____

_____

_____

If this happened, who made it happen?

Have you ever met a stranger, at a party or on a plane or on a train, and chatted, then found that stranger offering you – or helping you obtain – some golden opportunity? Has this happened to you? Make a note.

_____

_____

_____

_____

_____

_____

_____

_____

_____

_____

_____

_____

_____

_____

I

If it has, who made that stranger cross your path?

If you remain unaware, I invite you to notice. The Creator of these serendipitous moments, these happy coincidences, is your ultimate benefactor, God. He does it with love and affection.

Please don't misunderstand me. I'm not saying you mustn't be proactive and hardworking, or not follow through on tasks since "God controls everything, after all, so why bother?" I believe that God requires skill and concentration of us: he wants us to be result-oriented, determined and persistent to the point of stubbornness in the pursuit of our goals. He wants us to know that if we don't try our best and push our hardest, we won't achieve success, and when we do succeed, we need to be aware that the One who made this success happen is God.

How can this be?

This is what I meant by saying that we have a complex relationship with God. To work hard and know that He gives us the result; to know that if our hard work fails, to be certain that He has withheld the result, and to similarly be certain that this failure was best for us, even if our minds cannot comprehend why at the time – or ever; the point I want to make here is that the relationship with God is simple and complex all at once.

Is there anything more to be learned from the example of the child, the parent, and the car? One more thing. Imagine that the car was actually moving. Now imagine that the parent suddenly jumped out. How will the child feel? What will they do? Panic, right? And what will the child do? Probably nothing but scream and cry, ignoring that they are in a moving car, looking at the parent and begging them to come back, right? Why is that? Because, to a child, a parent represents security.

This doesn't apply to our relationship with God. For a start, God never leaves us; He is there for all his creatures. He is there for me as I write this, and there for you now as you read it. Whether you and I realize it, He is there; our awareness of His presence has no effect on the reality of it. Secondly, our sense of security in His presence never leaves us; He is etched into our subconscious, regardless of our conscious mind. Children feel safe when their parents are there; they seek freedom and run around, but out of a healthy instinct for that age, they look back from time to time to check that they're there, so as to feel secure.

The child does not *think* that their parents' presence affords security; they *sense* it.

Did their parents teach them that? No; they were born that way.

This instinct may become muddled throughout life, unless we remain aware. This can be seen in humanity's history: since the dawn of history, humans have sought a God for worship and shelter. If there happened to be a prophet around in their time, the prophet guided them to a correct understanding of God; if they lived in other times, they sought to devise gods to give them a sense of security in their worship.

There are a number of ways to approach this inner conviction: to be aware of God's presence 24/7/365, and enjoy that sense of security as we steer the vehicle of our lives; or not to enjoy this awareness, and be as stricken with terror as the hypothetical child left alone in the car.

This lack of awareness, manifested in the belief that we are in control of our own destiny, causes us to move, little by little, from God-centrism to self-centeredness. We think more of ourselves and less of God, which makes us more afraid, which in turn makes us more self-centered, and so on.

A final moral to the story: Does the child's lack of awareness that the parent is driving have any effect on the reality? Of course not. The same is true of our relationship with God. Living under God-centrism merely means *admitting* that God's will and purpose supersede our own; we don't *place* it above ours. Your awareness, or lack of it, has no effect on reality.

I am not asking you to read this in order to judge others, but to ask your own self: How do you search within yourself? This question is meant to help you seek within yourself the answer to this question: Do you want to live under self-centeredness, or under God-centrism? Do you want to feel secure all your life, or feel terrified from time to time and be reminded by this terror that God is always there for you, and only then be proactive?

What do you think? What will you choose? Will you achieve it? When? Lots of questions, questions you need to find more questions for.

When we say we have chosen God-centrism, we simply mean that we have chosen to believe that all of creation has only one God, that we have chosen to privilege His will above ours, and live by that belief through everyday practice, every day of our lives. When these practices prevail 24/7/365 in every area of life, we will be truly said to live in a God-centric civilizational paradigm, regardless of religion, language, ethnicity, race or culture.

The current civilizational paradigms, foremost among which are Western civilization, are excellent in practice, albeit self-centered. When I say excellent, I mean this: Look around you at where you are now, as you read this book, at home, in an office, a café, or a public conveyance. You will find that everything around you – clothing, lighting, air-conditioning, food and drink, entertainment, transportation, what the buildings around you are made of, etc. – are a product of Western civilization. The world's political and economic theories are a product of Western civilization. So is every labor-saving device known to humanity.

Asserting the need for a new paradigm is in no way an objection to this magnificent system. On the contrary, I insist on the need for what I have called civilizational cross-pollination, in which every civilization builds on the philosophical, cultural or even practical achievements of those preceding. Western civilization benefited from Islamic civilization, which borrowed from the Greeks, who built on Ancient Egypt. These civilizations all rose and fell in the Mediterranean basin, the heart of the Old World, long before Columbus set foot in the Americas. These were not the only civilizations: there were always others, in Asia and South America. This is why my ultimate ambition is a civilizational paradigm that completes the current one: that benefits from it and builds upon it.

There seems to be a global accord to fight monopoly in every field; anti-trust laws in Western countries, adopted by most countries, forbid any one company or its subsidiaries to corner the market. Having only one brand of, say, coffee, with no competition, ends up being unfavorable to the consumer. The same is true if there are four or five brands, all produced by the same company under different names. On the civilizational level, this seems to be absent; the Western paradigm of self-centeredness currently monopolizes world civilization. It has been offered to every community in different forms, under different brand names in the past 300 years: "European civilization," "Western civilization," "American civilization," and last but not least, "globalization." Different names, but the cultural product is the same, developed every now and then, and offered to the world under different names: ultimately, all the same product, all built on self-centeredness. This in itself is a civilizational monopoly, breaking the anti-trust laws of that very civilization that preaches the evil effects of monopoly on the members of the community. It abrogates their right to choose between diverse products. We need diverse civilizational products to choose from: this diversity is a global need, a natural alternative to monopoly that ultimately benefits all of us here on Planet Earth.

There are, then, two levels of God-centrism: the abstract, followed by the concrete. The abstract level is, of course, the easiest: a theory, which readers can accept or reject. It is much harder to achieve the latter, since its practices are absent on the ground. We want to create it, either by creating it from A to Z, or – more practical in many cases – engaging in master reframing. By master reframing I mean deconstructing everyday practices currently under self-centeredness, and reconstructing them to fall under the paradigm of God-centrism. The reader's role is essential, because these two skills – and any others needed – will be required in every field.

The first part of this book offered the theory, but of necessity cannot offer a guide to practical application: no book, indeed no individual or entity, can presume to know everything about every field, at least to my knowledge. However, your acceptance of this philosophy is only the beginning: the beginning of your application of a creative, innovative, inventive paradigm: your applications of living paradigms in joyful ease under God-centrism.

Two things are needed for God-centric living in this age, and in these civilizational circumstances. The first is initiative; the second is creativity. The first gives us the courage to confront challenges to God-centric living, and the second gives us the capacity to come up with civilizational systems and day-to-day practices that implement God-centric living. This is no simple task; it isn't even a project, or initiative. It is a new offering of a new way of life.

This new way of life begins with a philosophy: God-centrism means making God the center of your life and the ultimate goal of your actions. Your choice, with full consciousness, is to prioritize God's will over your own.

The difference between God-centrism and self-centeredness is the difference between waking up and asking, "What do I want to do for myself today, and will this please God?" and waking up to the question, "What is Your will for me, O God?" The first is asking yourself; the second is asking God. The first is thinking of yourself, then God; the second is thinking of God, not yourself. The first is seeking God's plan for you for yourself; the second is seeking God's plan for you for Him.

Freedom under God-centeredness

We have spoken previously about freedom under self-centeredness. Here, we shall speak of freedom under God-centeredness.

Once you choose to be free under God-centrism, you have chosen of your own free will to be free in the context of serving Him, i.e. you have chosen of your own free will to relinquish part of your own free will. Is there another choice? Of course: there is the choice of freedom under self-centeredness. Who gave us the choice? The benign, loving, compassionate God: he created us, and gave us the right to live in His world and eat of His fruits even if we don't believe in Him. He allows us to live with our own free will in this life, on condition that we bear the consequences of our choices in the next: our choice not to believe in Him.

What about those who *do* believe in Him, but choose self-centeredness – to prioritize their own desires over God's, to do what they want instead of what God wants? I believe they have the same choice: to live their lives however they want, and bear the consequences of this choice in the next.

You and I, dear reader, face such choices every moment of our lives. I believe that the best way to approach them is via the existential question, "Where is God's will in this? What priority shall I give it?"

"But," you ask, "isn't this a restriction on freedom?"

Yes. But your choice to limit your freedom is unrestricted. You can choose, and bear the consequences.

"But bearing the consequences is in itself a restriction, isn't it?"

Aren't you responsible for the consequences of your choices under self-centeredness? The only difference is that you are judged by society and your peers. It's not about absolute freedom; I doubt there is such a thing as doing exactly as you please with complete disregard for the consequences of your choices. The issue is choosing whom you want to be the judge: yourself, or God.

Please pause in your reading, reread the above, and take your time thinking about it. Digest it fully before we move on.

The above was profound, and requires time. Take your time. Taking your time, make a note of what is going through your head right now. Don't organize: just write.

Now you have taken your time, let's talk more about freedom under God-centrism. If you choose freedom under God-centrism, in every situation you will look for what God wants instead of what you want. God has been, and still is, generous to us: he has sent us His heavenly messengers to show us how best to accomplish His will in every situation in this world, instead of leaving us to ourselves to seek out His will. But, if how to behave in every situation is mapped out by God, where, then, is our freedom?

I believe that freedom lies in creativity.

"What kind of creativity?" you ask.

Being creative in achieving God's purpose.

"But you said before that God's purpose revolves around doing good for others."

That is what I said, and what I believe. I believe that God has created us free within the limits of serving Him; within these limits, I believe he didn't make us so we could serve ourselves and those we care about, but to serve others. This is the practical application of serving God: since God doesn't need anything from us, being the Creator and Maker of all, it is up to us to get creative in serving Him, and in achieving what He wants of us.

This is my understanding of freedom under God-centrism.

What's yours?

_____

_____

_____

_____

_____

_____

_____

Humanity under God-centrism

Remember, dear reader, that God did not create you like the angels, unable to sin or err; you are human. You make mistakes; you are allowed to err, intentionally or through oversight. His door is open for you to repent. All humans do.

I believe that disobeying God, while remembering Him, and under God-centrism, is better than doing His will while forgetting Him.

How can that be? Well, let's take two examples. First, imagine that one day, you are provoked to anger; you do remember God, but through human frailty, your reaction was motivated by a defensive Ego, not by what God willed. In other words, you prioritized your Self over God. While defending your Self, following your Ego, you said to God that this was the result of the human frailty He created you with. When you calmed down, you asked His pardon and begged for forgiveness, and asked Him to give you the strength to do what He would have wanted.

Second, let's imagine that one day, you are provoked to anger; however, you control yourself, because it is better for your Self, and more in line with the moral rules of your society – which God has nothing to do with, and which were not made to serve Him – and do the right thing, the thing that God would have wanted you to do. But you did not do it for God, but for yourself.

Which is a better path to follow, to repeat?

This is a deep and complex question. Your answer will indicate which paradigm you follow. Even if you can't or don't answer, merely thinking about this existential question places you in a God-centric, not a self-centered, paradigm: I believe this is the main purpose of life.

The Long Way and the Short Way

Imagine that both of us are farmers. Each of us has a field of wheat. In Egypt, where I come from, we plant wheat at the start of fall, and harvest it in the middle of spring. Each of us has started to plant. You plow the soil, and find me doing the same. "What are you doing?" you ask me.

"Plowing," I respond. "You have to plow to plant wheat."

Later, you bring the seed to plant. While planting, you find me still plowing. You ask what I'm doing, and I say, "Plowing. You have to plow to plant wheat."

Still later, you come to water your fields, and I'm still plowing. When you ask, I say, "Plowing. You have to plow to plant wheat." When you come to weed your plot, you get the same response: "Plowing. You have to plow to plant wheat."

At harvest time, which of us will reap a harvest of wheat?

Yes, you have to plow to plant wheat. But plowing is not an aim in itself. Plowing is a step on the way to a goal: a harvest.

If you don't plow your land, you can't plant your crop; but what is certain is that if you do as I did, and only plow, you will reap no harvest for all your trouble. I think our journey through life is the same, only more complex. God, I believe, has created two complementary paths to Him: the first is prayer, and the attendant rituals. The second is our indirect relationship with Him, which is daily dealings. The very term "dealings" presupposes another party to deal *with;* therefore, what He wants of us can only be fulfilled in the presence of another party. Your relationship with God, in this case, is fulfilled via another party, by treating them the way God commands that they be treated – not by treating them the way they treat you, and not by treating them the way your Self tells you to treat them.

Prayer and other rituals play a role not unlike plowing the soil: they soften and break up the soil of our souls, connecting them to God. Then comes the role of daily dealings – the indirect relationship with God, which is the planting of the seed. The soil is your heart. The plow is prayer. These steps *must* bear good harvest, a harvest produced for others, a harvest that will feed you and yours. Merely plowing the land without sowing seed is just as bad as never plowing it at all. What I mean to say is that it is not enough to merely pray and conduct rituals – a direct relationship with God – without making the effort to use that prayer to build a system of daily dealings that will create an indirect relationship with Him. The best indicator of success is the result. Look at yourself. If your prayers and rituals are perfect, but you produce no harvest for anyone else, and only serve you and yours, there is something missing in the way you are running your life.

The shortest – and most comfortable – way to God is through your prayers and rituals. The longer and more difficult path is through your daily dealings. But beware! The shortest path may well lead to your Self, not to God. Who benefits from your prayer, fasting and sundry rituals, other than yourself? No-one. Therefore, something is missing. Conduct your rituals. Then start your journey to benefit God's creation.

This means that your harvest must not only feed you, your family, your clan, or your tribe; it is not only for your people, not only for your race, not only for your species. "Creation" is not only humanity. It is people, animals, plants, and all creatures great and small, and all these are your responsibility. Both paths are necessary: prayer and practice. They are complementary. Don't forget either.

Remember that the Self is a cunning trickster: it might very well lead you to revolve around it, and begin to convince you that the best path is to immerse yourself in prayer and religious ritual, saying, "Isn't this what God commanded?" Beware wolves in sheep's clothing. Your Self might be revolving in self-centeredness, and calling things by the wrong names in order to put you in a comfort zone of selfishness and egocentrism, deluding you into thinking you are serving God, while you are in fact serving yourself. Your Self might use God's name to lure you into only doing good for yourself and those around you. This might be a ruse.

"A ruse? How?"

Simply put, because the hidden meaning of your prayers might be, "I seek God's favor; I don't care about others. I want to collect good deeds against my afterlife, regardless of others. I want to go to Heaven, and I don't care about anyone else." If you think and pray this way, try examining the other areas of your life. Do you give anyone anything? Do you give in the real sense, 'give till it hurts,' meaning giving of what you really love, not merely what is surplus to requirements? Remember, prayer, however arduous, is easy: what takes labor, toil and sweat is working for God.

Your prayer, dear reader, is like an athlete warming up before starting a match: limbering up the muscles before starting the *real* work, the work that requires the most effort. Who ever won a match just by warming up? What about the prophets? Did they choose the easy way, or the long way? There's an easy way to measure it: using the question, "How much good do I do for others?"

I'm not asking you to judge others, but to look inside yourself. Your job isn't to intuit others' intentions, and dispense advice; your job is to examine your own life, your own thoughts and goals. The only person you can change is yourself. Are you operating from self-centeredness, or God-centrism? If what you do benefits yourself and no-one else, the probability is high that you are operating from self-centeredness.

In that case, I would urge you to find a third party quickly: this third party will benefit from the harvest of your relationship with God.

The most natural relationship, in my modest opinion, is threefold.

The Three-Point Paradigm

The three-point paradigm is the start of putting theory into practice.

To practice God-centrism, you need to find what God wants of you; this must be achieved by serving some other person, since God needs nothing from us. Our duty under God-centrism is to seek out another person to serve in God. The three points are: God, myself, and an Other. If my Self turns this into a binary relationship, it shifts automatically from God-centrism into self-centrism. God gets taken out of the equation, leaving the Self and the Other; the former will seek its own interests. Various scenarios are bandied about: win-win, win-lose, and win-? All these are self-seeking, even win-win, which is based on shared interests, as the agreement here is between two Selves, my Self and the Other (who, to himself, represents the Self). If the other Self is too weak to fight for its rights, we have a win-lose, or undecided relationship. Therefore, the absence of God has turned this relationship from God-centric to self-centric.

Strangely enough, the absence of the Other from this relationship, leaving just me and God, makes it self-centric as well. How does this happen? The relationship becomes just me enjoying my relationship with God; taking from God, and giving the Self, where all I do is take – as we have said, there is no question of me *giving* God anything. Since all I can do is take, then the relationship becomes self-serving.

To achieve a healthy relationship with God in practice, therefore, there needs to be a third party. The relationship between myself and God has to be supplemented by a third party, one of God's creatures whom I serve in God. The three elements then are as follows: a servant, myself; a party being served, an Other; and the Ultimate One for whom we all strive, God.

In conversation with eminent men of God, a great many of them said that there was no such thing as Self, or Other, only God. "Certainly," I agreed; "the Divine Spirit in me serves the Divine Spirit in the Other, and there is no such thing as God: but we need guidelines on the ground!"

The prophets in all their greatness had direct access to the glory of the Lord; yet, with all the pleasure they took in communing with the Divine Spirit, they never let it become their sole intention. They always sought to fulfil His will through an Other. They preached His message to those around them, enduring ridicule, rejection, and sometimes actual injury. They remained strong and steadfast; they were patient and strong in the service of the Other to whom God send them. None of them sat around communing with the Lord.

This is what I mean by guidelines on the ground; what I mean by the three-point paradigm in applying God's purpose to everyday life, towards creating an integrated civilization.

Trust and Belief

On the philosophical/theoretical side, there is a dimension to which we must adhere in all honesty, or else risk destroying the application, or else making it more hypocritical than truthful. That dimension is trust and belief. Whom should we trust and believe in? God is whom we should trust, since we have chosen to worship Him. We must worship him on our terms, not on His. What happens in most religions is that we pray as He has told us to pray, but live the rest of our lives according to systems where God is not a priority. Sometimes we choose the easy path to worship, saving our hard work for the area of self-centeredness, encouraged to do so by the impressive success of our efforts under self-centeredness. When required to move from this familiar ground to the unfamiliar place of God-centrism, we are filled with doubt, and drag our heels. After all, the alternative is readily available, and requires no effort. On the other hand, living under God-centrism requires effort, courage and creativity, as there are currently no practical guidelines, no instruction manual. We also doubt God and lack trust in Him – I apologize for being so shocking, but I ask you to ask this to yourself in all honesty: do you trust in God? I have many examples where one doesn't believe God, or trust in Him, but I would prefer for you to search for examples in yourself, not in others.

Don't fear to ask. Seeking questions is far more important than finding answers. Others have answered before you, and you may well have adopted these answers as your own without sufficient research, but we're not seeking pat answers here. Again: Do you trust God and believe in Him enough? Be brave. Face yourself. Ask honestly. Without a correct diagnosis, the best medicines must fail. This is your start – if you want – to move from self-centeredness to a place of God-centrism.

Once you've had the courage to be honest, set down your impressions and feelings, then make a note of any questions you may have.

Him From Whom All Blessings Flow

This can be a stumbling-block to trust and belief. The Lord God has told us that He is the source of all good things: if you trust him, you must also trust and believe that everything in your life is for the best, even if painful.

A parallel with a mother's love may make it clearer. Why would a little child, six or seven years of age, with only token resistance, let himself be dragged out of their warm bed in the morning cold, stagger half-asleep to wash, made to leave their pleasant house full of toys, carry a heavy bag full of boring books and go off to an even more boring place, to be crammed into a room willy-nilly with other uncomprehending children, supervised by a stern taskmaster, and taught boring subjects? No child would willingly allow that to happen to them unless they were 100% sure that their mothers loved them and wanted the best for them, even if all the talk about doing well in school and securing a good future went right over their heads. Children *know* that their mothers want the best for them, even if their capacity for understanding and comprehending is insufficient. Feeling trumps knowing.

This is a partial representation of the relationship I think we ought to have with God, even in painful experiences: to know that nothing bad comes from Him. Despite our pain, we need to trust that what happens to us is a good thing we do not yet understand; and first, we must trust that God loves us more than our mothers. When we become adults, we start to use our minds; if we're not careful, mind will eclipse heart. We start to calculate material gain and loss, which gives us no tools to measure love and trust. The heart, not the mind, measures these; if these are muddied, we can't use them for their intended purpose, which in turn affects the love and trust in our relationship with God.

From a place of less-than-complete trust and belief in God, we can see no good in the pain we go through. Any painful situation will have no good in it, except insofar as patience in adversity is a virtue and will be rewarded. Which is not untrue, but it isn't the only choice. You need to rethink the painful experience. We can't control what happens to us; we can, though control how we react to it.

- Abandoning the Victim Role under God-Centrism

- Moving from reactiveness to proactiveness.

- Moving from passivity to action.

- Moving from patience to thankfulness.

These are the three steps for liberation from victimhood and moving to a place of healing.

There is a difference between what happens to us and how we react to it. We may have no choice in what happens to us, but we have a choice in how we react to it. Under self-centeredness, the ego becomes active, affecting our lives: one of the Ego's important roles is that of victim. All of us (one of the few times I feel secure in not qualifying the 'all') have had pleasant and unpleasant experiences. In point of fact, the above is not entirely accurate, as each experience is made up of two parts: (1)the event, (2)our reaction to it.

1. An Event: This is a painful event, such as falling ill, losing a loved one, our company going out of business, losing one's home or car, or a happy one, such as the return of an absent loved one, a birth, recovery from a serious illness, landing a dream job, meeting your intended, etc.

2. Our Reaction: How we store experiences affects us: some generate happy thoughts and thus are stored as 'good experiences', and others sad ones and are stored as 'bad experiences.'

There are two paths to dealing with the second type: reactive and proactive.

Reactive: You are a rudderless boat, tossed by the wind. You feel pain: this pain manifests as rage, denial or pain; you are unable to control your feelings, and remain in this state until another event pushes you into another place. The same happens with joyful occasions. You may go so far as to be held hostage by your pain, constantly ruminating on the wrong done you and those who wronged you, and slowly but surely slide down the slope to victimhood – the ideal place for those who want to remain reactive. All you need to do to stay a victim is to sit there, waiting for more bad things to happen, and accumulate more bitterness, creating an ever-deepening vicious circle of victimhood, auto-activated and set to self-destruct. The same can happen with happy events: one can become a virtual lotus-eater, lost in memories of good things. In both cases, you are an object; in both cases, your feelings are subordinated to past events.

If, for example, a reactive person finds themselves in a traffic jam, they may find themselves thinking they deserve better than this life, and this job, and how much luckier others are, and ending up sighing, saying that at least God will reward them for their patience.

Let's analyze what happened. You find yourself stuck in traffic; you gave in to the situation, and let it control you. You have become an object *par excellence*, neck-deep in reactiveness: you burst out into negativity – not without cause – that completely surrounds you, and makes it almost impossible to break free. You then slipped into the victim space, with its delicious self-pity, tempting to stay there. After your Self has submerged you deep enough in all this, and steeped you in it, it goes on to announce, "I am patient!"

An analysis of the above will show how false our claims of patience are, concealing a negative attitude and a deep sense of victimhood. But how could anyone react differently? Well, they couldn't. But is there another *choice?* Of course; there are many things you could do instead. You can choose to rise to another place – I use 'rise' advisedly, as it is an uphill climb, unlike the ease with which one's Self can slide into victimhood – namely, a place of proactiveness/subject/healing/ thankfulness. How to move towards it? Let's take the same situation as an example.

Proactive: The first thing to do is keep your head. True, the traffic jam may be beyond your control, but you *can* control its effect on you. Just by doing this, you move from reactive to proactive. Next, you can choose to be active, by doing positive things in a negative situation. Find positive things to make use of the time: first, look for your smile. Smile. Isn't this an opportunity to admire the view of the city? You can't very well do that when zooming by in the car. Look for a piece of music you've been too busy to listen to for a while, and do that. Think of an old friend you haven't spoken to for a while, and call them. Call someone you care for, and tell them you love them.

Enjoy their happiness when you tell them that. Smile at the driver of the car next to you, and try to relieve their frustration with some positive gesture. You will be the first to feel the positive effects. In this manner – being proactive, seeking positivity – you are the captain of your Self, not its victim. Now you can be thankful to God for inspiring you with the right thing to do: now, if you thank Him for your affliction, you will have been truly patient, and will be genuinely trying to move from a place of patience to a place of thankfulness. That's how you move from patience/being an object – to patience/being a subject, and being thankful.

Still on the subject of patience: If you are playing some sport, and receive a bump or bruise, you can choose to keep playing, or give up. Which choice do you think will make you feel better – to keep going, or to give up? I believe the former. There is a saying "A victorious soldier's wounds heal faster than a vanquished soldier's." Probably because of the beneficial effect of the positive energy of winning. You have a choice as well: to remain 'patient' in a victim-place, wallowing in negative energy, or to be patient in a proactive, thankful place. The choice is yours.

This applies to almost any situation you may face. I believe there is always a positive side to everything. One of the most positive things in painful situations is that they drive you – if you are aware – towards God, not away from Him; your attempts to be thankful and proactive will make your life all the sweeter.

However, there are painful experiences where no light can be found, such as losing a loved one in an accident. We can still be proactive, but not through seeking the silver lining. To be proactive here is to deal with pain in a healthy manner. Denial is unhealthy, and a reaction. Turning pain into anger is also a reaction. Facing up to pain and turning it into grief, not rage, is the least harmful path in such circumstances. The only difference between raging rapids and a calm river is the path taken. A raging river surges forth because it has nowhere to go; a river flows calmly and harmlessly through the path carved out for it, either over millennia by nature or over years by humans. Such is the case with rage and grief: rage is explosive pain, for which no channel has been cut. Grief is pain flowing through the path we make for it to leave peacefully. Creating a channel for our pain is being proactive.

Under self-centeredness, running from pain may make us forget God, and run from Him. Under God-centrism, we run from Him, to Him.

The above has been a number of examples provided by me. I suggest you apply the theories to your own examples; things that happen, and have happened, to you. Make a note of them here.

I

Beauty and God-Centrism

Taking pleasure in beauty under God-centrism is a means, not an end: a means to nourish and recharge your soul to make it more capable of doing God's purpose. Under God-centrism, you are not living aimlessly; either you have found out what God wants you to do at this stage in life, and are busy doing it, or you are seeking it so that you can start. In this context, your enjoyment of God's blessings recharges us for working for others in the service of God. The true enjoyment of beauty is for your soul, not Self or Ego; there are no boundaries to this simple pleasure. Most probably, your soul will need to enjoy as much beauty as you truly need, not what the Ego imagines it needs to be special, and starts to hoard.

Also, when truly nourishing your soul, you will find a clear divide between the enjoyment of beauty in all its forms and attempts to monopolize it. Your soul does not need to possess beauty in order to drink its fill; your freedom to visit different sources of beauty is in itself food for the soul. In the absence of the Self's panicked greed, there is a sense of peace; tranquility enhances our enjoyment of beauty and makes it more profound.

Beauty speaks to the Divine Spirit inside you, bypassing your conscious will, whether or not you are aware of this fact. How do you experience beauty? Let us examine the phenomenon.

You encounter a beautiful thing, and interact with it through your senses. You see a beautiful place; you hear beautiful sounds; you smell wonderful perfumes, taste delicious flavors, and touch tactile pleasures. Observe the stages of your interaction with beauty. First, your eyes, ears, nose, tongue or fingertips sense it, and feel momentary pleasure. Then, you start feeling this beauty's effect on you; you delve deep into the beauty of this sensation, for as long as your senses are interacting with it.

When I say "on you," what part of you am I talking about? Not your mind, this isn't its job. Not your body; that has its own needs. Is it your heart? Definitely! When you enjoy beauty, your will recedes; you have no control over its impact on you. When you see a beautiful place or creature, you can't very well command your mind to interact with it. Your heart is what feels this beauty, bypassing your mind. The same thing happens with your other senses. We don't choose what to like or what to enjoy; we simply fall in love, without meaning to.

This is what I meant by the title of this section: beauty speaks to the divine part of you, the Divine Spirit within you, in spite of yourself.

Note, also, that each sense can only enjoy the part it is equipped to sense, whereas the heart enjoys them all. Your ears, nose, tongue and so on cannot sense what your eyes enjoy, and vice versa. Your senses are all rivers that flow into the lake of your heart.

"Well, all right; but what does beauty do for my heart?"

I believe that the heart becomes more tender and compassionate the more it is affected by beauty.

"What are the symptoms of being deprived of beauty?"

Deprived of beauty, I believe the heart becomes hard and cruel.

"What is the difference between having a kind heart and a hard heart under God-centrism?"

It is my belief that a kind and compassionate heart is better equipped to commune with God and to sense Him. God has said that He cannot be contained in all the heavens and earth, yet a believer's heart can hold Him. Simply, a heart that can contain God, sense Him and commune with Him, can hardly be cruel; when your heart is full of God, you become more compassionate with all his creatures. His spirit within you rises above the Self; you are more in tune with the Divine Spirit that resides within your fellow-humans, and more compassionate with the rest of God's creatures on this earth of His. When you feel this way about those around you, it becomes easier to want to work for them and serve God in them.

Passion, too, resides in the soul. Passion is an endless fount of energy to do what you are passionate about. I believe that the more compassionate your heart, the greater your capacity for passion. In other words, you become more able to work for some Other, and so achieve what God wants of you. Naturally, the sense of beauty is not the only thing that leads to all this, but I do believe that it leads to a more compassionate heart.

There is a great difference between the effects of beauty and those of luxury. Luxury impresses us; it does not speak to the Divine Spirit within us, at least I think not. I believe that luxury is better-equipped to speak to the Self. In the discussion of luxury under self-centeredness, we mentioned that we never turn *beauty* into *luxury* for ourselves: we only do it to impress others with the slice of beauty we have appropriated. The minute "Them" and "Us" appears, we see the work of the Ego, individual or collective. As I have mentioned, the Ego's activity is a good indicator of self-centeredness. Under self-centeredness, there is no inner peace. Luxury goods hardly ever inspire one with inner peace, transcendence, love, compassion and fellow-feeling. Beauty, on the other hand, produces an uplifted, passionate, compassionate heart, easily directed to God-centrism.

Make a note of the effect of the above on you, and the difference between it and what you have read in the section on "Beauty under Self-Centeredness." Write down your questions.

_____

_____

_____

_____

_____

I

(Images of) Heaven under Self-Centeredness and Heaven under God-Centrism

We are constantly bombarded by commercials and advertisements for luxury housing developments. Swimming pools, wide open spaces, luxurious living spaces, nanny service, anything and everything to make life easier and more pleasant: all this and more is promised us. All well and good; the disturbing thing is that I've started to notice the same kind of advertising – in much the same tone – for Heaven.

There is a certain type of religious discourse that promises, as a reward for obeying God, a certain number of mansions in Paradise, with gardens, lakes, servants, nymphs for the men, et cetera. All well and good; but I think it is missing something basic. In housing developments, after you have signed your contract, you take possession of your home; you never expect someone to be already living there. I believe that some part of this has been planted in our minds as a result of the way Heaven is publicized. Some of us have genuinely visualize Heaven as a lovely housing development, built for us to enjoy in the afterlife, being bought and paid for here on earth. The thing is, when we buy a house, we don't expect to have to share. This may be why all our thinking revolves around the benefits we'll enjoy: *my* mansions, *my* orchards, *my* lakes, *my* fields, *my* nymphs.

Where's the problem? I believe that all the above is not the main reason one should want to go to Paradise; they are pleasant fringe benefits, whatever form they may take, but not the main ones. Naturally, first on the list is not going to Hell; but after this, there is still, I think, a more important reason. It lies in your response to the existential question: "Where is God's will in this? What priority do I grant it?" Under God-centrism, God comes before Paradise, and the true reason to aim for Paradise is that it is the appointed place to meet Him. Since God has stated that Heaven is where we will meet Him, that is where we strive to go, in order to meet Him; and, this being a joy unparalleled in any plane of existence, God uses similes and metaphors drawn from our worldly pleasures. But since self-centeredness currently rules, the Self makes everything revolve around itself; it makes even Heaven all about fulfilling its desires, while meeting God becomes secondary. The fringe benefits – metaphors from God for our ill-equipped minds – become the main event.

But the main event is meeting God. All the similes and metaphors describing Paradise are only to aid our understanding and whet our appetites. For the literal-minded, I offer the saying of the Prophet Muhammad: "[In Paradise], there is what no eye has seen, what no ear has heard, what no human heart could ever imagine."

I repeat: The greatest joy of Heaven is being reunited with God, an incomparable, unimaginable pleasure. It is the place to meet Him: to meet God. Yet under self-centeredness, the Self imagines Heaven as a place to enjoy everything – including God – for ourselves. This is the height of confusion.

To clear this up, let's imagine that instead of only Heaven or Hell, there were three choices instead: 1)Hell. 2)Heaven without God. 3)A place to meet God, but without the full benefits of Heaven.

I doubt that (1) would be most people's choice. In this imaginary trifecta, two choices remain: Heaven without God, or God without Heaven. What choice do you think you ought to make, (2) or (3)? Your genuine response to this question will be an indicator of which paradigm you are currently living under, self-centeredness or God-centrism. This is, in truth, an important step in finding out how you see Heaven and God.

If, when working for our afterlife, we concentrate (consciously or not) on ourselves instead of on God, then it is doubtful that we are doing the right sort of work. A good look at what you want in the afterlife, and what that reflects, will help you organize your priorities in this world.

Let me remind you that your life, in this world and the next, depends on the choices you make now. Not making a choice is a choice. What will you do? Think. Observe. Make notes.

Belonging under God-Centrism

In the section on self-centeredness, we spoke of belonging vs. prejudice. I said how they resemble one another to a great extent, and how healthy belonging can turn, under self-centeredness, into a kind of destructive prejudice. I gave some characteristics of healthy belonging. Under God-centrism, these characteristics take on another, deeper, dimension. A list of them follows, followed by the effect of God-centrism upon them.

1. We belong to things or entities because we want to, not because we need to. This is because we don't need an Other to feel an intrinsic sense of completeness.

2. When I meet a strange Other, I am eager to learn from them, and offer what I know. I am strong and integrated, and I see strength and integration in others. I don't feel threatened at others' allegiances, or lack thereof.

3. My main motivator and essential value is love: love for what I belong to, and love for the Other.

4. My allegiance reflects my inner peace, calm and assurance.

5. Your relationship with the groups to which you belong is non-exclusive: "and" supersedes "or." I belong to X, Y and Z. No-one and no entity monopolizes me. (Under God-centrism, you belong primarily to God, and secondarily to all His creatures.)

6. There is no room for abuse of patriarchy.

7. I am open to the Other; I am prepared to accept them and have them accept me.

8. We seek common ground with the Other who belongs to other entities, and try to build on this shared space.

9. I am usually proactive, both with those I belong to and with those I don't.

10. In negotiations with the Other, there is always room for compromise.

11. I have an independent existence, and opinions of my own; I may differ from the other members of the entity I belong to.

12. In the words of the late Imam Shafei, "what we all think is right may be wrong; what others think is wrong may be right."

13. What I belong to is not sacred; it may prove right or wrong.

14. I value criticism, and attack on occasion, of what I belong to: I can see the flaws in my chosen allegiance, and work towards developing it and correcting its flaws.

15. There is room for everyone. We can all coexist. (Under God-centrism, your sense of completeness derives from your connection to the main source of completeness, the Almighty.

Under God-centrism, no Other is a stranger. We all share the Divine Spirit. Your love for all God's creatures is a manifestation of the One who created them. Under God-centrism, you not only feel God's peace and tranquility, you spread them to those around you. There are no barriers between you and God with the potential to turn into a graven image via the abuse of patriarchy. You are always in tune with God, open to all of His creatures. Under God-centrism, your life is not aimless; either you are doing God's work, or seeking it so as to carry it out. Your life is a symphony played by every part of you and every aspect of your life, led by a great conductor: the Divine Spirit within you. This symphony is heard and enjoyed by others, including you and yours. Your relationships and the circles of belonging also play their part. They are a means to achieving what God wants of you.

Little by little, your relationships with other entities may – I say may – take on a new dimension. These entities may feel as though they belong to you, instead of you belonging to them. Your relationship to them starts to feel paternal; in contrast to patriarchy, which only allows for one father figure, we can have many children, love them all deeply, and feel responsible for their care and well-being. Your own belonging to God, and your path to Him, is the religion of your own choosing, your guide along the way your prophet.

Under God-centrism, the choice is yours: you can change the way you relate to everything you belong to, and have *them* belong to *you,* like your children. You can love them all, treat them all fairly, reconcile them if they quarrel. Your only unfettered state of belonging is to God: that is strong, direct and constant, with no need of intermediary. Just try to start this relationship, and let its kernel be love. This love will limit the fear that accompanies approaching God; it will let you come closer and closer. In this way, your belonging to entities will turn into them belonging to you, which means that you have risen above belonging to any earthly structure: you are ennobled by your greatest affiliation. God makes you great. God places you in the service of all His creatures.

Observe the effect of the above on you, and any differences from the section titled "Belonging and Prejudice." Make a note of your thoughts.

Ownership under God-Centrism

"What does the house think?"

The question occurred to me as I sat happily in the garden of 'my' house, thanking God for His blessings. I was remembering how I designed 'my' house, how I built it, how I planted my garden, and so on: all memories of this house assigned to me, and therefore 'mine.'

"What does the house think?" it occurred to me. Going by the average age of things, the house will long outlive me; others will sit in this garden in the coming years, and each of them saying, with complete truthfulness, "This is my house."

I thought of the magnificent buildings that Khedive Ismail, ruler of Egypt, commissioned 150 years ago; I thought of the buildings in Grand Place in Brussels, with plaques on them bearing the dates of their construction: 1760-1780, if memory serves, that is to say about 250 years ago. Imagine how many people lived within these walls and said, again in all honesty, "This house is mine"? Dozens, right? What do you think these houses would say, if they could speak, in response to the statement, "This is my house"? They'd probably burst out laughing. If they could speak, they would say, "Who owns whom? You leave; we stay. How can you say you own us?"

This shook the foundations of my sense of ownership. I began to reconsider the term as it applied to my home. 'Ownership...' I looked for something else that I could truthfully say I owned, something that no-one would use when I was gone. I finally found it: my body. My body and yours will be shared by no-one in life, and will be buried in the earth after death; it will disintegrate into dust. Then, my body and yours, dear Reader, are our sole property.

How can it be 'my' body, though, when I can't stop my nails from growing as I write this? How can you call it 'your' body when you can't simply command your hair to stop or start growing? When we buy a new TV, it comes with a remote control, doesn't it? How can this body be ours, when someone else is holding the remote? We can't control simple things like growing our hair and nails, let alone complex processes, like breathing or digestion. Knowing this, is it still accurate to call it 'my' body?

We are handed, so to speak, our bodies when we are born, working perfectly. The entire focus of modern medicine since its inception is simply to return the body to its former undamaged state. When our Creator decides that our time in this body is up, he ends our relationship with it. From this angle, how can we call our bodies 'ours', or say we own them? I think it would be more accurate to say we are licensed to use it for a certain period?

"But it's my body!"

We can call our body 'ours' as a hotel room is ours. "What's your room number?" I ask, and you respond truthfully that *your* room number is so-and-such. But imagine the hotel's reaction if you demanded they paint it a different color and change the furnishings: it's *your* room, isn't it? You can't do that; you're only using it on a temporary basis. The difference is that, once you leave your hotel room, someone else will take possession; once you leave your body, no-one else is going to live there.

If you are with me so far, then we don't even own our bodies. They are the property of the ultimate Owner, God. Knowing he has granted us the right to use them makes us change our philosophy of life. Your body's Owner did not create you frivolously; you were created to perform certain functions, for which purpose he gave you a heart, brain, lungs, etc. This is the meaning of ownership under God-centrism. Under God-centrism, the sense of ownership recedes; your relationship with all the things you own is that of temporary usage. You can use and enjoy them while knowing that they were not only created for your use and enjoyment.

There is a difference between a taxi and a private car. With your own care, you can do as you please. When you work for a taxi company, you drive a car but do not own it. The owner is the head of the company, who gives you a number of tasks to carry out with this vehicle. The owner sometimes lets you use the car for personal errands, with the understanding that it remains their property, and that, in driving it, you work for them.

The question is this: Are you a taxi or a private car? If your answer is the latter, then do as you please, and bear the consequences. If your response is the former, then waste no time doing anything other than the purpose God created you for, and gave you this body. I call this purpose 'what God wants of you'.

The road to finding out God's purpose is long, and will be covered in this book. Under self-centeredness, your happiness in this life is an end in itself, but only a means under God-centeredness, whose end is fulfilling God's purpose for you.

Take a moment to think about the above. Make a note of your feelings about being property. Then write down your thoughts and questions.

I

Render Unto Caesar The Things That Are Caesar's, And Render Unto God The Things That Are God's

In my stints as a board member in several companies, I have faced different challenges. There was, however, one challenge that I and my fellow board-members had in common in every company: disengaging ownership from stewardship, and removing any confusion between the role and capacities of the shareholders – the company's true owners – and the board of directors chosen by the shareholders to act in their interests. This challenge was complex. I sought out workshops on Corporate Governance Code and hired consultants. Nevertheless, the same set of problems seemed to keep cropping up in publicly traded companies.

The Chairman of the Board, or Chief Executive Officer, is chosen by the majority shareholder(s), and appointed with a clear mandate of the board's duty to the shareholders according to a number of Key Performance Indicators, by which they can be evaluated. As long as the Board is achieving what it is supposed to, the shareholders re-elect them. One of the challenges for a big company where there are no major shareholders, and the board is making good profit, the Chairman of the Board and the Board of Directors start to feel that *they* own the company, not merely manage it. This causes trouble over time, and often leads to the CEO and part or all of the board of directors being replaced by the shareholders.

The above example may shed some light on what the Self does to us. In management terms, if each of us is a business, the sole shareholder is God. God's spirit is your CEO, carrying out your mandate, God's purpose for you. The Divine Spirit within us knows full well that it is the manager, not the owner, never losing sight of this fact: the shareholder is God, and it must earn his approval as long as you live under God-centrism.

The confusion starts when your Self takes over as CEO. A classic delusion of the Self is that it presumes itself a joint stockholder with God, and treats the Almighty as though He were a fellow member of the board; all through the Self's term as management, it maneuvers and machinates, using the excuse, "render unto Caesar the things that are Caesar's, and render unto God the things that are God's," rejecting, ignoring, or willfully disregarding that Caesar and the things that are Caesar's are both God's. They ignore or pretend not to know that an emperor can only become a despot by God's will, for a wise purpose only He knows, that He may reveal to us or not as He wills, and that an emperor can only rule justly by God's will. When the Self starts to imagine itself a shareholder, it takes steps to protect its interests. It makes you work for yourself, not for the benefit of God, the Ultimate Shareholder. Such a system provokes the individual and collective Ego, with a measurable surge in activity of the Ego and Us.

Your self takes the driver's seat in the absence of awareness, heading for self-centeredness. Under God-centrism, you and yours belong to God, and he permits you to use them for a reason: fulfilling God's purpose. Seek out that purpose: start today.

Observe and note your reactions.

Religion under God-Centrism

First, allow me to offer a brief review of the concepts in "Religion under Self-Centeredness." Religion is one of the most lucrative pursuits for those who use it for personal gain. In primitive tribes, any good tribal leader exploited people's need for a god to worship by employing an individual of great influence, the witch doctor. The witch doctor's role has always been to convince the common people that the tribal chief is a god, a demi-god, or the god's shade on earth, and that divine will and the leader's will is one and the same, and to anger the leader is to anger God. Sacrifices must be offered and money paid to ward off the wrath of the gods. Accepting the sacrifices meant God's approval – whose prerequisite was the chief's approval. The gifts went to the chief's coffers. The chief, in turn, paid the witch doctor generously to secure his services in fooling the rest of the tribe. This state of affairs ultimately culminated in the worship of the Chief as a God, with the witch doctor interceding for the people with the holy chief, and so it went.

Even societies where heavenly prophets had spoken were not immune: if the people were ignorant and superstitious enough, and their rulers despotic enough. The rise of the Tribe of Religion was virtually guaranteed, so long as the main players were present: the Tribal Leader, the Witch Doctor, and Members of the Tribe, in different forms and numbers.

The Tribal Leader may be replaced by some economic, political or military power (or all of these). No matter; the important thing is the role of Tribal Leader. The Witch Doctor is always there, in the form of an individual or an institution, serving some ruling power. The Members of the Tribe may be asked for money if the Leader is a businessman, or votes if the Leader is a politician, or their mandate if the Leader is a military man bent on war for personal reasons and in need of popular support and religious credibility to cover himself. Indeed, all of the above may be present: the Tribal Leader may need the money, votes and mandate of the Members, aided and abetted by the Witch Doctor, the cleric.

Does this mean, however, that there is no such thing as a cleric who works only for the love of God? On the contrary. Most clerics and theologians down the ages have been good; the examples I mention are a minority. In fact, it is precisely *because* the majority were good that clerics and theologians acquired a kind of cumulative credibility in the popular consciousness, so sadly exploited by the unscrupulous minority. The question is, what is the difference between a setting that produces an honest cleric and one that produces a Witch Doctor who uses his power to equate worshipping the Leader with worshipping God?

The difference is one between religion under self-centeredness versus religion under God-centrism. Let us examine how a few charlatans have appropriated the credibility cultivated by the good intentions of most clerics to serve those in power, whether they had a direct share in that power or not.

Religion under God-Centeredness

God has said that He is too great to be contained in anything in the heavens and earth, except a believer's heart; since He has said this to us, this must also include revealed religions.

History has shown that God has sent thousands of prophets to us with methodologies and instructions on how to relate to Him. These methodologies are revealed religions. I believe that this is the best way to deal with religion: as a path to God, and his prophets as guides.

Religion as a guide was sent to your self so that it might avoid losing the way, and beginning to revolve around its Self. Religion under God-centeredness is a path, and the prophets an infallible guide. So are clerics: but they are not, however, infallible. God has set out the ways and means we must follow in our worship of Him. Religion is an instruction manual for life, very much like the one you would get if you bought a new electronic device. The Maker is God; the device is us; the recipient is, also, us. Religion is the manual sent to us by God to show us how best to use ourselves.

"To use ourselves? For what?"

This is the great difference. When we buy a device, it is for our own use; however, we are not supposed to use ourselves for our own purposes, but for His. God has blessed us by removing any mystery surrounding how we should use ourselves in his service, sending us the manuals to tell us how best to use this precious device, ourselves, for its intended purpose. Religions throughout history are these manuals.

"What is the purpose that God wants us to achieve through use of ourselves?"

There are the major answers He has given us: that we were created to know him, to worship him, to multiply.

"Why does God want us to do these things?"

The answers to this high standard of questioning are beyond our comprehension. God did not grant us the capacity; He only prepared us to look for answers to the first level of questions.

"How can we look for answers?"

This can be thought of as an open-book test. We can find the answers in the books.

"But that means our answers will all be the same!"

Not necessarily. Different answers will emerge in different times and places, and different people will answer in different ways.

One of the signs that our religious feeling is under God-centrism is our tolerance of those of different religions, and the constant search for common ground; another sign that we are operating under God-centrism is our devotion to fulfilling God's purpose for us, or to searching for it. This is why we have no time to focus on others and judge them, nor fill with resentment, wishing failure on them; we don't gloat over their missteps, but wish them well, and extend a helping hand to all, as the prophets did.

Look around you. Some who insist that everyone different is surely going to Hell, are implicitly certain that *they* are going to paradise. Says who? If we *were* to lend credence to what they insist, who's to say they won't join them in damnation? Do they think Hell has a quota – that if Hell is full, we'll escape? –to say nothing, of course, of the presumption to play God and decide who is damned and who is saved.

From all of the above, we can learn that when our center is God, religion is a path, a way, a methodology, to reach our goal, and our goal is God.

Being Religious vs. Being Godly

The way the term 'religious' is used in our time shows how confused some people are. A religious person used to mean someone who had dedicated his life to studying religion, what we would call a theologian today. The current use, though, muddles our relationship with God, causing our compass to point to religion and not God. It makes religion into an end rather than a means. 'Religious' now applies to the religion of the person it is used to describe, as in 'a religious Christian/Muslim/Jew'. There's nothing wrong with that – *as long as it is understood* that religion is a path to God. The implicit meaning is that this person uses religion to draw closer to God. But if that meaning is unclear, the term comes to mean 'becoming immersed in the minutiae of religion, and forgetting the reason for its existence' – which may lead to it being used as an end and not a means. Eventually, religion becomes an end.

History is full of tales of holy personages into virtual idols worshipped instead of God. This is a gradual process. First, statues of these people are made, as a means to draw closer to God. With the passage of time, the means is confused with the end, and statues become an 'auxiliary god' of a sort, a means to earn God's favor. Then it gets another promotion in our consciousness, and so on. I believe that the confusion that gave rise to modern idolatry is the same thing that has turned religion into a Tribe, and the problem with some people's relationship to religion.

A Godly person is someone, quite simply, whom God loves.

Godly people try to reach Him 24/7. They observe God in everything they do, and love all of His creatures in Him. Their compass never wavers; even if they are forced to change direction, their awareness is always with God. The aim of godly persons is God; anything else is only a means to that glorious end. They are from God, with God, to God.

Contemplate. Think. Observe. Write.

I

Comfort and Contentment

There is a certain lifestyle where you seek comfort; in another, you seek contentment. We may seek comfort right now, working hard to buy our comfort in the form of homes, cars, vacations and so on. These and others are means to our physical and mental comfort. We work towards a comfortable lifestyle in the future, through judicious investments to make us as comfortable as possible when it's time to retire and enjoy our leisure.

Sometimes, in life, we fall victim to stress. Nerves and exhaustion become permanent houseguests. Some of those around us advise strenuous exercise or extreme sports to 'work it off'. These do work to burn off stress, to a degree; in any case, the ultimate goal is to seek comfort.

It's also possible to choose a lifestyle where our goal is to be content with our lot, and to work hard to find means to this end. Most, if not all, roads to true contentment lie in working to serve others, where one's true aim is making others comfortable. This is not to say that you should stop seeking comfort for you and yours, nor to stop working for a good life; but they should be in parallel.

"But that will be exhausting!"

No doubt; but you can get enough rest if you consciously plan for life's challenges. You must organize your life to plan for times of rest using the same tools mentioned above. However, enjoying your rest is not to be seen as an end, but a means to recharge and renew our energies for the journey of life. If your main goal in life is to make yourself and your loved ones comfortable, you will probably get what you want; if you seek contentment by working to make others comfortable, you will probably manage to get it done. You will also probably be able to get enough rest, using the tools mentioned above. In the first case, your goal is your comfort; when you get it, you're done. Contentment doesn't have to follow. In the second, your contentment – being able to look yourself in the mirror – is the goal, and getting enough rest is a means to an end, like way-stations on your life's journey.

It may be noted here that it is hard to achieve contentment if one's life is exclusively dedicated to seeking comfort; in contrast, seeking contentment may hold a certain comfort. Getting a great deal of both is extremely difficult if not impossible.

"But what's this got to do with life under self-centeredness or God-centeredness?"

I believe that living self-centeredly is in direct proportion to the search for comfort; the one leads to the other, and practicing the one the one reinforces the search for the other. When you choose your life's goal as making you and yours comfortable, you provide the ideal climate for self-centeredness; if you already live that way, knowingly or unknowingly, your priorities will be your own self and your comfort, and thus they will feed each other. There is also a high probability of achieving the pinnacle of comfort, i.e. becoming so well-off that you can slow down to enjoy your free time. This is the phrase 'retirement age' and so on, where we work less and enjoy more.

A choice to live under God-centrism, on the other hand, is to try to be content with oneself via achieving God's approval, by making others comfortable. Interestingly, the reverse is not always true. We can seek to feel good about ourselves through doing good for others, without doing it for God: that is to say, charity for the sake of charity. "How?" you ask. Well, just as seeking the ability to look oneself in the mirror *may* yield a physically comfortable life – while the reverse is not true – life under God-centrism *must* include doing good for others. However, seeking others' benefit is not always for God. We have spoken of this in the section on charity and God.

Under God-centrism, we never arrive at the terminal, the final stop where we can said to have *enough* contentment, the point where we slow down in our service of God in order to reap the fruits of having done "enough" good, or feeling content "enough" about ourselves – this doesn't arise. This is a scenario from which you cannot retire; you can enjoy your achievements while doing your very best to achieve the next thing. You cannot retire, because you don't work for other people, but for God; your work for God only ends with the end of your life, at a time known only to God.

Which brings us to the inevitable question: What is your choice? Do you think you must choose between comfort and contentment? Do you see yourself as lacking initiative if you don't make a choice, or not? If you plan to choose between them, what kind of life experience do you want, a life glutted with comfort, or a life striving for contentment? Think; observe; write. Make a note of your questions. These may lead you to your choices.

Death

Death is one of the very few things that most of us can agree on. If you think about it, the number of people who believe in death is far greater than those who believe in God. Religious people have their own conception of it; the followers of non-revealed religions have theirs; and atheists, too, believe in death, if not in an afterlife. The overwhelming majority of people worldwide believes that death is the end of life. Under self-centeredness, the fear of death colors every aspect of life. Under God-centrism, the fear of death is not as extreme.

The introduction to this book mentioned five components that, in some worldviews, make up a person: the Spirit, the Self, the Body, the Mind, and the Heart. The leader of these, I think, is either the Spirit or the Self. The mind, heart and body follow the leader: their performance and status change depending on who is leading. For those who believe in God, as I have stated, there are two choices: self-centeredness or God-centeredness.

Death Under Self-Centeredness: The Wall

In the first choice, the Self conducts the quintet. The Spirit is isolated, deprived of the chance to play its role; the Self dies after a while, and is aware of its own mortality. Every Self is aware of its own mortality; therefore, its actions in the world are a kind of 'get what you can while you can'. The Self's passion is transmitted to the other parts, Body, Mind and Heart, each of which takes to grasping for whatever can nourish it. The Body seeks out as much nourishment as it can, food, drink, sex, etc. When the Self is leading, it forgets that the Heart needs to be full of God and quenching its thirst for God, so the Heart feels empty, trying to fill the void as the Body fills its stomach, by overcompensating and hoarding sensual pleasure, a bit like a *nouveau riche*. Too much music, art, perfumes, food and drink and other sources of beauty are hoarded to fill the empty heart: over time, hoarding turns into greed and desperation, like a thirsty person drinking from the sea. There is no substitute for the heart's main food, God.

The same applies to the mind. Under the leadership of Self, Mind oversteps its bounds: God has permitted us to use our minds for learning, while creating a ceiling, or limit, to the Mind's abilities.

Smartphones, for example, have a large memory capacity; but I can't ask someone to download all of, say, NASA's server records onto an iPhone. This is an *impossibility of quantity*. Yes, the phone has a large internal memory, but within the bounds of its intended use as a mobile telephone and mini-computer. Similarly, I can't ask someone to put five tons of potatoes on his iPhone, "because it has lots of storage!" This is an *impossibility of quality*. That's how we are: under self-centeredness, the human mind breaks through all barriers, and tries to download NASA and the spuds! Time and energy are wasted on fruitless matters; if you try to protest, you will be accused of apathy.

"What's that got to do with death, though?"

Death is the threat from which there is no escaping, the end of all the Self has hoarded for the mind and heart and body. Death, in this case, is the wall we are hurtling towards and *must* hit, sooner or later, and will deprive the Self of everything it has hoarded. Death is a source of fear and trepidation, because it is the end of the Self that is aware of its mortality.

In addition, the Self's preoccupation with the world distracts it from thinking of life after death; it treats life after death as "the Unknown," and that moving to the Unknown must be accompanied by a sense of alienation. The Ego's overweening preoccupation with its job of defending the castle allows the Self not to spend too much time thinking of the Event, death; it merely remembers death from time to time. Death usually comes as a shock, which only increases the panic attached to the End, the Wall: Death.

Death under God-Centrism: The Gateway

Under God-centrism, Death is a gateway through which we pass from a time and place we know, to an unknown state; passing through the gate is accompanied by some awe and trepidation, but also anticipation.

Under God-centrism, the Spirit leads the quintet: the Self, Heart, Body and Mind follow its lead. The Spirit disciplines the Self, not letting it control Heart, Body and Mind. Why this difference? Because the Spirit is immortal.

The Spirit has been immortal since God breathed His spirit into Adam, since He made us self-aware. The Spirit is immortal: it knows that when it moves from this life to the next, it will live forever in its new home. It is immortal, and it knows it, even here. The Spirit is immortal, and the Body is only its clothing, which it can change. It may not know what the new costume will be, but it trusts its Creator, and is aware of this change, and secure in it.

To the Spirit, Death is a change of clothing; it is a crossing from one state of being to another; Death is only the gateway. The passage is a return to where the Spirit instinctively knows it belongs, to its half-remembered origins. Here, there is no sense of alienation, no fear of the Unknown; the Spirit is coming home.

In this world, the Spirit is in a state of calm assurance. It has no use for the Self's perpetual state of emergency, its hoarding and greed and fear of the End. The Spirit looks forward to returning home, and is eager to meet God. This eagerness eases the fear and stress of moving from one state to another.

The Heart, filled with God in this world, only increases this eagerness. The Heart's main reassurance in this world is to be filled with God; so fed, it is tender and full of love. It looks on life with a loving eye, appreciating beauty. Its inner divine beauty is reflected in all the senses: the senses seek beauty in all they see, hear, touch, taste and smell. Because it is filled with God, the heart is always content; it seeks beauty for enjoyment, not out of desperate need, a bit as we would enjoy a cup of coffee after a big meal. If you have ever been in love, you know how it affects us: we see beauty in everything, and seem to be in seventh heaven. Something not unlike this occurs when the Heart is filled with God, only many orders of magnitude greater.

"But what's that got to do with eagerness to meet God?"

When the Spirit is leading, and God fills your heart, you are in love with Him and with everything, and see beauty everywhere. The Spirit knows that the bliss it is experiencing is only a tiny part of the joyous ecstasy awaiting on the other side of the door. It knows that the main source of all this is God. It becomes more and more thirsty for that sensation, more and more passionate to meet him, more and more eager to meet Him.

Make a note of your feelings knowing that one of your components is immortal; seek out your thoughts and questions and write them down.

I

Dying for God under God-Centrism

Life, I imagine, is the most valuable thing we have. When we give our lives for a certain goal or cause, it is only natural to view this as an honor to be respected and appreciated. When giving our lives for God, honor, respect and appreciation are supplemented with ennoblement and inspiration: we are giving the dearest thing we own for the highest goal. In addition to appreciation in this world, we are also certain of a heavenly reward. Throughout history, God has sent prophets to preach His message through kind words and smiles, then through warnings of the wrath of God. There are many tales in history of unbelievers tormenting believers, of battles led by prophets with unbelievers. In all of these, self-sacrifice was an essential component. The very presence of the prophets was proof of the validity of what they were fighting for: all these early fighters had to do was go and ask them, "Hey, if I die right now, does it count as dying for God?" and get a yes or no.

After the prophets died, their followers took up the banner, following their instructions closely at first, then distorting the message, until God sent a new messenger to set people straight. In the absence of the prophets, their followers worked hard to preserve the concepts they had introduced. History tells us how a minority managed to dupe people into sacrificing their lives for so-called holy wars, from which they then made immense political, social and material gains. These dupes gave their lives willingly, with the certainty that this sacrifice of their dearest possession was for God, victims of their own gullibility: millions died on the altar of ignorance and conspiracy, believing they died for the Almighty. This is a thorny issue, and it would take too long to discuss; but there is one side of it I would like to talk to you about.

Living for God

Do you remember the section on "Dying under Self-Centeredness" earlier in this book, and the alternative, living for God? Let's build on it here.

I think living for God may be more challenging, and take more work, courage and resolve, than dying for Him. Life is difficult when your God-centric paradigm is only a theory with no practical applications, while the opposing self-centered paradigm is flourishing on the ground.

When your paradigm, though admirable, has no real-life application, it is like owning a fabulous late-model Rolls-Royce in the middle of a forest: before you can drive it, you need roads. Our first duty, then, is to pave roads; and creating roads is definitely much more work than driving a Rolls. But how can you drive without doing this work at the outset? The same applies to a paradigm with no applications. First, we have to get creative in turning the theory into practical applications on the ground, in the form of day-to-day practices, starting with how we greet our neighbor on the way to work, through how we treat our business rivals, all the way to opening your heart in acceptance to your human siblings of different races, ethnicities, nationalities, creeds and religions. These new applications require original thinking, which leads to innovation. Innovation requires the courage to fail dozens of times. Strength, determination and fortitude are necessary to deal with failure, and these in turn require a high degree of initiative and willpower.

Living with initiative and willpower make life a series of challenges. But why all this backbreaking labor to create ways to live God-centrically, instead of self-centeredly or Us-centeredly? The reason is to fulfil God's purpose for you: to live for God, for others, and those around you, not only for you and your tribe. Such a life requires courage, initiative, and will. Do you have enough?

When you do this, you will be living for God through serving others, searching for His purpose. You are living for God. If you die while living like this, you will have died for God. This is a life worth living.

Make a note of any thoughts and questions you may have.

_____

_____

_____

_____

_____

From God's Destiny to God's Destiny

Since nothing happens without God's will, and being closer to Him is a source of divine strength, it is very important to discuss a common misconception: escaping destiny.

We need to know that we do not run to God when afflicted with poverty, injustice, disease, enemies, etc.; we run to God from God. This reinforces your sense that everything comes from Him and returns to Him; it makes us aware that He is our only refuge, which increases our sense of God-centrism. However, if we box God into the role of the protector, to whom we run for help in times of trouble, we unwittingly establish the notion that there is some other power capable of harming us, and that God can save us from it, unintentionally detracting from God's omnipotence.

There are many reasons, I believe, for this confusion. First, an ignorant and naïve if well-intentioned belief that God cannot be the source of anything bad, which leads us to assume that bad things come from some Other Source, against which we ask God for protection. Second, the concept that there is an eternal batter between Good and Evil, and that God is on the side of Good, which means that Evil can come from some Other Source, which has nothing to do with God. This led people to think that evil has some other source independent of God, leading to the confusion I have just mentioned. This was lent credibility by the writings of the Greeks and Ancient Egypt, bursting with intra-pantheon struggles, fights between gods and men, and clashes between good and evil, where good gods were depicted as no more or less powerful than evil gods, et cetera.

There is a third reason: the presence of a very successful civilizational practice based on self-centeredness: the empirical method. The search for causes, without looking for the Ultimate Reason, has achieved stellar success, only increasing the confusion. People have a very good understanding of only half the truth – "we are fleeing FROM God's destiny" – without seeing the other half – "we are fleeing TO God's destiny." It is essential that we establish an awareness that everything in this universe occurs at God's command. Everything comes from Him. Everything goes to Him.

This covers the questions and answers. What about the challenges we face?

If we want to control how adversity affects us, the source of strength, power and energy is God, and approaching Him gives us the change to allow Him to support us. When we are in pain for some reason in life, we must know that the One who allowed it to happen is God, and that the One we must turn to to ease or take away our pain is also God.

The same applies to our relationship with fear. We fear pain; if we turn to God to help us deal with pain, we can turn to Him to help us deal with fear. You can check the accuracy of all this, using your consciousness and awareness, to establish yourself firmly under God-centrism. If that is absent, we are at the mercy of the Ego, under self-centrism.

Think about this, and make a note of your impressions.

I

Competition under God-Centrism
Inclusive Competition

Inclusive competition is based on success. Both of us win, me and the other. The phrase "win-win" has become a buzzword in recent years – a phrase that urges both parties to achieve mutual success and mutual gain. I believe that it can apply to life not only under self-centeredness, but also under God-centrism.

Under self-centeredness, we will adhere to win-win principles as long as there are opportunities for mutual profit and success, opportunities that are plentiful if we choose to seek them. If resources are limited, however, I will scramble to crush the other and get them all for myself. Opportunities multiply when there is little room for competition, and become scarce when the Self and the Us activate competitiveness. For this reason, I have a name for Win-Win under self-centeredness: the fragile pact.

Under God-centrism, I care about my interests *and* the Other's interests. I care for the Other because my dealings with God and relationship with Him are through this Other. Our relationship with God, I believe, has many levels: We fear God; we trade with Him; we love Him. You are free to choose any form of these relationships, and practice it via your interaction with the Other. If you choose fear, that will make you always alert to the Other's needs, even in competition, fearing that God may take your profits away if you forget to serve Him in the person of the Other. If you choose trade, you know that the more you give to God in the person of the Other, the more your profits will multiply, and thus serve his interests, even as you compete, knowing that this will increase your profits. If you choose love, you are thanking God through the Other, enjoying the company of God as you see Him in the Other – for your love for God makes you see Him in everything, living the verse, "he is with you wheresoever you go." You are in God's company 24/7/365; therefore you are always careful of the Other. You always love the Other. You have boundless love for God and for the Other: your fierce competitiveness shrivels and all but disappears. You are partners with the Other; you seek others' interests perpetually; you always feel God's care and His blessings, which in turn heightens your gratitude to Him, making you want to thank him by doing good to His creatures, all His creatures, human, plant, animal or mineral. You know that all things praise Him; it is just that you don't speak their language. You are constantly communing with God, praising Him, thanking Him through the Other. The tools for praising the Lord are the tongue and the heart, i.e. direct contact with Him; the tools for thanking Him are working and loving all His creatures, i.e. indirect contact with Him. In this case, you care about the environment, since everything in it is God's creation, and because all God's creatures benefit from it: in God's love, you care about His creation for the sake of His creatures – known now as being an environmentalist – but you do it out of love for God, not out of fear of what the hole in the ozone will do to you and your interests.

I have no practical concept of what inclusive competition under God-centrism would look like at the moment, but I imagine the following: Your search for inclusive competition strategies motivated by the fear of God will be a challenge, but you will constantly seek out ways to benefit the Other even as you compete with them, since the awful fear of God's wrath motivates you and points your compass to the right path. In the trade with God, like any good businessman, you will seek the highest profit. You are aware that your profit increases so long as the Other is doing well: your creativity will be at its highest in the search for ways and means to achieve this. As for the love of God, you are in contact with Him. There is scarcely any competition in the matter. God is the source of all things; all things must also be for Him. You are always giving because you know that you do not really own anything, but that He owns all, and you live through His generosity, compassion and love. You ask Him directly for help, for you and for others: where, then, is the competition, if all you have to do is ask? Anything that comes from Him, profit or loss, is for the ultimate good. In this state – the love of God – you are achieving God's purpose. You see His purpose in your competitors. But what if they don't see it? You alert them to it, allowing them to achieve God's purpose. You are no competitor, but a servant: a servant to all God's creatures. A servant does not compete with those he serves, but merely does their duty; they only compete to serve God, and is in constant communion with God.

There are many examples of competition in life. Write down three competitive situations: at work, in the family, and among friends. Set down your ideas of how to turn it into an inclusive situation if you wanted to.

Women under God-Centrism
A Miracle

From my perspective, this is the most expressive term for a woman. Why do I say this?

God created women with amazing ability to do many things in parallel, and do them all competently. It is natural to find a woman conducting two conversations, one with a person with her and another on the phone. It is the most natural thing in the world to find a woman supervising her son's homework, making dinner for her family, writing a letter about some social cause she is passionate about, while giving strict instructions to the housekeeper and making a phone call about the job she left not an hour earlier, followed by a chat with a friend on the phone; then, with a broad smile and a heartfelt greeting, she welcomes her husband home, and listens with real sympathy to his complaints about how hard he works! All this, note, while she is in the final months of pregnancy. (The final addition is my personal, ongoing experience which I use as an example: my life with the miracle who takes care of me, my beloved wife Hala, carrying to term our latest blessing from God, Ahmad Widdallah, born in the same month I finished this book, November 2014.)

It is only natural for the helpmeets of the "influential few" men in the world to be women. She manages his life and his family's for him, in addition to her relatives' daily lives. It is natural to find the success stories of the influential few men and women in history linked to a central role played by some woman (wife or mother), either by raising them, caring for them, supporting them, leveling obstacles, or all this together.

In poorer societies worldwide, female breadwinners are common; single mothers are common in richer societies worldwide. Both represent a single phenomenon, regardless of financial and social differences: a young woman shouldering full responsibility for a child, or children, abandoned by their despicable father, who planted his seed and decided he wasn't up to the responsibility. It is only natural for charities to seek out the most responsible person in the families they assist, and that person is usually a woman – a mother, a sister, etc. – for fear that the fathers or brothers will spend the money on their own pleasures, ignoring the what family needs. It is natural to find two-thirds of the attendees of development workshops are women;

the same ratio seems more or less constant in workshops on recovery and healing. A Canadian friend once told me, "I realized that most of the attendees in my lectures and workshops are women who had been hurt [sic] and they insist on standing on their feet again; as for men, if they got hurt, most of the time they cave."

Naturally, women had an important role in the lives of the prophets. Is it natural to say "naturally"? Not unless you agree to my description of women at the start of this section: a miracle. Let's look at this miracle more closely.

The miracle of womanhood may be summed up in one word: Life. Everything women do, as wives and mothers, are a means to give part of her heart, part of who she is, part of the life inside her. Regardless of her financial, social and cultural status, she shines. When a man does what a woman does, he may do it very well, but he lacks that unique flavor of womanhood: the flavor of life. Man builds and produces, but what he builds and produces is meaningless until his Miracle arrives and blesses it with the flavor of life. Woman builds and produces as well, but her magic touch is in everything she does.

Before a woman finds her man – the flower of her garden – she is ready to shine, but has not attained her full glory. When a woman finds her man, he is everything to her: his presence renews her energy, helping her give more life to everything around her. If he disappears for any reason, she keeps giving, but she loses her source of energy, and starts to drain her soul dry in order to keep giving.

Man does not radiate life as his woman does. He isn't made for it. He is only the fuel for a magnificent life-giving machine.

Before moving on to the next section, please make copious notes about a wonderful woman (or more than one) in your life – whether you are a man or a woman – whose effect on your life matched what I said after "natural" above. (I hope you thank the miracle herself for being in your life, and then thank God for sending her to you).

_____

_____

_____

_____

I

Another unique facet of these miracles that walk among us: her special relationship between her and her Maker.

God breathes the Divine Spirit into men in the womb, while they are still embryos and cannot sense the miracle of their creation. What about women? They have the same experience in the womb as well. But God has blessed her with a unique ability: after it was only a collection of cells, God breathes life into the embryo *in her womb*. I'm not talking about the miracle of life, but this woman: God has breathes his spirit into her. Can you imagine it? She has had contact with another world, the Unseen that is God's alone, at an age when she is aware and conscious of it. Can you imagine its impact on her?

Since it happens all the time, to all women, we don't pay this much attention. But it is enormous in impact: this second contact is another miracle with which God blessed this miracle that walks among us. Unfortunately, history tells us that men have always tried to oppress women. I believe that God's holy books are enough to restore the balance: I also believe that there will always be men who try to abuse religion and twist it into a tool to oppress women and impose restrictions on their freedom. This always happens in self-centered societies, where the "I" and the "Us" manifests in a lust for power, and an attempt to control those around it: the relationship between men and women in such societies is prime breeding-ground for that in self-centered societies.

A different angle may give us a different perspective. I think the individual male ego is constantly threatened by women. Why? Men can only concentrate on one thing at a time; they prefer to do things consecutively, not concurrently. Women's ability to multitask disturbs, frightens and threatens men.

Men are result-oriented, not process-oriented. Women prefer to succeed via interpersonal relationships, an avenue not usually open to men through their chosen pursuits. Women are more capable of dealing with loss and pain. In the presence of ways and means, women can get back on their feet when they fall down, and overcome adversity, while men often limp through life, unable to recover. These all combine to make men feel threatened and inadequate.

When panic overtakes the male ego completely, it scrambles to defend the male identity. The first line of defense is depriving women of ways and means. History tells us that this was done by stripping women of their rights and treating them as inferior. In the microcosm of society, the family, an unbalanced relationship between male and female can upset the balance of the family. It is like a business where the Chairman of the Board feels threatened (whether truly or out of his own insecurity) by the CEO, and seeks to hobble the CEO and limit their freedoms out of a sense, conscious or unconscious, that the CEO's success somehow makes a mockery of the Chairman's own, and makes him look inadequate. The CEO tries to do their job bypassing the Chairman, and the company is thrown into disarray.

In a healthy nuclear family, men and women plan together: usually, the male is the Chairman and head of the company, and must provide the operating budget, while the mother/CEO manages the day-to-day affairs, as well as contributing financially to the treasury. The man stays out of the daily running of the family, while the mother does everything.

If the man – the Chairman – feels threatened that the CEO is more competent than he is – whether or not this is true – this insecurity makes him flustered. He starts to corner his spouse and limit her role; she responds by trying to push past these restrictions, whereupon the family unit collapses.

If a family breaks apart, most women find it easy to play the roles of both Chairman and CEO, sailing the family ship alone, whereas men find it hard to do the same. They end up either leaving the children to the woman to raise, providing only financial support, or find a woman as soon as possible to do the job. This is a characteristic of this miracle, the ability to adapt to circumstances easily.

Is this the only way for men to treat women? Well, as long as a man's Ego is active, he will view women as a threat, greater or lesser depending on the era he lives in. Under self-centeredness, the relationship between men and women can be classed as a competitive relationship. I believe men are lucky that women realize themselves through relationships with people, because the success of a woman's relationship with her man falls into this category. This explains why women try so hard to make relationships work, as opposed to men who give up more easily when there are challenges. Women are also more forgiving than men, which gives the relationship many second chances. But such a relationship is nowhere near peaceful, loving and giving enough: which is why under self-centeredness, a lot of married people seek peace, love and understanding outside the marital relationship, which increases infidelity and puts an ever-increasing number of marriages at risk.

Another point is important: the trap that modern women have walked into of their own free will.

The Trap

In women's search for equality, they have fallen into the trap of seeing the symptom, not the ailment: they have attempted to deal with men's urge to compete with them, not with the reason for this competitiveness. Women have asserted their ability to succeed in every field, using the same tools and methods as men: this too is a trap.

An example may help. It is generally accepted that pentathletes – athletes who take part in the modern pentathlon, which includes fencing, swimming, show jumping, target shooting, and running – will have lower scores in each individual sport than those who train for that sport alone. What if a pentathlete decided to compete with the world swimming champion, while still training for the pentathlon, by devoting more time to swimming? Most probably, they still would not beat the exclusive swimmer's times, and exhaust themselves in the process. What should that athlete do, then?

While you think of answers, let me share mine: there seem to be only two paths, either to concentrate on the sport they are most suited for, by dint of being good at five sports, or else retire from pentathlon competition, and concentrate only on swimming. But even if a pentathlete has slightly lower scores than their counterparts, the world champions who have dedicated themselves to one sport, they are still superior: they are good at 4 additional sports of which the respective single-event world champions know nothing!

This, I believe, is what happened to women when they entered into competition with men on their terms.

Before I go into this example and how it relates to what I am saying, let's not forget that the entire society we live in is patriarchal, constructed by men over centuries, if not millennia, for men's convenience, to serve men's needs. Women have been systematically excluded from constructing any social, economic or political systems. The criteria for success and failure, the ground rules for business, even working hours, dress codes and vacation times, are all created to serve a masculine order. Women entered the workplace as women, but working within a system designed exclusively for men: they had to 'act like men,' 'compete like men', and generally pretend to be men if they wanted to be taken seriously in the workplace. At the start they may have had no choice, but now it seems imprudent to keep going along the same path.

Women are like the pentathlete: they have the ability to do many things at the same time. But women don't have the choices open to the pentathlete; a pentathlete can choose to become a swimmer, but a woman cannot easily – and in most cases would rather not – turn into a man. What remains is three unenviable choices: (1) give up work; (2) give up her other roles; (3) do both, and exhaust herself in the process.

Who put women in this fix? I believe they are responsible for this situation, even though they had no part in creating it. Women became responsible by agreeing to play a game whose rules and tools were tailored to the convenience of another player. First, men had been refining the system to suit themselves for hundreds of years; any modifications to it are bound to be unsuitable for women. Second, the concept of women's liberation appeared at a time when self-centeredness was the dominant paradigm.

Under self-centeredness, competition is exterminatory, not inclusive. Men would never, in a win-lose system, change the rules of the game so both parties could win. What happened on the ground is that men clung more tightly to the rules of the game, pushing women into the corner of "be like us or get out." Women became even more determined to beat men at their own game, and let themselves be forced into competing on men's terms, and being judged by men's criteria.

Does this remind you of anything? It's our old friend the Ego: male ego vs. female ego, the male "I" vs. the female "I", the male "Us" vs. the female "Us." Nobody wins in this battle; there doesn't need to be a battle. Battles provoke the ego, and everyone loses. What do we lose? We lose love and compassion. We lose the essence of life. We lose family. We lose love.

It is a misdiagnosis to blame the breakdown of families and the disintegration of society on the liberation of women. This is short-sighted. Yes, women have fallen into a trap; but the path to the cure is to treat the illness, not the symptom. A bird's-eye view will help.

The true illness, I believe, is self-centeredness. The start of a real solution is to move into a God-centric place, where things are completely different. Under God-centrism, the male Ego is under control. Men no longer feel threatened by women; they feel grateful for women's care, and admiration for their marvelous abilities, and they complement one another. Under God-centrism, complementariness is the name of the game: men will help women to succeed, because her success is one of his life goals. Under God-centrism, women complement their men, not compete with them. Men and women will ask each other for help; everyone plays their part. There is room for everyone to succeed. If part of God's purpose for us is to help others achieve their own part of God's purpose, shouldn't we help our spouse tenfold?

Under God-centrism, women will have no need to escape the trap: they won't have to. Men will be there for women, helping create an alternative to the trap, and, more importantly, they will work together to eliminate any future traps.

Question: Why not do all this under self-centeredness?

An important question, with an important answer. The reason is that when we do the right thing for the wrong reasons, it doesn't last very long; it may well collapse under the slightest pressure. The Ego, I believe, is the root of the problem; most of the complex disagreements between men and women can be traced back to an overactive ego. Even one overactive Ego is enough to make life miserable; and the only thing that can truly curb the ego is God-centrism.

This is not to say that God-centrism is a magic pill to end all marital disputes. They will always be a part of life. But under God-centrism, disputes will be genuine, not a distorted by-product of an overactive Ego. Plus, I sincerely believe that we can only escape from the issue of competition, not by patching up and modifying competitive male-created dynamics, but by changing our strategy. In strategic language, changing the dynamics keeps women trapped in the "red ocean" – that is to say, the traditional 'female' framework –whereas I believe the solution lies in both men and women seeking a "blue ocean," a creative new ideology to create a society that can accommodate both, where we can use our God-given gifts in the service of each other.

We need to know that life without the Other is impossible. The choice is ours: to compete with one another under self-centeredness, or complement one another under God-centrism.

That's what I think. What do you think, dear reader? Make a note of what you think regarding the issue of women.

I

PART TWO
God's Love

Remember the teacher at school who was firm but fair? The one who, you felt, truly cared about your future? Take a moment to think of them. What about your mother? She, too, cared about your future. Both of them sometimes got mad at you; both sometimes punished you; both smiled and praised your success. Despite that, did we feel the same about both? I doubt it; the difference was that our mothers loved us unconditionally.

Which of the two was, and still is, closer to us? The answer is a foregone conclusion. Nothing can compare with a mother's love.

Based on the above, how do you want your relationship with god to be? Based on love, or fear?

"You mean we have a choice?"

The choice is yours. In His generosity, God has given us the choice. The Prophet says of God: "I am what My servant assumes me to be." This can be applied to many situations, but I limit it here to the type of relationship one wants of God. Which do you want – the Teacher or the Mother? There are a number of possible choices:

1. A loving relationship.

2. A business relationship.

3. A relationship based on fear.

4. Not knowing there is even a choice.

From 1 - 3, I respect your choice. If you chose (4), I strongly urge you to make a choice. Think of your relationships: your mother, your teacher, your workplace. Which is sweeter? I think a loving relationship with God is the best by far. That is what I think: what do you? What is your choice?

If you choose a loving relationship with God, don't make a businessman of Him.

Make notes here of your current relationship with God, and what you would like it to be.

_____

_____

_____

_____

_____

_____

_____

_____

_____

_____

_____

_____

_____

God Is Not A Businessman

We have spoken of the possible relationships you may have with God: love, business, fear and ignorance. Some people prefer to organize them in a hierarchy: fear, then business, then ultimately love. This is not bad as far as everyday life goes; sometimes, though, an exceptional circumstance can confuse our priorities, and we need to be alert.

This exceptional circumstance is the dominance of the self-centered paradigm in the past few centuries, to the pretend. This has confused the fear-based and business-based models of interacting with God, leading to profoundly negative consequences. This particular danger reminds me of another exceptional circumstance: ocean rip currents, which can carry even the strongest swimmer for long distances parallel to the shore, but can be survived if you know not to resist them and let them carry you to a point where you can swim safely back.

Self-centeredness activates the individual and collective ego (and vice versa, that is to say, when the ego is overactive, we unconsciously slip into self-centeredness). Since fear is the primary motivator for the Ego, there is a danger for fear to be centered around your Self.

In the business relationship, there are always dangers. The effect of self-centeredness makes the central question always, "What's in it for me?" This is the very core of the self-centered paradigm, a universal concept *par excellence* that has negatively impacted the old values of altruism, chivalry and valor, and also love. Since almost everyone is agreed on this principle, it has become acceptable to offer a financial return for services that, long ago, were rendered out of simple human decency. But has this affected our relationship with God?

I believe it has. I believe that it has changed the nature of our business relationship with God to fit the "What's in it for me?" paradigm. This has always been there, but not so blatantly. This makes our relationship with God primarily – and exclusively – self-serving. Each of us pulls out a little virtual pocket calculator, on which we tally up the profits of serving God. "I have done ten good deeds," such a person says, "and a good deed, according to the Qur'an, is worth ten of itself, so I have earned 100 good deeds!" Or perhaps, "I have prayed in the Holy Mosque of Mecca, and each prostration there is worth 100,000 prostrations, so I have tallied up one million prostrations." The 26th of Ramadan, Laylat al-Qadr, is said to be worth a thousand months, so, in a simple calculation, several million good deeds are added to the Self's bank account. And so it goes. (I have used examples from my own religion, Islam, but I'm sure you can find examples in your own.)

Does this mean that I'm saying you shouldn't pray, do good deeds, and so on? Of course not; these are all good things, but what I am saying is that the exceptional circumstance I spoke of earlier has transformed noble notions into cheap calculations. As with the rip current in the ocean, humanity has been drawn inexorably into self-centeredness. We perform the same rituals in that space, but every beautiful thing they meant – to our fellow-humans and even to God – has been stripped from them. Do you think that formerly, under God-centrism, matters were conducted with such flagrant materialism? I doubt it.

"But what can we do about it?" In my opinion, the best course currently open to us is not to follow the hierarchy of fear, business, and love, in relating to God. The ocean rip current is simply too strong in the business relationship, and will drag you into self-centeredness without your knowing it.

What practical steps that can be taken to achieve this?

First, if you are just starting out – or advising young people – in building a relationship with God, I strongly urge you to bypass business and fear, and move straight to a loving relationship with Him. I have held open discussions on this subject titled "Free Your Will" at my organization, *Baladna*; they included Imams and priests, as well as dedicated youth officials, and youth-oriented human resources trainers, and focused strongly on this point.

Second, for those who are in too deep with the business relationship with God, a fundamental change is required.

"You mean stop doing good deeds?"

Not at all: keep doing them, but for the love of God, put away the calculator!

"But how?"

Don't calculate. That's all I have to say. That's the fundamental change I propose.

"What should I do?"

Do your best to do everything you used to do, and more, but don't calculate the rewards/profits. This is a way out of self-centeredness and towards God-centrism; it will open your door to God's love.

"I don't get it."

Calculating focuses you on quantity, whereas doing good is more about quality.

"Quality and quantity? We're back to calculations!"

It's true that I believe you should give God everything you can – quantity – but the most important thing is to have a profound relationship with God – quality. The way to God's love is to give your all, without calculating the profits.

The above may need some time to take in before you set down your impressions. Take your time.

Self-Love under Self-Centeredness vs. Self-Love under God-Centrism

Most of us take good care of our tools. We've all seen taxi-drivers who keep their vehicles in tip-top condition; farmers who take care of their machines reap impressive harvests; workers who oil and polish their machines tend to enjoy smooth running and a positive experience, and so on. If we want a positive experience with our smartphones, tablets and other devices, we give them the attention they deserve, upgrade their hardware and software, and so on.

A positive relationship with our equipment is a recipe for success. If these devices constantly let us down, we would get rid of them in frustration, and replace them with equipment that actually did what it was supposed to do. I believe that your relationship with yourself, dear reader, is the same, only on a more complex level.

In the section in god-centrism, we spoke of not owning your body but having a right to use it and its resources. You need to find God's purpose for this miracle of which He gave you stewardship, and to know that his purpose is achieved by doing good for others, and for you and yours. In this system, you are responsible for the care and maintenance of this magnificent machine, to achieve the best possible results, mentally and physically. You must also love this miraculous device, as a means of fulfilling God's purpose. You need to love yourself, while knowing you do not own it – while knowing it is merely held in trust.

To feel at peace, your Self needs to know that you love it and care for it. Selfishness is not the answer. Egocentrism is not the answer. Loving yourself is loving God's tool. You cannot change yourself; therefore, accept yourself and love yourself, the equipment that God has given you.

"But how can I tell the difference between the healthy state of loving myself in God and loving myself out of self-centeredness?"

Your results will tell you the difference. If the good you do is confined to you and yours, then you may need to take another look at the way you're doing things. However, if you do good for others as well as yourself, then you probably love yourself under God-centrism. This opens the door for you to love God and ask Him to love you, not just for your joy, but for your use.

Fear and Love

Imagine a room with the following people in it: a prince and a pauper, two rival clerics, a pair of managers of opposing football clubs, two CEO's of leading multinational corporations, a prominent leftist and a prominent right-wing politician, and so on. Now imagine that these people's children, all about three or four years of age, are together in the next room; they speak different languages.

The parents' room will be a powder-keg; immobilized with tension, everyone will be avoiding everyone else's eyes, taking refuge behind a newspaper, or finding some ally in the room to complain to. If it comes to confrontation, it will be violent and intense, with veins popping out and screaming and cursing.

If we go into the children's room, it will be full of noise: the prince's child will be playing in the mud with the pauper's, and so on with all the opposing factions' children. As children do, they will fight over a toy or game, then make up a few moments later, and go back to their play, forgetting their conflict as if it had never existed. The cycle of fight and play will continue as long as they are in the same place, together. Language is no barrier: language is never a barrier for children to laugh and play. They can invent a shared language, and have fun together in moments. They know nothing of religious factions, football teams, business rivalries, and so on. This is not untrue: but it is incomplete.

The parents' room, with its fierce rivalries, is full of something: a basic instinct, the main thing which causes all the tension and anxiety in the room.

That something is *fear.*

There are two kinds of fear: fear *of* something or fear *for* something. I fear *for* my possessions or achievements: I am afraid *of* poverty, humiliation, competition. Fear is the main motivator in the adults' room; love is the main motivator in the children's room.

We are careful to teach our children to fear the Other: a legitimate fear within limits, a destructive fear without them. We don't need anyone to teach us how to love: we were born knowing how to love and be loved. We need to learn fear: without it, we die. We learn to fear the fire, wild animals, and so on. If we are passive followers all our lives, we eventually let fear overcome the love within us; when this happens, the part of us activated by fear – the Ego – is activated, and eventually takes over. This leads to self-centeredness, with all its consequences.

If we are aware and proactive in life, love will always be in control, even in the presence of fear. When this happens, the part of us activated by love – the Divine Spirit – is activated, and takes over. This leads to God-centrism, with all its consequences.

It's easier to make use of what is already within you, rather than the thing you have acquired. When I say 'love' here, I mean it not in the narrow sense of affection but something far broader: a loving way of life, creating a loving environment and atmosphere, a loving relationship with those you interact with (including of course your romantic partner). Such a way of life provides an inexhaustible source of energy for doing our life's work.

"Find a job you love and you'll never work a day in your life." Imagine if every day of work was a pleasure. Instead of cursing fate and waiting for opportunity to knock, know there is another choice. Create this way of living, for yourself and for others. Be the maker of this civilization. Be the subject, not the object.

What's your choice? To be motivated by fear, with all that implies? Or by love, with all that love implies? The choice is yours. Remember, not choosing is also a choice.

Observe and make notes.

Fear

There is a difference between fear under self-centeredness and fear under God-centrism. In the former, it is a motivator of Ego, and one of Ego's tools to convince the Self that its interests are being served; in the latter, it is a passing circumstance to be dealt with. Under God-centrism, when frightening things happen, they will not turn into terror or panic: we have a greater opportunity for self-control and calm handling of the situation.

Being in a place of God-centrism allows you to feel close to Him; this not only prevents fear from becoming unmanageable, but assists you in dealing with the cause. It puts you in the driver's seat. Even while afraid, you control yourself, curb the Ego, and prevent it from engaging its defense mechanisms. You hold the reins. You are aware, and proactive. This is how you deal with fear under God-centrism, provided this is the place you have chosen.

The main motivator in Divine Spirit is love: it uplifts the spirit, and colors every other instinct, especially the Ego's default, fear. When Divine Spirit is leading, and we are fully aware, deciding consciously to place it in the driver's seat, Love leads. Affection, fondness, confidence and fellow-feeling rule the day.

Since I have spoken so much about Love, let's quickly be clear about what it means or does not mean. As a result of the supremacy of Western civilization, love has been reduced to a young couple kissing on a screen. This is a shameful reduction of the overpoweringly broad meaning of the term. Love is part of every person; it is a human, divine value that colors our every interaction. Under the umbrella of Western literature, this reduction of love to romance has had negative results: "I love your dress/car/house!" have become common phrases; however, if you want to express non-romantic fondness for another, the acceptable phrase is, "I like you"; anything else might be open to misinterpretation.

The exclusive use of 'love' to denote a romantic relationship – and other circumstances – has led to a decline in the amount of love in society. Language plays a role in constructing our emotional makeup. It is precisely because love has been called by other names that the currency of the actual emotion has declined among us. The use of 'love' has declined, and with it the part of our emotional makeup that was once watered by that marvelous value, Love.

This has also led to a reduction in the main source of love within us, Divine Spirit. This in turn leads to the reduction of the space Divine Spirit occupies within us, losing ground to its rival, Self. Since Ego is Self's Captain of the Guard, the result is that we are primarily led by Ego; because of this, many human relationships are starved of love. How many of us tell their same-gender friends "I love you?" Our parents? Our children? (I mean saying the words, not giving them a gift with a Hallmark card.)

There are two questions I want you to ask yourself, and yourself alone. Do you tell the people listed above of your affection, using the magic words "I love you?" If you do, remember how many times you say it. Think of the last time you said it. Now, stop reading. Find something to write on and set down the names of the people you love. Now, make a note of how many times you told them the magic words, and the last time you said it. I venture to say you will be shocked. You have no idea what these words, sincerely spoken, create in the person you address them to; you have no conception of how they will affect the relationship between you, unless you try. I advise you to try, in spite of the difficulties you're even now thinking of. I promise you it will repay all that awkwardness and discomfort, and more.

I believe there is a complex relationship between two camps: Divine Spirit and love in one, and fear and Ego in the other. When God's love is leading, love is our default. When Ego is leading, fear is our default. In any case, a default cannot do away with the other instincts, but colors them. when love is leading, fear doesn't disappear; but it becomes colored by love. Instead of fearing those around us, we fear hurting their feelings; instead of fearing they will hurt us, we fear hurting them. We fear that others may not have what we have, instead of fearing that they will take it away from us. This is one of the applications of the threefold paradigm we mentioned earlier: the one that makes us view others under God-centrism.

We perceive the Divine Spirit inside whom we deal with; God is not the exclusive property of those who believe in Him. Our fear of and for things turns into fear for others, in the love of God.

We need to remember that everyone has the Divine Spirit within them, even those who do not believe in Him. Do not presume to judge. He loves them, gives them their daily bread and is caring for them as you read this. Don't play God with anyone. Only God is God.

A Loving Relationship with God

We have spoken above about your own relationship with God and your love for Him. All well and good. There is another level to this: to seek God's love for you.

Different religions view God's love differently. Some believe that God's love for them is unconditional; some see it as a path to follow. We will be speaking of the second: the path to God's love.

To get a college degree, one must study a number of subjects and take a number of tests; this is an intellectual and practical endeavor. There are creatures that make us love them effortlessly, like our instinctive love for babies; this is an endeavor of the heart. I believe that the path to God's love combines the two. First, let me tell you what I believe to be the controlling rule: Only God can lead us to God. We can only reach Him with His permission, no matter what we do. We can only attain God's love if He wills it.

You must keep this rule in mind. You must also start out with the certainty that you will achieve your desire. Don't limit what you ask of God to your own puny imagination: ask of Him what He can do. Base your certainty on your trust in Him. "I am what My servant assumes me to be." You ask in trust and faith, not on your own merits, but because He is generous and giving.

Here are some divine sayings, by way of the Prophet Muhammad. Don't take them literally; look at what God is trying to tell us. "God was pleased with them, and they were pleased with him."

"I am what My servant assumes me to be."

"If My servant approaches Me at a walk, I approach him at a run."

Behind these simple phrases is a profound meaning: God gives us the opportunity to ask of Him what He can give, not what we deserve, and that we must make use of it. I believe the best use you can make of it is to ask Him to raise you to that place – the place where He loves you.

If you ask it, certain that God will grant your request, this is yet another chance for you to live in a place of gratefulness – gratitude to God. Start from a place of gratefulness for the present, and anticipation of God's love in the future. Your certainty and trust in Him will be self-perpetuating.

Pause for a moment in your reading and think of the last paragraph. After this pause, make a note of your thoughts and questions.

A Place of God's Love

Living from a place of thankfulness is the practical application of life in a place of God's love. I believe that thankfulness can only be realized through fulfilling God's purpose for you, by serving His creatures. Living in God's love gives you the chance to see Him in all His creatures, and gives a new meaning to the concept of being a God-fearing person when dealing with others. This concept is linked in most people's minds to treating our fellow-humans and fellow-creatures fairly and kindly, out of the fear of God's wrath.

Please, try to think of a situation with someone else where you thought of God, and avoided acting badly, i.e. acted like a God-fearing person. In this situation there were: you, an Other, and a situation of some sort. In the process of settling on some reaction, you thought of God, and remembered that He is watching you. You therefore decided to act like a God-fearing person in this situation.

If this is what happens, you sense that God is hearing and seeing you, watching you from Somewhere. This Somewhere is outside you and outside the Other, isn't it? Well and good; but isn't there another possibility? Don't we all have a breath of Divine Spirit in us, as God has told us? Can't we then add to the previous meaning, of treating others like a God-fearing person, namely, having reverence for that part of Divine Spirit that resides within every one of our fellow-humans? From a place of God's love, it is easy to add that meaning.

"What does that give us?"

If you see every one of your fellow humans this way, won't that make you respect them more? Make you kinder to them should you disagree? Won't others, even those who do you wrong, have more credit with you, simply by virtue of the Divine Spirit that resides within them? Won't that give the lie to Self's whisperings that God is on your side alone, not on theirs? Won't that make you wary of the Self when it tempts you to play God and decide that this person is going to Hell, that one is going to Heaven? So many things would change if you started looking at your fellow-humans this way, seeing that each of them contains a breath of Divine Spirit.

In so doing, we follow the example of the prophets, who were always forgiving of their long-standing enemies. No matter the wrong these enemies did, they always saw the Divine Spirit within them.

Once you choose this perspective, it gives you the opportunity to build new relationships based on the shared Divine Spirit between you and the other. It will fire your determination to serve God's creatures. However, this is merely an opportunity. To make use of it or not – that is up to you.

What I think, though, is this: Living in a system of serving God's creatures, fulfilling God's purpose from a place of thankfulness and God's love, will give your life a unique, wonderful and profound flavor; a flavor that nothing else can ever give you. Take note: this is a system where you must work, not merely enjoy the flavor. Enjoying the flavor of communing with God without fulfilling His purpose of you satisfies your Self alone: and it puts you on the slippery slope down to self-centeredness. Enjoying this flavor through a system that fulfils God's purpose, through serving His creatures, places you under God-centeredness. It is here that you have the chance to enjoy your life while you live it.

Enjoying Life

Have you ever seen someone whistling while they worked? Perhaps they hummed a happy tune, enjoying their tasks. Have you ever wished you were one of them? Would you like to be?

You can. You can not only hum a happy tune while you work – you can live your entire life humming a happy tune. That is what happens when you live your life from a place of thankfulness, regardless of the challenges that come your way. Why is this? Because it's your heart that's humming a happy tune.

When Your Heart Sings

In the section on appreciating beauty, we spoke of how beauty makes the heart more tender, more sensitive and refined. It is the heart which fills us with joy at the beauty around us. And in a place of thankfulness, your heart is at its healthiest. This reflects on your dealings with others: you become more cheerful, more friendly.

One of the prerequisites for wisdom is to have a gentle and compassionate heart. Wise folk see and hear more than others; they have a heightened awareness. This, in my opinion, is because they see and hear, not only with the senses, but with the heart. They use their insight, intuition and discernment, which can only come with heightened vision – a matter of the heart *par excellence.*

To work with a singing heart, we must care for our heart and nourish it with healthy food. The heart's main nourishment is communion with God; it fills the heart and slakes its thirst. One of the signs of a satisfied heart is a sense of peace and tranquility; there are supplements for a healthy heart, such as an abundance of beauty for the senses, as we have said before. A deficiency in its main source of nutrition – communion with God – confuses the heart, which starts to try to make up for this deficiency by consuming a large amount of supplements. Have you noticed the explosion in producing music and movies worldwide? Has it occurred to you that they would not be produced unless there was a giant, greedy, ravenous market for them?

I believe we must consider the possibility that this superabundance of art would only find a market if the heart, deprived of its main nourishment, took to a ravenous consumption of supplementary food in order to fill the void. This didn't fill the emptiness inside, so the heart turned to more consumption, and still more, but nothing could fill the void. New music comes out every day; Hollywood has spawned Bollywood (in India) and now Nollywood (in Nigeria), and the demand for new films never wanes. The amount of consumption is less notable than the sheer speed of consumption; I can't help being reminded of someone searching for something and not finding it, like taking painkillers.

There are also levels to the heart.

The ocean north of the Pacific collects tons of flotsam and jetsam into giant islands of garbage, random objects jumbled together, disgusting from the aerial view. A deep dive, though, shows clear, calm and peaceful water. The flotsam and jetsam is too light to penetrate into the depths of the ocean.

The same is true of the supplementary nutrition I spoke of just now. Music, art and beauty only penetrate the surface of the heart: they form islands of random objects jumbled together, sound and visual pollution creating a great deal of surface noise. What happens when the heart's surface levels suffer from this sort of pollution? I believe it confuses and muddies your access to the depths of the heart.

God has told us that he can be found in the hearts of true believers: that the earth and sky cannot hold him, but a faithful heart can. This means you have many opportunities, and many ways, to commune with God: externally through treating His creatures well, and internally through reducing the noise that muddies your communion with God in your heart.

I believe it is possible to recognize when someone is stuck in the surface levels of the heart.

Mothers smile and whisper to their babies in the gentlest of tones. Loving couples gaze into each other's eyes, listening to each other's voices, drinking their fill of each other's presence, talking in whispers. When they do listen to music, they play romantic music. And what is romantic music? Calm, soft tunes, playing in the background. Who is in the foreground? The one we love. A baby is loved deep in its mother's heart. Lovers know they are at the heart of each other. They enjoy their presence in each other's hearts, and feel safe, and secure, and loved, knowing that this is where they belong. Loud concerts, being a secondary food for the heart, also bring enjoyment; but it is a superficial kind of enjoyment, filled with noise, laughter and loud sounds.

This is not to say that the satisfaction art and music brings is a negative thing: I just want to alert you that it might obscure the real source of fulfilment, security and true joy, communion with God. Music and art do nourish the soul and refine the senses, but they are no substitute for the main sustenance of the heart which nothing else can provide: the love of God. They are a supplementary form of nutrition: don't give them too much weight, and damage your heart in the process.

The presence of God's love reinforces the Divine Spirit within us: it elevates it, making it worthy to lead the system of self/body/heart/mind, settling us comfortably under God-centrism, in a way substitutes or supplements cannot. It makes the heart tender, like turning over the land, but fails to provide the seed to plant. The heart needs to be close and connected to God. The Divine Spirit within us yearns for its source: the branch longs for the tree. And then, the heart hums a happy tune.

When every part of you is enjoying fulfilling God's purpose, or else actively seeking it – that's when you live your life humming a happy tune.

Think about the above paragraph: make a note of your thoughts and questions.

Close to God

I am endlessly fascinated by mothers and children. One thing I notice is when a mother rebukes a child of three or four for doing something dangerous, perhaps something the child has done many times before. She bends and shouts at the child, who cries and looks about for some safe place to hide, and ends up pushing its small body into her legs and clinging to them.

This fascinates me. The child runs from its mother, to its mother. Two things become apparent on analysis: first, the child does not really fear its mother, but her punishment; and second, the child grasps for the only source of safety: its mother. Nobody taught the child to do that: it is entirely instinctive. This instinctual behavior of the child's, to seek refuge in a place of love even if it is a source of punishment, bears a kind of wisdom that many adults lack.

In moments of adversity, we feel pain and fear. If we lack awareness, the Self may drive us to turn our pain into rage, and fear into defeat, whereupon we self-centeredly slip into that most beloved of roles, the Victim Role. All this, unfortunately, draws us away from God: the Self makes us run *from* God, instead of *to* God.

If we allow the Self to control us, we let it pull us away from the only source of love and security, of healing. When we do this, we show less wisdom and awareness than the three-year-old in the example. Being close to God is the only guarantee of healing from fear and pain; to guarantee this, you must always monitor the Self and its games. God is always close by; you must exercise awareness to remain close to Him. He is the source of power in the adversity He sends: He is the source of strength and peace; and simply, there's no other choice.

God has left it up to you how close you are to him; not being aware of this is to shirk your God-given responsibility, and you alone are responsible for your distance from God.

Freedom, Power and Closeness to God

The degree of closeness to God is closely related to how much freedom is in a given society. In societies ruled by restrictive or oppressive governments, people relate to their governments through fear. This relationship serves to reaffirm the fearsomeness of its power: this fear and trepidation create what is known as a large power distance, which turns into a psychological barrier over time. Nobody wants to approach the seat of power, out of fear.

This state of affairs reflects on our relationship with God: we may well unwittingly turn him in our minds into a Higher Power in the governmental sense of the word, a tragic curtailment of our relationship with the Merciful, Compassionate God! Our fear of God outweighs our faith in His compassion and mercy, which makes us hold God in fear and awe rather than love him. Because of the enforced distance between us and those in power in the societies I have mentioned, we unconsciously put space – a power distance – between ourselves and God, feeling it would be somehow inappropriate – or forbidden – to come too close. He is, after all, the Supreme Authority, and we are used to shying away from authority. This is at the root of many negative relationships with God.

Do you have any experiences with this? If so, make a note.

I

Communicating with God

Once you become dissatisfied with your communion with God, and want to go deeper, I believe there are several starting-points. Two of these are to be convinced you are not connected enough and want to go deeper and take steps to; or to be convinced that the connection with God is continuous and permanent, and all you need is to hone your receptive skills and do away with interference.

One of my old teachers used to say, "Always learn from children." My little son, Muhammad Hobballah, had a song he was very fond of: he always asked me to play it over and over and over again, as children do, until he was satisfied. One day, we were in the car, and luckily, his favorite song came on the radio. When it was over, he said, "Play it again, Daddy!"

I embarked on a long explanation of how the car radio was different from our CD player at home, and how in the radio, there was a person playing the song, and we received it through waves, and so on. "You mean," he said, "there's someone playing our song somewhere far away, and we're listening to it on the radio here?"

"That's right," I said, "we and other people can hear it, and only that person can play it again."

"What happens to the song if we don't listen to it? Does it stay up in the air?"

"Yes," I smiled, "the songs stay up in the air, until we turn on the radio and hear them."

Suddenly, an idea sprang to my mind. "What happens to the song if we don't listen to it? Does it stay up in the air?" In other words, "Where do ideas and inspiration come from?"

Why do different questions come to different people's minds in the same situation? Thousands of apples must have fallen on thousands of heads before Sir Isaac Newton's; why was he the only one to be inspired with the thoughts on motion and gravity that changed the course of history? What was the Power that made him think of it?

Again, where do the thoughts that "occur to us" come from? Are we a CD player, or a radio?

As I was explaining to my child, I think there is a transmitter operating for each of the seven million people on this planet, creating what we call "our" thoughts and ideas, whereas we are actually only receivers, doing nothing but accepting incoming messages.

We can even imagine playing two roles: a radio, receiving transmissions; and a recording device, recording the thoughts and images that come to us, in our memories, via pen and paper, computer, or various other means. We then call them "our" ideas, writings and inventions.

This presents an opportunity: We can either remain absorbed in our daily life and wait for inspiration to strike, by pure chance; or try to hone our faculties and seek inspiration proactively.

As a young architecture student, our professors taught us a number of steps to inspire creativity:

1. To read or scan every design we could lay our hands on with a similarity to the design we were asked to produce.

2. To rack our brains day and night thinking of the project and what innovations we could produce, but not start production until we had slept on it, so that the ideas could percolate through our unconscious.

3. Wake up early with a clear head and uncluttered mind, and start scribbling with pencil and paper, to call on what our subconscious mind had come up with while we were sleeping.

To tell the truth, this simple method often bore wonderful fruit.

There are now more advanced and complex methods that no doubt produce deeper and more wonderful results. Most of what I have read about inspiring creativity revolves around 'accessing' ideas, whether in the conscious or subconscious. This is what led me to the question about Newton and the apple: What made him think that way? Or should the question be: *Who* made him think that way?

This brings us to the same old question: "Where is God in this?"

I would like to suggest another possibility: Ideas and inspirations are with God, like everything else. It is God who nourishes and sends our subconscious all these ideas and inspirations. I would thus like to add an extra level to the method outlined above, namely to strive to be more connected to the main source from whom all ideas and inspirations flow: to be connected to God.

My suggestion: Use whatever means you prefer. Ask God to provide you with ideas and inspiration to create things that humanity needs. In such a case, you have two choices: either to ask God for innovations and inspirations to serve you and yours, or to ask Him for ones that serve His purpose for you. Needless to say, I strongly recommend the latter.

When you commune with God, you can dream big. Seek big ideas. Ask big. Aim high. The sky's the limit. Your constant receptiveness to God's offerings, and your certainty that his loving gifts will bring you closer to Him, are the source of a great gift that is yours for the asking: communion with God 24/7/365.

In the section titled "Close to God", communion with God brings you closer to him, and vice versa. When there are constant efforts to commune with God, your receiver is always on, which reduces interference.

Remember to use your communion with God to find, work towards and achieve God's purpose for you (which makes your life God-centric), not only enjoy communing with Him (which has the potential to make your life self-centered).

Ask of God what you will. Ask, ask, ask, ask and you shall receive. Asking and dreaming big is a sign of your trust in God. Ask according to what He can give, not according to what you think you deserve.

God's Kingdom

What if I asked you to look at things from a new perspective?

What if I asked you to look at our planet, our solar system, our universe, as part of God's kingdom?

What if I asked you to look at the country borders on the map as an attempt by some of God's creatures to organize a part of His creation?

Try, then observe the following:

When you look at the world and humanity as part of God's creation, do you feel we have more in common than not, or vice versa? No doubt if you live in a time of peace, this will greatly influence your outlook. I believe that the younger one is, the closer one can come to common ground, whereas the reverse is true.

Borders are a great idea for security, but they come at the expense of freedom. This brilliant idea is no more than 200 years old; it has served us well, but it is on the way to its inevitable decline. The tools of this era have made it obsolete: this obsolescence is clearer to the young than it is to the old.

I'm not so optimistic or so utopian as to imagine that all borders will soon disappear. I do believe, though, that sooner or later they will need to be replaced with *something* that better fulfils the needs of this era. Young people are naturally closer to imagining such future innovations than older people. I do invite younger people to view this beautiful blue planet as part of God's creation, holding all we know of God's creatures: this global view will affect you, your orientations, your responsibilities, your horizons, your dreams, and most importantly, your view of God's purpose for you.

Alone With God

Try, from time to time, to be alone with God. Try to do this in an isolated place, away from the city. After you have found some peace, pour your heart out. Not just in prayer, although prayer is essential: I mean speak from the heart. Just start, and it will all come pouring out. Everything you cannot say to another person, say to your Maker.

It doesn't matter if you can't afford to go on a wilderness journey: there is some place you can go to get away from the city for a while. The fields around your village; the desert some way away; the forest close by; a beach some way away; any place on God's green earth that you can afford. Just get out of the city and be alone. You need some time alone with your Maker, without company to cloud it. Plunge into His creation: purge the noise inside you, and start your communion with God.

Time is helpful in this, too. You can commune with God when everyone else is asleep; in the most crowded places, when everyone is sleeping, you have a moment to be alone with God.

You also need solitude to contemplate God's creatures.

God's Creatures, Love, and Compassion

Contemplate and commune with God's creatures. Give your soul free rein to sense everything around you with all your senses, slowly, deeply, for a long time. Everything around you is a miracle of creation: contemplate this miracle. This brings you closer to God; it nourishes the Divine Spirit in you, and makes your heart tender.

A tender heart is more compassionate, and begins to see God's creatures in a divine light. God has told us that He is the most compassionate of all, so let His compassion into your heart. This will give your life a different flavor, the flavor of compassion for God's creatures mingled with your appreciation of them.

Remember a time when you were compassionate. Remember how you felt. There are two levels of feeling when you practice compassion, not to be confused. The first comes from within, uplifting you and filling you with peace and tranquility. The second is your reaction to the positive emotions of those to whom you have shown compassion. There is also the joy of giving inherent in the practice of compassion. Enjoy this as well.

Who gave all the above its wonderful flavor? God. This is His bounty. Your feelings and emotions when practicing compassion bring you closer to Him. Under self-centeredness, Love is the emotion closest to being an end in itself for the heart. But love under self-centeredness may or may not inspire us to compassion, whereas under God-centeredness, Love is a means, not an end; it inspires us to compassion, and to work towards fulfilling God's purpose for us.

In the latter type of love, there are three levels to the sweetness of the world: the love of God within you, the love you feel for your beloved, and the compassion you practice with God's creatures. All of these make your heart tremble with compassion and tenderness: compassion *must* hold love within it. Your love becomes deeper and sweeter and wider. You are full of love for all God's creatures and for your beloved as well. You become more compassionate; this reflects on your work in gratitude to God, in the service of His creatures, which makes your heart even more tender and loving, filling you with more thankfulness, in an ever-widening circle of thankfulness, compassion, and love.

I will leave you, dear reader, with your feelings of love and closeness and communion and compassion and solitude and thankfulness. Here's a little space to write down how this all reflects on you.

I

PART THREE
The Divine Spirit

By this, I mean the divine part of every one of us, the one the Lord breathed into us. Specialists and scientists have researched this and arrived at a more precise definition, but for this book, the simple meaning will suffice: the divine part within every human being. The how and why of it is not the issue under examination; there is no need to delve deeper. Divine Spirit is meant not as an adjective but as a possessive, as one would say God's land or God's creatures.

Here is the definition of Divine Spirit offered by Dr. Amr Wardani, Secretary General of the Egyptian Fatwa Council:

The Divine Spirit is gentle, placed by God in human beings, and made by Him to be the repository of all good things and virtuous behaviors. It is one of God's creations; just as hearing is created within the ear, souls are created within bodies. It is pure and untainted ….It is not, as some might believe, part of God placed within His creations; it is claimed by God in His Word, "I have breathed my spirit into it," thus honoring the spirit, and doing honor to us as well.

It is beyond the scope of this book to define Divine Spirit: there are specialized fields of theology for this. What I intend to do in this section is to discuss the relationship between the Divine Spirit, the Self and the Ego. I believe that under self-centeredness, the Ego takes the reins and leads the rest: spirit, mind, body and heart. When we take our consciousness back and decide to live with awareness and choice under God-centrism, the Divine Spirit within us takes over, and leads the rest.

Signs the spirit is leading: a sense of safety and security so strong they radiate out to others. Our mere presence among others spreads a kind of peace and security. Have you never met such people? That kind of person, whom we feel comfortable at seeing and secure in their presence, people who make life's troubles seem insignificant – people whose smile brings reassurance, to themselves and those around them. They are positive, look on the bright side, and see the positive side of the problems we find negative, a side we might not have noticed. They feel as though we've known them for years, even though we've just met. Is the term "that kind of person" accurate? Actually, I doubt it. It would be more accurate to call it "this state of being", not "this kind of person." I believe these people have achieved this state of being by letting the Divine Spirit lead the rest of the elements that make them up, including the Self.

Many of us have experienced a state like this, although not on purpose: we feel it when we devote time and space to communing with God. Space, such as spending two weeks in Mecca or Medina or a mosque for Muslims, or the Vatican or the Church of the Resurrection or a monastery for Christians, a kibbutz for Jews, and so on; time, such as Ramadan for Muslims, Lent for Christians, Hanukkah for Jews, and prayer times in mosques and churches and synagogues. Think of how you feel at the end of these periods, when resuming your normal life. You may find yourself uplifted, full of peace and contentment. Your relationship with others – friends and strangers alike – is more intimate and connected than normally. I believe the reason for this is that our presence in holy places – more accurately, the places of constant communion with God – energizes the Divine Spirit in us, activating its effects, namely the state of peace and contentment I have just mentioned. This is one of the most important characteristics of Divine Spirit, lying dormant, just waiting for us to wake it up.

Our presence in these places and times not only energizes the spirit, but calms the Ego; the Self loses its defensiveness, whereupon the Divine Spirit with us can shine. This doesn't necessarily mean that Divine Spirit is in the driver's seat; all it means is that the Ego is calmed, and the Self along with it, allowing our spirit to shine through. This reflects on others: we lose our shyness and open up more, breaking down barriers of language and culture with those around us, thanks to the shared element within all of us, the Divine Spirit.

"Why does this happen in these places?"

Because there is no room for the Ego to be active there. Communion with God activates Divine Spirit, leading to communion.

"Is it true of everyone?"

Actually, no. Some of us have been so overpowered by our Ego that it doesn't leave us even in these holy places. This can be seen in travel agencies' competition for luxury tours to holy places, and in pilgrims' boasts about this and that five-star hotel where they stayed on their pilgrimages. Here, the Ego is firmly in charge. People who feel the Divine Spirit tend to mingle with like-minded – like-spirited – folk, and avoid those still controlled by their ego.

Adherents of revealed religions have no monopoly on this state of mind. In Buddhist temples and meditation centers, we find the same peace and inner tranquility, security and communion with those around us. Not only in revealed religions does the Divine Spirit within us sense its counterpart in the people around us; whenever the conditions are created, the Divine Spirit activates, the Ego and Self are calmed, and our souls commune with the souls of those around us, even if one or both of us don't believe in God.

I repeat, this feeling is not necessarily an indication that we have made a conscious decision to put Divine Spirit in the driver's seat, and let it lead the other components. It is merely a temporary state related to a particular time and/or place, and disappears in its absence, whereupon we hope circumstance will activate it again. This is the very opposite of being proactive; we're about as proactive as a sailboat on the high seas, letting the winds take us where they will. This is a state of passivity *par excellence*.

If we're not proactive about it, the state of being will vanish with the circumstances that created it; we go back to our daily routine, the Self gets up to its old tricks, the Ego plays its part, Divine Spirit loses ground, and we lose that wonderful temporary feeling, until the time comes to go back to that specific time and place.

Have you ever heard it said of someone returning from a spiritual retreat, that they "glow"? Over time, we take it as a fact of life that this glow is just a phenomenon associated with a specific set of circumstances, not unlike a summer suntan.

But is there another choice?

The Glow and the Source of Light

An important point here is that there is no specific *type* of people with a monopoly on love, peace and tranquility; it is a *state of being* they have arrived at consciously, by enabling the Divine Spirit within them to lead the other parts of them.

This is my point: you don't have to be some special sort of person. It's a state anyone can achieve. You and I can be like those people whose company we enjoy, if we use our free will to enable the Divine Spirit within us to lead the Heart, the Self and the Mind. The Divine Spirit naturally chooses to live under God-centrism; this leads you to the same peace, tranquility and security you feel when around these people. You will glow with inner light, but you will also become a Source of Light, bringing illumination to those around you. The light comes from the same source, the Light of God.

Every Source of Light glows, but not everyone who glows is a Source of Light. A Source of Light always takes the initiative, is always positive, always helpful, always in communion with God, 24/7/365; God supplies them with light to offer to others, and uses them to light others' lives: therefore, they are Subjects.

A person who glows is not proactive, and takes no initiative. They glow as a result of limited moments of communing with God, or when they meet a Source of Light to illuminate them: therefore, they are Objects.

The former and the latter are yours for the choosing: which will be your choice? To be a subject, or an object? A Source of Light, or a person who glows? God-centric, or self-centered? The choice is yours. Not choosing, or neglecting your right to choose, is a choice in itself.

Please note, dear reader: This is a complex and interrelated system. When you choose to live under God-centrism, the Divine Spirit will lead you. God's love will creep out of you to color the value system by which you interact with God's creatures... What a wonderful life!

Think; observe; write.

PART FOUR
God's Purpose

It may be safe to say here that all that has come before has been a preparation for this: God's purpose. (In fact, this issue was so important that it grew large enough – 150 pages – to warrant a book of its own, to be published later, God willing; the editorial team and I agreed that it would bloat this book out of all proportion to include it here.)

All the above, about conscious choice, the Self, individual and collective ego, God's love and God-centrism, was preparation for you to look for God's purpose for you and do your best to achieve it, if that is your choice. All the above may only support your self-centeredness, unless you seek out and work towards achieving God's purpose for you.

It starts with a question.

The Courage to Ask

Searching for God's purpose is in itself an enjoyable journey. Spending long hours contemplating how best to use God's greatest gift to you – yourself – keeps you in God's company, and you cannot know the joy of this until you try it.

As we said in "Close to God", being close to God should remain the rule, and being apart from Him should be the exception. This should apply even if the exceptions outnumber the rule. One opportunity to be close to God is the courage to ask.

When we speak of the courage to ask, we must speak of Abraham. The story of his life is filled with important moments, but the focus here is on his constant questioning: Was God the sun? The moon?

The stars? He always asked God questions, up to and including how He raised the dead, in order to increase his certainty. Whom did he ask? God. Who was asking? One of God's holy prophets, a man who experienced the miracle of being thrown into the fire without getting burnt. And what was the response to his question, "Show me how to raise the dead"? God answered, "Have you no faith?" Abraham simply answered, "Yes, but I want reassurance." Imagine it! Imagine being in Abraham's position, and receiving that answer – from whom?! God Almighty Himself! It wouldn't be easy to keep making demands of God if He answered you so. What gave Abraham the courage to persist? Think about it for a moment: I believe he must have felt safe in asking. Where do you think he got that feeling? Most probably because he was secure in God's love.

Why does God tell us this story in the Holy Qur'an? What is the moral behind it? What does God want us to know, to learn, to apply, through the story of Abraham? I believe there is more than one lesson to be learned, in the context of fulfilling God's purpose for us. I will list them from least to most important:

Third: When you ask God, ask Him for big things. Don't be afraid to ask for everything. Ask according to what He can give, not according to what you can imagine.

Second: To ask for much, you must be brave. You must learn the courage to question. Ask God, and fear not. Don't forget that asking God a lot of questions makes you closer to Him than someone who doesn't ask; and being close to God is one of life's main goals.

First: To be brave enough to ask God for things and question Him, you must feel safe. To feel safe, you must feel that God loves you. Do your best to love God; ask Him to love you, in words – by asking and praying – and in deeds – by thanking Him for His gifts. One way of thanking God for His gifts is wanting to do His work; one way of doing His work is serving others. That will come about by seeking and finding and achieving God's purpose for you.

Just as I urge you to find and fulfil God's purpose for you, I urge you to seek God's love for its own sake. God's love for you is everything. Of course, you can ask God for everything, great or small; but what I mean that in seeking God's purpose, be ambitious. Be close to Him. Be close to the endless Source of all. Closeness to Him is a joy; but don't enjoy that closeness so much that you forget to achieve His purpose for you. Be close; be ambitious; be big; this gives you the chance to dream, ask and achieve: to dream big, for you and yours and for others, to ask God for a wealth of resources, in order to achieve great successes for all of you.

This gives you the opportunity to be of God, with God, and for God.

Now think: What are the big things you might ask of God to benefit His creation through you? What big things might you ask of God to prepare you for this responsibility? What big things could you ask for those you love to make them happy? What else? Dream. Observe. Make notes.

_____

_____

_____

_____

_____

_____

_____

_____

_____

_____

_____

_____

_____

I

The Difference Between God's Purpose for You and Your Life Goals

Sometimes, we meet those who urge us to find our goal in life. They tell us to practice self-leadership, ask why we are here, and similar very positive attitudes that urge us to take the initiative and be active, not passive, participants in our life; to be proactive and not reactive. An excellent attitude for creativity and initiative, fostering the courage to innovate, avoid fear of failure, and have the courage to fail numerous times before we finally succeed. All of this leads to fresh and renewable systems of living, and to a more comfortable and happier life.

Is anything missing from the above? At first glance, it would seem not; quite the reverse. Results on the ground show that these attitudes have led to a lot of positive results: the progress in the last centuries is proof positive of that.

Allow me to propose that there are two ways to apply the above, similar in form, completely different in content.

The first is to do all of the above under self-centeredness. The beneficiary is "I," and those related to "I" and in its orbit. "My life goals" and "my self-leadership" are a fashionable way to express self-centeredness. The ultimate goal is achieving more happiness and comfort for my Self by means of improving my work skills so I can achieve my life goals, having a better relationship with my life partner, being closer to my friends to make my life warmer, to balance work, family, friendship, stability, physical fitness, entertainment, leisure, and so on, to satisfy my Self. In other words, my Self's pleasure and comfort is the ultimate purpose of my presence on this earth.

The second starts with the existential question: "Where is God in this? What priority do I give to His will?" This question moves me to a qualitatively different plane, so that I apply the above under God-centrism. Here, the beneficiary is God, what He wants, and what will please Him. The aim is for my Self to be happier and more comfortable through achieving God's purpose for it. First, I must find the big picture of what God wants of me, and spend a great deal of time outlining its framework and different aspects. My professional life is part of achieving the big picture of God's purpose. I must seek a life partner whom I can mutually assist in achieving God's purpose for us, and our emotional stability shall be based on this. Every step of the way will make us more secure in our footing and more loving towards each other. I search for friends who march to the same drummer: who play the song of God's purpose. Our friendship keeps us warm as we seek to achieve that purpose. We seek a balance in life – family, friends, mental comfort, physical fitness, leisure – to nourish myself so that it may better achieve God's purpose.

Both look the same from the outside. But what a difference in essence! In self-centeredness, my comfort and joy are an end in themselves. In God-centrism, my comfort and joy are a means to a greater end: achieving God's purpose for me.

In self-centeredness, I can live a great or a small life: I only serve myself, and I may want a little or a lot. But with God-centeredness, I aim to please not myself but God, and God doesn't need anything from me, which means I must serve Him in others.

The moment we start to seek out an Other to serve, our life undergoes a fundamental change. Our life becomes great; it can no longer be small from that moment on. We dream big, and set big goals, and create strategies big enough to serve them.

Goals

In self-centeredness, I serve and care for myself. In God-centrism, I seek another to serve in fulfilment of God's purpose, and serve and care myself and those I love while serving and caring for others. Serving others by no means means exhausting myself! On the contrary: I must take as good care of myself as I do of the Other I am serving. Indeed, I must develop and hone my God-given skills, and invest in them. In self-centeredness, such care could well turn into egotism or selfishness, no matter how thick a mask I wore to hide it. But under God-centrism, this possibility declines significantly.

The above shows the difference between your life's goal, and God's purpose for you. Your life goal is its only end, whereas God's purpose is big enough to encompass your life goals, and many, many others besides. That's because God's purpose has one main title: the common good. The common good very often encompasses individual interests, but the reverse is rarely true.

Try and set down your thoughts in the following space to remove any lingering confusion between the two things meant above.

God's Purpose for You

Trying to find God's purpose for you isn't easy, but it's worth every bit of effort you put into it. It's like filling out an application to work for God, an opportunity worth the effort because of all the positive change that will happen in your life. Not only in the afterlife, but in this world, in the sweetness and fulfilment of a life spent achieving God's purpose.

Why do you think job competition is so fierce for big-name, high-profile international companies? Most of us aim for local or, at the most, regional companies; we know that the employers who work on a global scale only accept the very best, the highest qualified. It's not only about qualifications and skills, or even drive and initiative: it's about making the necessary sacrifices, putting in the hours and effort, to achieve the extraordinary. You work far longer and harder for a global employer than your counterparts at middling or local companies. And the question arises: What for? Why all the blood, sweat and tears?

Naturally, the compensations. Companies that make billions are apt to offer very large salary packages to top talent; not only generous remuneration, but medical insurance, company cars, special apartment complexes, private schools for employees' children, and a host of other benefits. The compensation is not only material; no less rewarding is the look in people's eyes when you tell them you work for Facebook or Google. Their admiring glances, and their recognition that you must be a person of exceptional ability, make you feel special. This is why there are hundreds of thousands of applicants for jobs at famous companies, and only a few hundred are accepted.

All this from a company, even a big company! Now think about offering God your resume! One thing is certain: it's the best job you'll ever get.

You may need to apply several times before you're accepted, possibly pass a few tests to prove you're serious and understand the privilege. You might need to persevere in applying, try over and over before you finally get the job. Or you might get accepted on the first try; one never knows. My advice to you is not to benchmark your performance against anyone else's. Judge yourself on an absolute, not on a curve; you aren't competing with another person, but finding how to best serve God.

It all comes down to a choice between two questions. They seem the same, but between them is a world of difference.

It's the difference between waking up in the morning and asking, "What do I want to do today?" and following up with "Will what I want to do please God?" and waking up in the morning and asking, "What does God want me to do today?" This difference, which seems so tiny at first, is like a fork in the road, or a delta in the river: a small difference, a few inches at most, but it widens into a great divide between paths hundreds of miles apart.

In the first case, you put yourself first, then ask whether God will approve as an afterthought. There are two possible reasons for this: (a) a conscious choice, a proactive decision to put Self first, and a willing decision to live under self-centeredness; or (b) a lack of awareness of the consequences of your life decisions and of your unawareness, sending you sliding down into self-centeredness. In the second, you have chosen of your own free will to put God first, which can only be interpreted in one way: You are proactive and decisive, on the firm path to God-centrism.

There are several ways to live.

The first is not even being aware enough to ask the question. You spend your life following others by being a part of their lives and goals, in which case you are an object *par excellence*.

The second is asking "Will what I want to do please God?" while really wanting to please yourself. The aim of this question is avoiding any possible discomfort. The actual goal here is to reassure the Self that its desires will not displease God. To this end, God's will is twisted and misrepresented to indulge the Self's desires, secure from wrongdoing. The ultimate purpose is self-satisfaction, and God is a means to satisfy the Self. This is the start of a slippery slope of compromise that may lead you far astray. Aiming to just barely scrape through a test often leads to failure.

The third is starting with the question, "What is God's purpose for me?" and its attendant question, "What priority have I chosen to place on God's will?" This choice prioritizes God's will over yours, and makes the We and Us only a means to an end. The purpose is God, which means you are on your way to fulfilling His purpose not for yourself, but for Him.

This question is your compass. No matter how you veer off course, with this question you will always come back. It is your guide to God-centric living.

Beware of the Self's tricks. The first question makes it easy for the Self to lure you into self-centeredness, do what you desire, then rename your ungodly desires with ungodly names. The nomenclature of "sin" and "piety" is prime breeding-ground for the Self's games. The Self may well lure you into achieving what it calls "God's purpose for you", which is nothing but self-centeredness by a misleading name. You will know by the fact that the Self will limit the beneficiaries of this so-called "purpose" to your Us, you and yours, your political party, your business colleagues, in a word: your tribe.

When the Self draws you into self-centeredness;

When your main goal is to check whether or not something is a sin;

When you are often confused;

When you find yourself finding justifications and making excuses;

When you constantly find yourself compromising and making concessions;

You will find yourself in the position of one who, knowing what they are doing is illegal, hires a good lawyer to find loopholes in the law.

The second question, on the other hand, opens up your path to God-centrism. When you take the second path,

You will make god-centrism your way.

You will make checking for sinfulness your first step.

You will make your ultimate goal fulfilling God's purpose.

You will take the reins of your life.

You will make as few concessions as possible; and,

You will notice a lucidity of vision and a clarity of purpose.

This all occurs when you are achieving God's purpose for God. You will know by the fact that the fruits of your labor are not limited to you and yours; you are like a tree whose fruit feeds many, and whose beneficiaries multiply until you become an arbor. Yet you are not your own property: you are owned by God, and your fruits are all His property, which in His infinite bounty he allows you to benefit from, and benefit others, thereby being secure from His punishment in the form of taking your blessings away in this life, or worse in the next.

I repeat: in serving God, dream big. Ask much. Do much. It is not easy to find His purpose, but it is worth the effort. Living for yourself and your tribe is limited. Living for God is limitless. Truly great dreams only come with complete trust in God, that He can help you achieve your dreams. This will only happen if you truly trust in God, and truly believe His promise.

God, God's Steward, and Divine Purpose

Imagine that the Ambassador of a great country – the USA, currently the world's greatest power, or formerly the United Kingdom, the Empire on which the sun never set – called up the Presidency of a country, any country, and requested an immediate audience with the Head of State.

I believe it would not be going too far to say that a slot in the president's, or king's, schedule would immediately be cleared, even if it meant reshuffling or even canceling some previous commitments. After all, this is the world's greatest power we're talking about.

However, if the same Ambassador, now retired and vacationing in this same country, casually picked up the phone from their hotel, and asked for an immediate meeting with the President, or the King, well, you can imagine the reaction – that is, if they even got through to an undersecretary.

What's the difference? In the case, the Ambassador was not calling in their individual capacity, but in their capacity as a representative of the world's greatest superpower. The scramble to meet the request was not out of esteem for the Ambassador's person, but for the power that the Ambassador represented.

Let's further imagine that the Ambassador, in their capacity as Ambassador, requested this urgent meeting with the Head of State – only to ask for a personal favor for themselves or their family. Naturally, their employer, the Embassy, would be notified, followed by a reprimand or outright dismissal. Why? Because the Ambassador abused a professional capacity – that of official representative of their state – for a personal matter, instead of the state they are given the privilege to represent.

You have the opportunity in life to be an ambassador, but not for a country – for the Owner of all countries and of everything. You have a unique employment opportunity: to be an ambassador for God. He has told us so: He has said that we are "stewards" of the earth. As I understand it, "being a steward" ought to mean, "serving all God's creation in His kingdom." Being a steward of the earth, you have certain rights, I would go so far as to say certain duties. You must be strong in God, big in God, tenacious in God, perseverant in God. The stronger your certainty, the greater all of the above, and the more capable you are of achieving great things.

But this great choice carries with it great responsibility. First and foremost: You must not live only for yourself. Second: You cannot live 'small'. If you choose to live as God's Steward on Earth, live up to it!

Who ever heard of someone telling me they have chosen to live as God's Steward on this earth, and when I ask what they think God's purpose is for them on this earth, responding, "I want to start a business with my dad!" Or someone telling me they have chosen to live as God's Steward on this earth, and when I ask about their ambitions, saying, "Well, I'd just like to be free from want!"

I'm not saying that starting a business – or living free from want – are bad things. But it will not do to have this as the ultimate, most ambitious dream you can possibly think of! Your choice to live as God's Steward on Earth is far more weighty than the position of the US Ambassador we spoke of earlier; its responsibilities are also weightier. When you choose to live as God's Steward on this Earth, you also choose to be one of the Influential Few in the world.

The Influential Few

Alexander the Great; Napoleon; Gandhi; Sultan Muhammad Ali; Mandela; all people who profoundly changed the societies they lived in.

Most of them – with the possible exception of Alexander – were not a product of "the man and the moment"; on the contrary, they all lived in weak societies, at a time of decline. Their achievements were in direct contrast to their societies at the time. They may have created magnificence or they may have wrought havoc, but one thing is certain: they brought about what is known as a sharp turn in history, which means that they created irrevocable change – positive or negative – in the history of their respective nations. One way or another, they left their mark on history.

Now I have a question: What was it that allowed them to achieve what they achieved?

Whenever I ask this question, I receive answers to do with their leadership, and ambition, and their dreams, and the historical moment, all of which are accurate; but it's something else I'm looking for.

In the night, the last night before the first step, the first step each of them took towards achieving their goal, what do you think went through each of their minds?

Think about it.

I think it was: "I know I can."

Each of them, that night, thought of his dream and said, "I know I can."

They may not have known exactly what the ways and means of achieving it would be, come next morning; but what they did know was that this was their dream, and that these were the obstacles, but that one thing was certain: "I know I can."

And they did.

I have no way of knowing whether these men did what they did for God. (I'm not denying that they may have; I simply don't have enough information.) However, God allowed them to succeed even though they may not have believed in Him. Believing in God is not a prerequisite for granting success: in His infinite bounty, He allows us to succeed even though we may not believe in Him; consequences in the afterlife are a separate matter. Now, allow me to mention a second group of influential people.

At the time of the death and resurrection of Jesus of Nazareth, how many Christians were there in the world? A map of the world in that era shows a tiny dot on the map somewhere in Palestine, where there were maybe a few dozen Christians at the very most. Fast-forward to four hundred years later: the boundaries of the Roman Empire were also the boundaries of the Christian world. After a long time of tormenting and torturing Christians, the Roman Emperor's conversion to Christianity had ushered in that religion within the Empire, and it became Christian, from Central Europe all around the Mediterranean Sea, then the center of the known world.

Who achieved this mighty feat? No more than a dozen people or so, Christ's disciples, who went out to spread and preach the new religion. But did they live for two hundred years? Of course not; but they passed the torch to others, who passed it on to others, and so on until the Emperor's conversion, and with him the Empire. The disciples were not prophets; they were regular people like you and me. They believed in God and His Prophet, and they knew they could. And they changed the world.

These are the influential few.

Let us move to another period. History shows that the Prophet Muhammad preached Islam for a total of 23 years, 10 in Medina, and 13 in Mecca. Its twofold branches, worship and dealings (with others) were only completed in Mecca: for example, the final prohibition of alcohol, the structure of social relationships, and the Medina Document that organized the strata of society, were all created in Medina. Ten years later, 100,000 Muslims performed the Prophet's funeral pilgrimage, final pilgrimage to Mecca with the Prophet, meaning that the number of Muslims had increased from a few hundred to tens of thousands.

If the dealings branch was only completed in Medina, then what was Muhammad doing in Mecca? If the number of Muslims had risen to in 100,000 in ten years in Medina, how many had he converted in Mecca? The point is that the Prophet would have had to prepare a certain type of men and women. Note that the migrants from Mecca to Medina were not in the thousands or even the hundreds, but 68-72 people. In 630 A.D., the time of the Prophet's death, a map of the world's Islamic regions would only show a few points in the Arabian Peninsula. 200 years later, what do we see? Islam had spread to great regions, from Indonesia in the east to the Pacific Ocean in the west, as far northward as Central Asia and southward to the Sahara Desert. Who did this, if our Prophet had died in 630 A.D.? Only a few dozen people, at the heart of whom were the only 68-72 people who had accompanied our Prophet to Mecca, and had been prepared by him for the future. They were not prophets: they did not live for 200 years. They passed on the torch to others who spread their message. They were the Influential Few who changed the world.

They knew they could.

The above examples of people who changed the world show different reasons. Some did it for God; some did it for other reasons. God does not prevent people from making achievements in His name. He does not require belief in Him as a prerequisite for success in this life; in the afterlife, that is another matter. In any case, what brings these influential few together was that they were result-oriented. You need to be, too. Don't be seduced by the lure of motion – the idea that "as long as I'm doing something, I should be all right." A player who jogs on the sidelines of a football field for 90 minutes makes as much effort, or more so, than his teammate who is busy running and scoring goals, but is ultimately only running in place.

Don't run in place. Be result-oriented. You are the steward of God's greatest gift: yourself, with all your own infinite resources. Use them well. Get others to help you. Make things happen. The results you achieve will be part of something even greater: fulfilling God's purpose. Once you do this, be certain that you will be one of the influential few who made their mark on the world, in the name of fulfilling God's purpose.

I have not wanted, so far, to break your train of thought regarding God's purpose. I leave you now to pour out those thoughts onto paper. Let me help you: Have you made your choices? Will you live for you and yours, or for God? If the latter, are you currently on a journey to fulfil God's purpose, or are you about to start it?

_____

_____

_____

_____

_____

_____

_____

_____

_____

_____

I

Stern and Serious vs. Fun in Fulfilling God's Purpose

Post WWII, the most successful business model and business school was the US Army School of Management. The US entry into the war set the gargantuan wheels of American industry turning, and the Army influence seeped into the companies that did business with it – which were many. After the war, businesses flocked to it. This military school had a great effect on American companies, which in turn spread their way of doing business throughout the world. To this day there are military terms in use in business, "fire," "officer and the like.

Military management is completely dependent on blind obedience, iron control, rigid hierarchy, sternness and other principles without which no modern army can function. What concerns me here is the conflation of sternness with seriousness, making them conjoined twins in most people's thinking.

At a management seminar, I met a business heir from South America who had written many books on business. I chatted with him on his latest book on a new management model, and was struck by how much fun it was to talk to him. He was very natural, without airs and graces, with a ready laugh from the depths of his childlike heart. His new business model, in short, was to turn over the decision to the workers in his company of how much they should be paid and how much vacation time they should take; they were the ones who made hiring and firing and salary decisions *for their bosses.*

This must be a joke, right?

The proof of the pudding is in the eating. Profits soared; productivity was through the roof; and most importantly, morale and job satisfaction and just plain *fun* among workers and bosses alike was sky-high. The owner of the company bragged happily not only of profits and products, but of the diverse hobbies his employees enjoyed and the vacation time they took with their families: rarely, he told me, had one of them had to miss a family event or an occasion with his children because of work.

We spoke, I recall, of the US Military business school, of the success it had achieved after WWII, and the realization that it was not the only way; his own success was proof of that.

Why am I telling you this story about success in business, and enjoying life?

Because throughout this book, I have been telling you to dare to dream big, to work hard to achieve your dreams. I can almost see you already girding your loins, preparing for the heavy price you will have to pay for this: a grim and dim, stern and serious life, and I want to head you off before you do any such thing.

Yes, I do urge you to dream and work hard and pay the price, but I urge you to do so while smiling, enjoying life, humming a happy tune at how sweet and wonderful and beautiful life is.

Have you ever been somewhere wonderful, eaten something delicious, heard a magnificent melody, but been unable to appreciate it because your heart was heavy with some pain, or burdened with some great responsibility? And inversely, been able to enjoy them with a light heart? Yes, I'm talking about the heart.

Under "Beauty," we mentioned that beauty is perceived with the five senses: the final step, enjoyment, comes from the heart. If your heart is heavy, or burdened, or broken, no matter what wonderful sensations the senses send its way, it is blind to them. However, when you are exhausted, but your heart is light, are you not able to enjoy affection or comfort from a friend or partner, or take pleasure in the laugh of a little child? Forgive me for this long introduction. In plain words, I believe that if your heart is open to comfort and joy, then no matter your burdens, tasks and responsibilities, you will enjoy a beautiful life.

What is having an open heart?

Your heart must not be hard or cruel. It must be tender and gentle.

"But that's not a characteristic of those with iron will and steel determination!"

Says who? That's why I started with the US military versus the genius from South America. Being a grim and dim, lugubrious killjoy are not synonymous with seriousness and success; they are a choice. If you choose them and can still enjoy life, then fine, but that doesn't mean there aren't other choices.

According to some surveys, 20% of family businesses started from scratch required three generations to turn into giant companies. Three generations for a success rate of 20%. Think of that a moment.

Now think of the prophets, the ones who faced the greatest challenges, the most result-oriented, who most wanted to see results in their lifetime, who changed history, who paid the greatest price. Did they face down their societies with a scowl, or with a smile? Were their hearts filled with sorrow, or with joy? Were their hearts hard and cruel because of what they had suffered, or tender and gentle?

Don't say, "Do you expect me to be like the prophets?" We are expected to be like them, after all. Still, if you find this example weighty, here's another. Have you seen how children enjoy life? Children are not stupid or lacking in memory. But every day they laugh at the same songs, because they enjoy them every day. They are delighted at the sight of a bird, for they see it every day with fresh wonder. Children's hearts are unspoiled. If your heart is filled with the love of God, you can have the unspoiled wonder and joy of a child.

Never lose your wonder. An unspoiled heart is one that can enjoy a sunset over the sea; feel childlike pleasure in the first blossoms of spring; be filled with joy at the birds' dawn chorus; one, in short, that has not lost the capacity for wonder.

Do you want to be like them? The choice is yours. You can wear a forbidding scowl; that will certainly make you look Serious and Important. If you start caring about how you look to others, this is a pretty good path to self-centeredness. Having the time of your life while still being serious sounds incongruous at first, but if you can combine hard work with fun and pleasure, then why not?

One of the world's largest tech companies offers its employees all sorts of fun things in the workplace: exercise balls and even a giant hamster wheel, while still being the most innovative and fastest-growing company worldwide, with a budget exceeding the GDP of some countries. Would you say its employees aren't serious? I doubt it.

Serious and stern are not synonymous.

What do you think? Observe and make notes. "Life is not a battle; it can be an enjoyable journey, all the while fulfilling God's purpose." Comment. Jot down your thoughts and questions.

_____

_____

_____

_____

CONCLUSION

A New Beginning

As I started this book, I will finish it. I started by saying that this book was for everyone, and for young people all over the world in particular, being a book about the future. More specifically, it is a book that urges *action,* especially on the part of the members of Western Civilization and what used to be called Islamic civilization (of all faiths, not merely Muslims). It is a responsibility, since these two are the source of all the world's headache; and a call to action, because much needs to be done to get rid of this headache.

After this book's journey, now is the chance for what I call a new beginning: a vision of a new method of living under God-centrism. This method will lead us into the next phase of the current civilization. When I say "next," I absolutely mean building on what we have rather than replacing it.

I believe that most of the 7 billion citizens of the world, due to circumstances that have been described in detail, have the sense that it may well be possible, at this point in time more than any other, to come together into a single world civilization. Such a civilization would be inclusive, bringing together diverse and many things, but its building-block would be the will of its smallest component: the human entity. You.

A big thing like civilization is made up of many small everyday things, sciences, arts, work, life, earning, spending, etc., which take diverse forms based on differences in culture, religion, society and so on, to which the different "YOU's" belong. You have the choice to adopt my premise; to reject it; or to come up with a different one of your own. I respect your choice, as long as you make one. However, failing to choose on the premise that it's none of your concern, then calling your apathy a "choice" – that's fooling yourself. We live in an age where your silence inevitably means that someone will speak in your name, and interpret your silence as a power of attorney. In this age, your silence is a virtual blank check for someone else to act for you; your passive attitude means you probably won't even know who has stolen your voice and acted in your name. If this occurs, know that this too is your choice; your apathy has led to your will being hijacked, led to you being an object, and you have no-one to blame but yourself.

Another point is for *you,* to think of your*self,* and re-examine your*self.* Don't use the questions in this book as a tool to judge and find fault with others: this is one of the many tricks in the Self's arsenal to absolve you of responsibility and dump it on others in the guise of 'advice.' Don't fall into the trap. If you genuinely want to help others, have them seek their own questions, don't volunteer them for others. This is a book, as I have said, about questions, not about answers.

Before you start your journey into questioning – as I hope you may – I would like, in the best business tradition, to offer you some threats and opportunities. It may help focus your questions. The list, of course, is not exhaustive.

Threats

In the section on Islam, we discussed how an influential few had – unfortunately – turned the good and benevolent religion of Islam into the "Tribe of Islam", exporting a distorted image about Muslims to millions of non-Muslims, and thus offending millions of Muslims going about their lives in peace and quiet. Both parties have the right to their feelings, even though they were brought about by a falsehood: remember, perception is reality.

Similarly, the tenacious efforts of the influential few to transform the flourishing and successful concept of Western Civilization into the exclusive Tribe of Western Civilization were facilitated by the apathy of the vast majority, going about their lives while the influential few spoke in their names, giving the impression that they had full authority to do so. Again, this was a falsehood, but again, perception is reality!

The end result was that these few turned western civilization – on the verge of becoming *the* global civilization – into an exclusive social, political and economic club. Further, they see themselves as the founding members, and this exclusive club as being accessible by invitation only – from themselves.

The Civilizational Social Club

While the current civilization is wonderful, a handful of people persists in treating it like a private club, and themselves as the founding members; they see themselves as the owners and board members of this club, comprising about 20% of the world's population; they run it as though they had a power of attorney from the members to act in what they see as the members' best interests.

This is, as stated above, the largest tribe ever formed in human history, in the negative sense of 'tribe.' This minority has ignored the fact that the world all took part in building this civilization, either with the cumulative effects of their own civilizations, or in blood and wealth forcibly paid. The minority noticed that the rest of the planet admires their club, and wants to join. The pretend owners impose strict rules to join, with the excuse that they built the club from scratch and so they get to make the rules.

With the end of the colonial era, when these countries pillaged the world's countries for wealth and resources, they find themselves obliged to extend a hand to others – only when they need them, of course, as partners in their military ventures, as markets for their products, out of a need for their countries' resources, or for other reasons that definitely do not include a wish to live together. When they do reach out, they are careful to keep the boundaries of their tribe far apart from the others. They are virtually saying, "Welcome, fellow-humans. We need something from you: we need you to buy our products, and if you have any natural resources, it seems only right that we monopolize them, because we will manage and make better use of them than you. But please, not too close! Welcome, fellow-humans. We might allow you to join our club, on a simple condition: that you become copies of us. You can bring your culture, your heritage, and your religion; that's natural. It's a club for all of us, after all.

Welcome, fellow-humans. All we ask is that you pass through the filter and the mold on your way in. The filter will sift out your understanding of religion and heritage, while the mold will press you into our shape so that you look exactly like us. Once you have done this, we will do our very best to feel – and to make you feel – that you are nothing but a pale imitation of us. If you are ever obliged by circumstance to live among us, we will do our best to make you feel alien. We will mock your traditions, poke fun at your habits, ridicule your culture, and force you to retreat into ghettos and closed communities. These we will then call "little" followed by the name of your homelands, so as not to afford you the chance to integrate into our society. Finally, we will attack you mercilessly, saying you threaten our identity and our culture because you don't want to integrate. You don't want to be a pale imitation of us that, as we've told you before, and as you've experienced, we despise.

Welcome, fellow-humans. At every opportunity, if there is any conflict between us and your culture of origin, we will quickly herd you into isolated camps, and we may ostracize and humiliate you a little.

Welcome, fellow-humans!"

A bloated collective Ego has produced a despotic "Us" manifested in the largest tribe in history. Where to? I venture to say, to the same fate that humanity has experienced in past centuries: bloody and destructive world or regional wars.

Why bring this up now? Because anyone reading the world news can see the intimations of a new world war. The influential few speaking for Western civilization as a tribe, not a civilization, is forever seeking a threatening "Them" against which to define the "Us," and they have found it in the influential few speaking for what they sincerely believe to be a tribe and not a religion, in addition to some countries designated a "They", such as China, Iran, and others.

The world is on the brink of a destructive world war. No-one knows what small incident may set it off. What we do know is the destruction that will follow as a result.

Who beats the drums of war?

The people running these tribes.

How many are running the tribes?

No more than a few thousand.

How many people are set to fight in these wars?

Several billion.

How many victims are expected?

Hundreds of millions.

What will follow this tragedy?

The "Us" will need to expand its collective ego, and bring in a number of the battling parties. Prosperity will ensue for the former enemies who are now allies in the new tribe with expanded borders, as was the case in previous centuries.

Enough! Enough! Enough suffering cause by this narrow definition of "Us", represented by a Tribe under self-centeredness. The world has paid a hefty enough price, and it's time to say: Enough.

I say it to two groups: the first is the tiny minority who claims to own what they think is a social club, and the second, the rest of the members of Western civilization.

First: To those who claim to own it: Please, calm down. Have no fear. We don't want to hurt you. We don't want to demolish the great civilization that you have built upon the basis of our old ones. We have all paid far too much for the benefits you now enjoy. We are not minimizing your efforts: yes, you have done the building, but we have paid part of the price through trial and error in past centuries.

The ideal solutions you long for will not, unfortunately, come to pass: (a)All the Earth's inhabitants die, except for you, leaving you to enjoy the planet's resources exclusively. I don't see any signs that we're about to become extinct: we're staying on the planet with you, until God sees fit to destroy the entire planet. We are not going to be mere passive consumers and markets for your products. That was in another time. So we're not going anywhere, and you can't get rid of us, so please stop trying.

(b)You make us into carbon copies of yourselves, sincerely believing that you are the ideal. That's not going to happen either, however hard you try. It will end in the destruction of this magnificent civilization, and after that, all of us will have to start from scratch. We will have become united, true; but what a wonderful opportunity wasted.

These perfect solutions that roil beneath the surface of self-centeredness will not come to pass, but what *will* is the burden you have already made us bear in past centuries: bloodbaths.

Second: To the overwhelming majority of Western civilization, 20% of the world's inhabitants: This loyal minority is speaking in your name, and has been for centuries. They have brought you great success; they have brought the rest of the world greater calamity. This tiny minority is turning Western civilization into the Tribe of Western Civilization. They will keep speaking in your name as long as you remain silent, taking your silence as tacit agreement, and you will have given them the right to do so.

Dear Members of Western Civilization: Is there any hope of not repeating the disasters of centuries past? Your silence is a tacit agreement to repeat the past. If you don't want to, don't worry, you will lose nothing – on the contrary, we will all win.

Dear Members of Western Civilization: You are no better – and no worse – than the rest of the people on this planet. We are different, and diverse, and there is richness in it. A minority among you knows this; a minority of people in the rest of the world knows it. Most of you think you are the best race; most of the rest of the world thinks the same of themselves. But that doesn't matter. An influential few among you may form a seed for an influential few made up of all of us that can change all of us.

Borders and Armies

An old invention is slowly becoming obsolete: geographical borders.

In times past, geographical borders offered a measure of security in exchange for some obstacles to freedom of movement between countries. They were also drawn by colonialist countries between colonies to cause maximum confusion and disruption after they withdrew, impede progress, and guarantee the colonized countries would continue to need them.

When you began to do away with borders on the European continent, the rest of the world began – as usual – to emulate you, and form alliances, unite, or do away with borders. Even the secessionist tendencies of smaller territories, such as Scotland from the UK, or Catalonia from Spain, took place in the context of a desire for direct unity with the larger entity, Europe. If this goes on long enough, the question will eventually arise, "Do we really need armies anymore in their current form?"

I doubt that armies will ever be completely obsolete. There will always be foolish actions around the world, which creates a need for some form of armed forces. In addition, many powerful countries prefer to reinforce their status by maintaining an army, although they never actually use them. The balance of terror, too, will always exist as a deterrent for any would-be adventurers. Still, the question remains: In what form? What shape will they take?

The United States has no need of armies to protect its states from one another; Europe is the same within its own borders. What happened to get to that point? Apparently, these entities wearied of centuries of bloody war, and realized that cooperation and complementariness were better for their citizens. Another apparent reason was the spread of liberty and democracy. However, the real reason behind these developments was the curbing of the collective Ego and the Tribe of Us, which the influential few had used to brainwash their citizens and make them fear the Other – leading to bloody wars between European countries and the American Civil War. When the citizens of these countries became more aware, they managed to curb the collective Ego.

I put forward the suggestion that we emulate the United States, which did away with borders and hence with the need for national armies, and European countries, which did the same, becoming the

European Union, and therefore having no need for defense forces against one another. This might help us arrive at the same result and avoid global strife, possibly leading to World War Three.

What do you think of my solution? Do you like it? Does it inspire you?

Then let me tell you that it is an absolute failure.

Why? Because it's under self-centeredness, for the good of Us, with no thought of God, what He wants or His purpose. In short, an Us starts to annex sundry other Theme's, because a simple calculation has shown it that it is more profitable than fighting them. This is the same foolish reason why a great Us has now formed, and is currently seeking an opposing Them against which to define itself and thus support its position. Trying to follow the same path is a prime example of not seeing the wood for the trees, in other words, letting tactics blind us to strategy and acting without awareness of the current situation's opportunities and threats. If it succeeds, it is palliative at best, not addressing the root of the condition.

The issue is not in the details: the issue is that we are still working under self-centeredness. From that place, the collective ego – the sense of the Tribe – flourishes.

The Fragile Alliance of Us

Let me alert you to this very important point, which, I believe, demonstrates the necessity of finding a path other than expanding the circle of Us. When societies based on a large collective Ego – an "Us" – are exposed to an outside threat, they quickly lose the false unity built on mutual interest. US internment of Japanese-Americans after the bombing of Pearl Harbor is a case in point. In the language of this book, the fragile alliance was dissolved; they were excluded from the 'Us,' albeit temporarily, and became 'Them.' Have you followed the events of the Brexit scare? As soon as the 'Us' began to feel that part of 'us' constituted a threat, 'we' started to prepare a scenario to get rid of 'them' – Greece – to be implemented in case it became impossible to arrive at a deal guaranteeing the interests of the greater 'Us'.

I am not speaking from a political, economic or security standpoint, but a broader perspective, that of this book: the paradigms of God-centrism and self-centeredness. "Us" under self-centeredness is very fragile in its alliances. "Us" will be forever seeking a "Them" to

define itself against and feel threatened by, simply *because* there is no
"Us" without "Them." That will inevitably lead to the same results:
confrontation, then assimilation into 'Us', then a new conflict with a
new Them, and so on.

I urge you not to waste time and energy on the above. You must
make a strategic choice freely, then take your time devising tactics of
implementation. In fact, wait a moment – before that, you must make
an existential choice.

Choice and Heritage

From which place do you want to live, under self-centeredness or
God-centrism? Your response to this first question of all will indicate
the path you will take. Each path has its own questions and answers.
Choose what you will, carry it out, and bear the consequences.

Why am I speaking to the members, especially the younger
members, of Western civilization, although they hold a stake in
this? In fact, I am speaking to many more, but I am starting with the
most important and influential ones, the ones who bear the greatest
responsibility, the citizens of the Western world. Western civilization
is currently the victorious and prevailing one; as stated previously, it
is also history's very first potentially global civilizations. This places a
heavier burden of responsibility on its citizens, particularly the young
among them.

The rule that everyone follows and imitates the victor becomes clear
here: the easiest and shortest path for the world to adopt some principle
is for the global victor to adopt it, and the rest to play follow-the-leader.
It is by no means the only path, of course, just the shortest; there
are others that must be taken at the same time. If I had been making
this suggestion 600 years ago, I would have been addressing it to the
citizens of Islamic civilization; 2500, to the Greeks and Romans; 5000
years ago, to the Ancient Egyptians. At every stage of history, there
have been civilizational leaders, followed by the rest of the world.

Members of western civilization: You represent the victors. Your
decisions will be followed and imitated worldwide. You will be
followed by others down whichever path you choose to take. For a
significant amount of time, the world is going to remain reactive to
your proactive stance, because your young people currently lead the

world's creative efforts, linked to other young people in the world via communications networks via the new electronic language of youth.

Young people of the West: You are the generation with the weightiest responsibility to choose carefully, and not to blindly follow the heritage of your forefathers. Liberate yourself from that heritage; then choose, whatever your choice. Only choose, don't follow.

There is another challenge facing the members of what used to be called Islamic civilization.

Threats

First, I speak to those who distorted Islamic Religion into the Tribe of Islam. Dear sirs,

First, I repeat that no matter how good the cure, it is useless if the diagnosis is incorrect. You are reacting to a perceived attack on Islam. What you believe to be an attack on Islam, as a religion, is actually an attack on the people who live in parts of the world that used to be home to Islamic civilization. Millions of other people in the world, members of Islamic civilization, are subject to the same pressures, the same attacks, despite not being Muslims; millions more, in civilizations remote from us, East Asia, South America, sub-Saharan Africa, Eastern Europe and so on, are by no means Muslims, yet still experience the same pressures.

Second: Your reactiveness from a place of incorrect diagnosis, using the same tools and methods as those who threaten you, has created a distorted image of the refined religion of Islam in the minds of the rest of the planet's inhabitants: it is now seen as the Tribe of Islam, a great injustice to this valuable religion.

Third: Please note that your adoption of tribalism is merely a reaction to others' tribalism. This was not a choice made of your own free will; you are blindly aping those you consider to be your enemies and your oppressors, which in itself is their greatest triumph – even if you win at the game of Tribe Wars they started!

Fourth: No matter how pure, strong, and selfless your dedication, it will not turn wrong into right; it will not turn injustice into justice; it will not turn sin into virtue, nor doubt into certainty. Take your time and think before you start your dedicated journey in defense of what you believe.

Fifth: Gentlemen. Know that you will have been the reason, and bear the responsibility, if there is a repeat of what happened in Renaissance Europe. Soon enough, treatises will appear from adherents of the very religion you are fighting for, calling for its exclusion from daily life practices, and calling for it to be confined to ritual only. Soon enough, this will split God from religion, and turn the latter into mere spiritual exercises not unlike yoga and so on.

If you haven't noticed, we're pretty close to this already. It will come not from outside, but from within: from Muslims who no longer know what to do with their religion. The practices of the Tribe of Islam will have been the direct cause of it.

I also address myself to the general population of Muslims, who number in the hundreds of millions. In short, you're the next target. There are those among you who move in your name, claiming to act for you, imagining that your religion is under attack. They have declared holy war in defense of their religion; they are completely prepared to die for this noble cause of theirs. The Other is also preparing for this war. Your silence is clear tacit agreement with their ideas and actions: when you are hurt by others, you will not be blameless. When war comes, it will be like all wars, indiscriminate. Millions of innocents will die. There's no longer time to sit around letting others act for you, or in your name. Your duty is not fulfilled by giving someone else a mandate to speak for you, either, while you sit around sipping coffee! Move!

That was the threat. Before we seize the opportunity, I have one more warning for Western civilization and for Muslims, a sometimes obscure truth: Both parties in the influential few, on both sides, owe their existence and power to the corresponding few on the other side. There are conflicts that aren't easy to settle, without a clear winner or loser, but just drag on, and any victory is Pyrrhic at best. Unfortunately, we are in the middle of one of these.

Members of both civilizations: If you remain content with silence, don't claim to be victims!

Opportunities

First, the question begs itself: "If I'm happy this way, why should I change? Why move from self-centeredness to God-centrism?"

A logical and, I think, essential question. Allow me to first explain in the language of self-centeredness: Because you have nothing to lose, and everything to gain. First, I'm inviting you to abandon the concept that life is a struggle at which you must win; it's a lifestyle that is strongest under self-centeredness. Also, in the language of self-centeredness, you will be adding more profitable long-term dividends to your short-term investments. I say "more profitable," which is a vast understatement; I'm also saying "long-term," which refers not only to 'in the long run', but also means rewards that last forever! All you have to do is disassemble the paradigm by which you live from around self-centeredness and reassemble it around God-centrism; a simple act of master reframing. The vast majority of the things that make up your life will stay the same; you will merely rearrange your priorities. If you – and your Self – decide to take this opportunity, I suggest the first step be from a self-centered place to a God-centric place. That will make the rest of it much easier.

God-centrism is the Self's Kryptonite. It is much easier to control and curb the Self's urges under God-centrism. Once you do, the dividends and investments I lured you in with may well recede; they are certainly not the whole picture. What I'm inviting you to experience is a life spent humming a happy tune, the leader of your own band, or a player with another if you feel it forms part of your music dedicated to serving God's creatures, or a solo musician playing their own tune of helping and serving others.

I invite you to seek God's purpose for you, to taste a sweetness you can only sample under God-centrism, while fulfilling that purpose. Try a life where the Self is tamed, placed in your service in your fulfilment of God's purpose, instead of a mad endless panting rush to fulfil the ambitions and desires of that same Self. I invite you to cast out fear; to fill your heart with perfect love for God and for His creatures, an endless source of creativity, innovation, service, and productivity; to live your life filled with strength, knowing you can, content with yourself, with God's creatures, and with God.

I invite you to live free of fear of death, knowing it is not the end of life, but merely a gateway where you change your garb. To live your time on this earth experiencing the immortality of the Divine Spirit inside you. To live on this earth experiencing God in every detail of your daily life, speaking to Him, asking Him, leaning on Him, complaining to Him, and drawing strength from Him. To live big, big,

big; to be of great service to God's creatures; to use your Self in their service. To live out your life aware of the miracle God has given you: you – and using it in the service of His creatures. Please value it, care for it and nurture it; it is your most powerful tool for fulfilling God's purpose for you. I invite you to live out your life knowing that you and yours are God's creatures, deserving of service just like all others. I invite you to live positively and proactively, your compass directed at God's purpose, serving others.

There are things in this world we may consider goals, or way-stations: these are our criteria for success. Examples are graduating, getting a job, inventing something, finding a life partner, buying a dream house, and so on. There are other things that we may consider our lodestone, our North Star; anything achieved while moving towards them is a by-product, while our real aim is never to deviate from our path.

An Inclusive Society Centered on Love, Based on God-Centrism

This, I believe, should be our North Star. Even if we deviate for a time, we can recalibrate, and head north once more, towards God-centrism. It is naïve to imagine that heading steadily north on one's compass (easily accessible now thanks to the kind young inventors of smartphones) will lead one to the North Pole. The North Pole is the same as our path in life: an indicator of the path to follow. There is no Ultimate Destination where one can stop. One simply keeps working until one's time on this earth is done, enjoying the journey, and in the best possible company – that of God.

God's company grants you the opportunity to enjoy every part of life more deeply. Things you love and admire are felt by the heart, which can only fully open when you are in God's company. There are levels of the heart that can only open when activated by God. Your love for your parents, your partner, your friends, your children, your homeland, everyone and everything you know, is transformed when you experience it from these levels of the heart.

The smallest building-block of civilization, yet the most influential, is the human being. This is why I invite you, the human being, to live under God-centrism: so that this paradigm will color your civilization with this divine hue. When we say that civilizations include many diverse religions, cultures, languages, ethnicities and races, we may note that all the above depends on the choices of the smallest, greatest building-block, the human being. Civilizations will keep their differences and specificity and richness and diversity and multiplicity, but be divine in essence. Religion will be finally rid of its idolatry and tribalism, and once again be a path to God.

The best of it is that the moment one decides of one's own free will to change one's compass, there is an immediate shift to God-centrism, which is an existential choice. All that follows is just tactics, ways of realizing this wonderful existential decision. These details will spawn entire life structures, all colored with divinity. Your choice to live under God-centrism grants you the ability to see all of life's details differently: like special glasses that conduct a master reframing, reconstructing everything in life around the Almighty.

Many wise folk say it is more enjoyable to give than to receive. The charitable organization, The Giving Pledge, started with Bill Gates and Warren Buffett pledging half their wealth to charity and encouraging the world's wealthiest families to do the same. So far, 81 multi-millionaires and billionaires have pledged to give at least half their wealth to charity.

An examination of the reasons for this will be helpful. The most fascinating thing, to me, is that they *instinctively* did it *simply because they felt if they did it, they would feel good.* Why do we feel good when we give to charity? It would be just as easy *not* to feel good when giving, wouldn't it? Who allowed that feeling to creep into our hearts? That is a good question. I believe that when we give, we are giving ultimately to God, and it is that communion with God that creates the good feelings. Naturally, God could have chosen not to grant that feeling and merely to require charity, but He is a loving God, and so kind to His creatures that He grants the good feeling to all those who give to charity, even those who do not believe in Him.

This is a small example of what I call decoding things to see their reality. I suggest, dear reader, that you use this method throughout your life: to try and acquire the ability to decode, and to see the true center of creation – God – and the relationship of everything to Him. Ask, as Abraham asked, only be careful of the Self's tricks and don't get so lost in questioning that you spend your life asking and not doing. Keep your eye on the prize, the main question: "What is God's purpose for me?" This is the question that allows you to live creatively and innovatively, to make magnificent and great plans, and to live up to your responsibility as God's steward on the Earth. Under God-centrism, you are responsible for *all* His creatures in *all* His land, people, plants, animals, all of it, responsible for them to be able to be fruitful and multiply. You are in the service of every person – those who resemble you and those who do not; believers and non-believers alike – and of the environment. You are responsible before God for the oceans and rivers and forests, not merely so that they may remain as a source of food, oxygen and wood respectively, but because God's creatures live in them. You are responsible for protecting wildlife from extinction, not only because we will lose them forever once they are gone, but because we are responsible for their right to life. Under God-centrism, you are responsible for _____, _____, and _____ fill in the blanks.

Under God-centrism, what used to be called "calamities" can be viewed as challenges. You can take the initiative and face them proactively, instead of being an angry victim. You can control pain, instead of pain controlling you. More than that, you have the chance to explore how you might relieve the pain of others in your situation. You can try to decode the situation: what is the coded message that God is sending you through this pain? This might be a new step in your service of His creatures. Your sole concern is no longer to break free of despair; despair is never an option.

Under God-centrism, you are innovative, creative. You search for new ways and means. Under God, you are a Source of Light, inspiring those around you to be like you, filling them with strength and hope, giving them the courage to dream, and then taking their hand to help them make their dreams a reality.

I invite you to live under God-centrism: you will find all of this here and more, plus everything you enjoy currently under self-centeredness, after a master reframing. You will have everything you had before, plus more. I would say it's an offer you can't refuse.

But even these tempting benefits will pale into insignificance next to the glory of living in communion with God, of living for God, for living in the company of God. What an indescribable joy. Believe me, it's worth trying.

A Chance to Reconsider

Members of Western civilization, I believe it may be time to reconsider the reactive stance your ancestors forced you into all those centuries ago, a result of the unholy alliance between money, politics and the Church. God had no part of that alliance. They had reasons – not excuses – for doing what they did, but those reasons are no longer valid. It may be time for groups of people to reconsider, to reexamine past events, to reassess and reject the self-centered paradigm established by your ancestors as a reaction. It may well be time to free yourselves from your unreasonable rejection of Almighty God.

Most Renaissance thinkers, in politics, social sciences and economics, rejected any role for God in the treatises they wrote, as a reaction to the Unholy Alliance. But what we have now is a paradigm of thought that has rejected God. God is in no need, of course, of our recognition. He has nothing to lose. We are the potential losers if we continue to burden Him with the results of this historical circumstance, a product of centuries ago, that still holds us trapped in its orbit.

You have nothing to lose by reconsidering. If, at the end, you decide that you have no desire to change it, and remain under self-centeredness, this will be a renewed vote of confidence in self-centeredness, a consummation devoutly to be wished; if on the other hand you decide to reframe your lives under God-centeredness, it will be a choice of your own free will. I repeat: whichever you choose, the rest of the world will follow you. That is the fate of the victor.

In the past, what I say would only have been addressed to a small intellectual and cultural elite; however, in this age, we all have the tools to start this reconsideration and reevaluation, question ourselves and discuss it with others. Social media need not only be for current events and kitten videos – as much fun as they are.

Opportunity: Lateral Flow of Information

We have said before that the technological innovations of the 21st century have made the world into a village, bringing us closer and deeper than ever before. Now, as you read this, this minute, a past system is dying and the future is taking place. One of the most important revolutions of the communications age is the death of the old hierarchy of information transfer – not in business and government, but in civilization and what creates it.

In times gone by, the overwhelming majority of people on this planet lived in a constant state of anticipation. They were always waiting for knowledge from some person, some source, from prophets and priests and thinkers to intellectuals and theorists, to newspapermen, military leaders and captains of industry: an individual would first explain his (almost always his) theory to a small circle, who would then spread it to their own inner circles, and so on until a pyramid of information was formed, the original leader at its top, and the base expanding over time. The future of this call depended on the small circles that formed the stratum immediately after the individual theorist in the pyramid. Without their help, the idea would be stillborn.

This meant that any new idea must necessarily be geographically limited in scope. When it reached the next stratum, it was inevitably colored with the embellishments of the reteller. This was true of new ideas in economy, politics and sociology; it was equally true of inventions. The first great innovation, of course, was Gutenberg's invention of the printing press, which democratized the spread of information to a great extent, but even then, the decision of *what was worth printing* was taken by a relatively small circle of elite publishers. The hierarchy of information transfer was still firmly in place. Even when an idea crossed the first few barriers, that was no guarantee; sociological surveys tell us that for every idea that became popular, there were a good four ideas and inventions that did not, despite early adopters' enthusiasm.

Now, for the first time in history, the rigid old information hierarchy is giving way to what we may call lateral information transfer, or lateral information flow (due to speed and fluidity). An inventor has only to sit at their computer, tablet or even smartphone, and share their innovation with a single click. There is no longer any need for the small circles at the top of the hierarchy; there is only a lateral motion, growing every day as the number of Internet users grows. The effect of this, socially, economically, politically, is incalculable. The waiting game that people were once used to has already all but disappeared. No intermediary is needed to usher in new ideas. The world is in a constant state of dynamic flow of ideas. The relationship of thinker or inventor to audience is direct. Not only can an idea be presented as its innovator chooses, but it can also be presented as a work in progress, and audience input requested, which for the first time gives the opportunity for a truly global flavor – in the positive sense.

This also offers – and please think carefully about what I am saying – a mechanism for virtually instantaneous and direct selection between inventor and audience. This gives people the opportunity they have lacked for so long. Before this capacity existed, a select few controlled what information got through, whom they wanted to get it through, how they wanted their audiences to react, how best (in their opinion) to use it in the public good – that was even assuming they let it become public, or refrained from using it in their own interest. Now, every individual in the world can be effective; every interaction can be truly interactive.

The waiting game is on its way out, if not actually over, being replaced with interactivity. This means that you – yes, you – are stronger and more powerful, if you want to be; you are also more apathetic and passive if you refrain from seizing this opportunity. The static gap you hid behind is disappearing rapidly. I urge Western civilization again to use this lateral motion to reexamine the existential philosophy of the Renaissance, and reframe your wonderful self-centered civilization under God-centrism. You have nothing to lose, and everything to gain, including a response to a great many questions concerning the spiritual emptiness of modern life.

A Chance for Justice

I urge you to reframe the current self-centered civilizational paradigm around God-centrism. You can do it; you just need the will to start. Your ability to do so is clear from your magnificent civilization's characteristics. I believe you have already gone a long way down the road that God tells us to take when dealing with others, in all His divine messages since the dawn of history. Your wonderful value system of justice, accuracy, honesty, cleanliness, dedication and creativity that you have achieved after a hard road full of thorns has created an environment rich in scientific, artistic and ethical progress. It was a hard road because it was guided by trial and error. It was full of thorns not because of the "how" but because of the "whom" you did it for: You achieved a great deal of what God wants, but you did it under self-centeredness, not God-centrism. For this reason, if you should have the notion to add this final element, it will not be hard: on the contrary, it will be easier than you think.

To the members of this civilization, I repeat: You are closer to a master reframing than you imagine. You've done the hard part; all that remains is the core. You're so close, you need only want to – because you certainly can. If you do, you will save yourselves and the world. You will defuse the self-destructiveness that self-centeredness has planted in your society alongside progress and prosperity. You will uproot the injustice that self-centeredness has planted under the soil of your society alongside the seeds of justice.

It is my belief that any value system, no matter how good, just and noble, will always be missing something if it is not based on God-centrism.

Let's take the value of justice, for example. Any wonderful justice system under self-centeredness will always serve an "Us," some Us, no matter how broad, and exclude a "Them," however few; and that in itself is an assault on a principal tenet of justice, its blindness. Justice is supposed to make no distinction based on sex, race, color, or any other characteristic. The magnificent justice system in the Western world is one of the best, if not the best, in the world today; the vast majority of its citizens have recourse to the law, a principal instrument of justice. We have said before that any civilization has certain central countries; we may claim at this moment that the US is a central country in Western society, if not *the* central country post-WWII. The relationship of its citizens to the justice system is strong and direct: the most important question governing the moral compass of day-to-day interactions is, "Is it against the law?" An admirable practice, one that has made this country respected and emulated all over the world. However, since the justice system is based on an "Us," and the consensus of an "Us," it achieves justice only for "Us."

In the early twentieth century, the US justice system produced a great deal of excellent legislature governing the interactions of the "Us" it served. The issue was that women were not yet considered part of that 'us'; women had to fight – doing a great many things that were illegal at the time – to be included. Similarly, not many decades later, African-Americans, a large part of American society, were also excluded from protection under the law, and had to fight civil rights battles before they were finally included within the "us" of the law. In both these cases, the people who made the law believed in God, but under self-centeredness, as I discussed earlier, what Self wanted took priority over what God wanted.

In many – unfortunately, in most – societies around the world, despite their belief in God, some tribe reigns supreme and the collective ego is in control; in addition, what this Us wants out of the law takes priority over what God would want. From history, we can draw the following conclusion about justice: Under self-centeredness, however fair the justice system, its fairness will always be limited to Us – whoever 'us' happen to be at the time. There will always be a Them excluded from justice.

"Wait, if history is full of examples of this, all over the world, why are you only addressing Western civilization?" That's a good question. Since the dawn of history, human civilizations have centered around a particular 'us', and consequently, people have needed prophets and religions to help them answer the existential question, "What would God want? His will or mine?" and help to establish truly equal divine justice. This is where Western civilization now finds itself. It has one of the world's most refined and humane justice systems; yet that system is confined to a certain 'us', however expansive. In short, history allows us to say with great confidence: "Only under God-centrism is there no 'us and them' in the justice system. Only then can there truly be justice for all."

A Second Chance for Others

From Indonesia in the east to the Maghreb in the west, from Central Asia in the North to the middle of Africa in the South, millions of people live, with different religions and cultures, in the lands of what used to be Islamic civilization. With all their diversity, they share one thing: belonging to the broken civilization.

This is a chance to get rid of the humiliating adjective 'broken' that has haunted us since the start of this book. Brokenness is a state of mind and spirit, which can be overcome. Unfortunately, I doubt that the members of this civilization have the resources to overcome it just yet. We hardly play any role in world civilization at all as it stands. Not achieving much isn't evidence of brokenness: the true evidence of brokenness is not even trying. Not trying is evidence of a lack of confidence, both in ourselves and in what we have to offer.

To make matters worse, let's look at some of the urban legends shared online, which clearly express not only brokenness and inferiority, but a sense of worthlessness. The form differs, but the content is similar: Some Western genius or inventor goes to Mecca, sees the speed and order with which Muslims line up for prayer in neat rows, and converts to Islam on the spot.

Really?

Is there no sense of worthlessness at play here?

Let's take a closer look. Firstly, the story is always about a European or American scientist. No Indian, Chinese, Japanese, etc. need apply. Second, the scientist is always white. No other ethnicities are mentioned. Third, the scientist is always male. No women ever star in the urban legend. What is this picture? Simply, the colonial stereotype of the White Lord, who used to be regarded as the pinnacle of human and racial superiority. The aim of the story is not, as it might look, to praise Islam, but rather to beg for scraps of legitimacy for this religion in the form of a member of the Master Race converting to it!

Who needs this reassurance? Mainly Muslim members of what used to be Islamic civilization, suffering from an inferiority complex. They have lost confidence in themselves and the legitimacy of their religion and civilization; hence the urban legend, an appeal for legitimacy from those who make them feel inferior.

I mention this not out of self-pity or self-blame, but as a diagnosis, followed by opportunity. Dear young people of Islamic civilization, you have the opportunity to join the fast-forming global human civilization. What do you have to add? Your wonderful selves; your modern ideas inspired by your rich civilization and heritage; you have your creativity and initiative. What you lack is confidence. The difference between you and previous generations is that you have not had direct contact with a colonizer, with a White Lord. I claim that the lack of confidence is only the legacy of previous generations, crushed beneath the victorious Western civilization. The Jews who wandered in the desert for forty years were a lost generation, with no hope of creating a civilization. The difference between them and their descendants – including David and Saul – was that the younger ones, being spared these factors, were capable of achieving what their fathers could not have even dared to dream of.

Dear young people, a great many of your fathers are like the Jews of the wilderness, useless and hopeless: love them and care for them, but don't waste energy trying to change them, and don't let them pass on their crushed and cringing natures to you. Wonderful young people, rebel against those who came before: rebel against their obsequiousness, their submission, their fear. Let your imagination take flight. Communicate with young people like you all over the world. Share what you have; you will never learn the true value of what you have unless you show it to the young people of the world. Don't be content with merely learning; conquer your hesitation; seek what you have; share with your peers. Share your heritage and values. Share your initiatives, your innovations, your crazy ideas. Share your most valuable asset, who you are. The lateral flow of information is at your service as well: use it in the future, to build, to create a new civilization with young people like you all over the world.

To the rest of the inhabitants of this beautiful planet, especially the younger ones: Don't be lured into a reactive stance against the Tribe-of-European-Civilization camp. Don't react in fear; don't let that minority provoke the worst in you. In fact, you possess a great strength, which works as a powerful tool to bring out the best in them.

What is this strength, you ask? A glance at a map of the world will show you. Since the dawn of history, throughout Asia, over half the world's inhabitants have founded rich and refined civilizations. An essential cultural component of these was wisdom and peace. People from the West seek spiritual regeneration in these civilizations and cultures, but I believe they must be used for far more than spiritual retreat: they must form an essential component of future civilizations.

I can feel your surprise. Here I am, talking about common ground and accepting the Other and coexisting, while all over the world, real events in the news warn of the danger coming from the Tribe of Islam, and the Tribe of Asia. I don't blame you. After all, this is part of their heritage, but it's as good as useless if it isn't used as an essential building-block for the civilization of the future.

Why not use it, then? I believe that their faith in the values of their civilization is deeply shaken. Although they make up around two-thirds of the world's population, and a rich heritage of ancient culture, in recent decades, some members of Asian civilization have responded to a call from some members of Western civilization to attack and destroy their own cultural and civilizational heritage, for the benefit of modern Western civilization. The reasons for this would take too long to explain, but today is not yesterday, and the past is not the present. The younger members of this civilization, armed with confidence in themselves and in their own heritage, are not like the children of yesterday whose confidence is crushed. This magnificent legacy will languish in books and history if it is not used by the young people of these civilizations to add their own values and civilization to the new world civilization currently forming.

"But we're talking about God-centrism. How can that happen with so much religious and cultural diversity?"

All this, I believe, will only enrich such a diverse civilization. All this depends on the youth of these cultures reclaiming their self-confidence and their confidence in their own civilizations.

"But but but violence and extremism!"

That's their choice. Those who use violence are being reactive (to past injustices). Those who become extremist are being reactive (to past extremism against them). I believe now is the time for the youth of these old civilizations to move away from reactiveness and towards proactiveness; to choose freely, whatever they choose. They must shake off the overwhelming influence of some powerful people in Western civilization who have created defensive tribes – religious, ethnic or otherwise. By submitting to tribalism, by being reactive, they only hand over victory to a tiny minority in Western civilization.

A Chance for Integration

Let's look at US ghettos or ethnic 'towns.' The USA is a nation of immigrants. Everyone who lives there, with the exception of Native Americans, came there as an immigrant. Still, you will find there a Chinatown, where you are in Beijing or Shanghai as soon as you set foot in it, culturally, architecturally, religiously, linguistically, and so on. The same goes for Koreatown, Vietnam-town, and so on. There are areas populated by people of other ethnic origins: Iranians, Arabs, Mexicans, etc. Who lives there, then? American citizens who immigrated there from these countries. Why form these communities, then? Because they feel more comfortable there. In the language of this book, the controlling "Us" of that society forced them to create smaller "Us" units, communities and ghettos.

This is an opportunity for you, too, young people of these communities. Break out of them. Merge into the homeland where you were born. It's your home as much as everyone else's. The current situation is a product of decades of strife; it doesn't have to be that way. Just follow one rule: Believe in your civilization, and in yourself. Believe in your traditions and values, in your difference. No-one will respect what lies within you unless you do.

In addition, you bear a responsibility to your chosen homeland, the country where you live. If you choose a homeland, you must remain loyal to it, and give as much as you take. Taking from it to give what you take to another place is an implicit admission that you do not belong there. The more you give back to that country, the more confident you are that you belong.

A Dream

As I said in my Introduction, this book offers questions and not answers. That said, I am offering some suggestions, which we might entitle "Dream."

Most of humanity's suffering has been due to self-centered systems – civilizations, empires or states. It is these that spawned the Us, the Collective Ego, and tribalism. I believe setting our compass to God-centrism is the more correct path. It will give everyone a fair shake; make room for everybody; accommodate everyone's opinion, regardless of their cultural, religious, ethnic, etc., status. God-centrism offers an umbrella for invention and innovation, allowing those who wish it to live according to a different perspective.

Citizens of the World and All Of Us

These are new ways of looking at old things, from a God-centric perspective. Being a citizen of the world means seeing things differently, after moving from self-centeredness to God-centrism. It is a way of viewing yourself and God's gifts to you under God-centrism; a way of seeing all God's creation with the full awareness of the common ground you share, and with a sense of responsibility, as God's steward on this earth. It is a way of activating God's purpose for you. You know how great, strong and capable your divine side makes you. It is the way you view the earth, wind and water of this planet, and everything in it, as God's property and God's domain. These are your playing-fields, where you must go as far as you can; to visit, to know, to learn, to teach, to serve, in your achievement of God's purpose. Even if you are in a small, remote village, and your resources are limited, even if my words about travel seem like an impossible dream, please, dream and imagine that you will leave your small remote village to seek God's purpose in God's earth – which includes your little village. Don't limit your dream to your current resources: don't! Let yourself dream, and depend on God. You know that He holds the world in his hands, and that He can give you what you want to achieve what He wants, confident that if you ask, He will respond.

This is your starting-point to global citizenship. Your roots lie in your small village; your scope is the beautiful blue planet. Don't view the borders between you and other countries as towering walls or deep divides; view them as lines drawn to organize your life and the lives of others, no more and no less. The moment you start to view the lines dividing our planet as attempts at organization, you will start to feel you belong to this planet, that you own it. This is the start of your life as a global citizen. Belonging to God is global citizenship.

As a global citizen, you do not allow your Self to lead you in your dealings with others, conveying messages of fear and distrust and generating similar emotions in them. You curb and control your Self, and are aware of God's purpose for you and seek to achieve it. You send messages of confidence and introduction, of cooperation and inclusion. As a global citizen, you seek common ground with the Other, so as to build on your commonalities. You practice humanity continually, under God's continual protection. As a global citizen, when confronted with an Other with different beliefs, you are "All of Us."

All Of Us

I have thought a lot about a single phrase to summarize what I am trying to achieve. If I had to choose a slogan, it would be, "All of Us." By no means is that an erasure of our differences. All it means is to take a different view of the things that we used to fear as a threat under self-centeredness, when we move to a God-centric place. We will preserve our differences without letting them scare and threaten us. 'All of Us' means that our cultures, religions, mores and values, looks, races, and ethnicities will remain diverse, and that we can view this diversity as enrichment. 'All of Us' means curbing and controlling the collective ego. It means dealing with every new 'other' from a place of wanting to meet them and not needing them; the only One you both want and need is God. It means we no longer need a Tribe to defend us. It means we can all mix and mingle freely. It means we accept everyone, together. 'All of Us' means you must no longer pass through the mold of Europeanization in order to be allowed into the Tribe of Western Civilization.

'All of Us' means no more tribes. It means a broader framework for our civilization, with room for all our cultures, religions, habits, mores and values, yet allowing us the freedom to keep what makes us unique. It means curbing our individual and collective ego, to make room for God's spirit within us and allow it to take the reins of our life.

"But how?"

'All of Us' is nothing but a God-centric way of thinking. To translate this into applications in the world of things, and relationships in the world of people, it needs your creativity.

What I propose is for our diverse "us" to start thinking in completely new ways, under God-centrism. For those of us who believe in God, I believe it prudent to belong to Him in the ways that He has specified. I think it is also prudent to accept God's priorities and not impose our own. If we believe in God, it seems more prudent not to allow the Self to confuse us with the illusion that this life is everything and that death is the end of everything. This is self-centered thinking.

Youth in Western Civilization

Again, I address you: I ask you to adopt 'All of Us.' I place it in your hands for you to start.

I repeat: If you start, others will follow more easily than they would follow anyone else. You are a child of the victorious civilization. You inherited this victory; you inherited with it great responsibility. If an influential few among you adopts it, you will have the honor of being the ones to change the world. I place it in your hands to save time and effort, for the eyes of the rest of the world are on you. If you run with it, they will follow. That's how the world works now: they stare at you, starry-eyed, and what you do is convincing simply because it is you who do it.

At the same time, I offer it to the rest of the world. Working together is better than working in succession, even if one way is easier. I remind you again of the fragility of the alliance of Us, any Us, under self-centeredness. But under God-centrism, the relationship is stronger and deeper, being built on what God wants of us, not what our Selves want of us – and what a difference.

Us, All Of Us, Armies, and Borders

Imagine the future of armies and borders in this type of thinking. Borders offered security at the cost of liberty, an acceptable compromise. Armies, too, were invented to defend these countries, and especially the borders. What happens when neighboring countries decide to blur the boundaries between them? What happened to the EU? Does it need armies on the same scale, size, ability and privilege they occupied pre-WWII? Naturally not.

The EU created bonds with other countries which look, to its citizens, like an "all of us," don't they? A European citizen is that way regardless of their origin, and a global citizen as well in the context of Europe. What happened to the concept of borders and armies? At least in this context, they are transformed, as we have said also occurred in America, which became the "United" States, an 'all of us' to themselves, and a powerful Us in relation to the rest of the world.

Compare the borders between the states of the USA, the USA and Canada, and the US and Mexico. Each of these different arrangements was arrived at in an unhealthy manner, via a tribal Us disguised as an All of Us. This had nothing to do with what I'm advocating here.

I believe we have a chance to achieve the same results, the best possible, by taking the healthy road: by making "all of us" the essence, not the form, of our actions. This can only take place under God-centrism. I suggest you think outside the box, try thinking in a different way, abandon "Us" and the collective Ego. I suggest you take the path of God-centrism.

"But that doesn't sound very practical."

True. This is a new way of thinking, nothing more. Thinking from this perspective requires the courage to be imaginative, then use the imagination to think of creative and practical new plans. Then it will take another burst of effort to turn these plans into tangible results on the ground. The plans and blueprints will come from you, the reader, if you choose to think from this viewpoint. I trust your – our – creative ability, once we choose to live under God-centrism.

If you choose this path, avoiding war will not be the main goal I presented, but a by-product. The main goal will be an inclusive civilization based on love, built on God-centrism.

Is this an idealistic dream?

Certainly. But every great change in history started with a dream.

God, "I" and us

I hope you have made your choice and decided to buy my wares.

I hope you have decided to live under God-centrism.

I hope you have decided to make God your first priority and to prioritize "self" and "us" the way He has ordained.

I hope you have decided to make the following existential question your constant companion in life:

"Where is God in every situation? Am I truly prioritizing His will over my own?"

I hope you have decided to become part of an inclusive civilization based on love and on God-centrism.

I hope you realize that, in life, we adopt an illusion of there being many "I's", while there is really only one "I" and only One with the right to declare it: God.

I hope you realize where the letter "I" belongs:

"I ... for God."

I hope you choose not to prioritize what your "I's" want, making your and our lives difficult. I hope, instead, that you choose to prioritize God's will and to spread internal and external peace among us all.

I hope that when you say, "This life is mine," that you choose, of your own free will, to offer it to God and not to your self.

I hope you are reminded of the golden rule: that everything in this book has been geared to inspire you to question things and to question yourself; not for you to question and judge others.

Dear reader,

Now I leave you with what I believe is your responsibility.

God Almighty has told us that He will judge those who know differently from those who don't know.

Know this:

"Now you know."

I

ABOUT THE AUTHOR

Waeil Borhan is a leader of unity and peace... Borhan's life path has lead him to realize the innate readiness of human beings for love, harmony and oneness and he is now investing all he's got to promote a living paradigm that enables collaboration while safeguarding measures of efficiency and achievement... He's advocating for performance through realizing your Devine purpose under a sky of abundance and joy that eradicates competition brought around by the illusion of scarcity.

Borhan studied architecture, then as an entrepreneur he built business ventures in real estate development, farming and later, venture capital investment in the technology field. He excels as a strategist and master reframer. He has participated in establishing many social institutions. Baladna Foundation, for example, holds a special place in his heart. Baladna is the runway where Borhan's philosophy land on carefully selected influential figures. The inflicted impact on them transforms them into purposely driven leaders in their areas finding more common space for collaboration with peers of very different religious, political, economic and social views bringing around significant potential for a better world.

This book "I" tries to pose some existential questions that might make you revisit and revise some personal and collective believes about what you define as "others" and will help you to clearly define your position towards collaborating with people or groups that you could've placed earlier out of your circles of concern; thus bring you closer to your innate design and allow you to live effectively and blissfully.